music 3.0

A Survival Guide for
Making Music in the Internet Age

Second Edition

music**PRO**
guides

music 3.0

A Survival Guide for
Making Music in the Internet Age

Second Edition

Bobby Owsinski

Hal Leonard Books
An Imprint of Hal Leonard Corporation

Second edition published in 2011 by
Hal Leonard Books
An Imprint of Hal Leonard Corporation
7777 West Bluemound Road
Milwaukee, WI 53213

Trade Book Division Editorial Offices
33 Plymouth St., Montclair, NJ 07042

First edition published in 2009 by Hal Leonard Books

Printed in the United States of America

Library of Congress Cataloging-in-Publication Data
Owsinski, Bobby.
 Music 3.0 : a survival guide for making music in the new music industry / Bobby Owsinski. -- 2nd ed.
   p. cm.
1. Music trade--Technological innovations. 2. Music trade—Computer network resources.
3. Music and the Internet. 4. Internet marketing. I. Title.
 ML3790.O968 2011
 780.68'8--dc23
                                                                    2011029663

ISBN 978-1-4584-0289-9

www.halleonardbooks.com

Contents

Introduction

The music world has changed a lot in the two years since I wrote the first edition of this book, but we all knew it would. While we anxiously wait for the music industry to find some point of stability, instead we find it moving ever faster past that point of equilibrium. Which is exactly why this update is so needed.

I originally decided to write this book precisely because the music world was changing so much. Oh, it's always been evolving, but the speed of the industry's remodeling has increased at a rate previously unimagined. It would be nice to say that this change is brought about by a leap in musical creativity, but that's not the case. This metamorphosis has been caused by technology.

The Internet has brought us so many conveniences and so many new ways of living our lives, having fun, and communicating with those we know and don't know that we sometimes don't appreciate how quickly it's all come about. It's also brought us so many choices in the way we make music and ultimately make it available that, unfortunately, it's also left most artists and music makers dazed and confused with all the seemingly endless options. What should I do? How can I do it? Who are my customers and fans? What do they want from me? How do I reach them? How do I take advantage of all these choices? These are all questions that an artist might have had previously, but the relevancy and urgency have only increased with the current times.

I came up with the concept of Music 3.0 after writing a post on my production blog (bobbyowsinski.blogspot.com; there's now also music3point0.blogspot.com) in which I discussed the current woes of not only the music business but especially the artists who are just trying to do the thing they love most—play music. I know that some artists have grand ambitions to be the next Justin Timberlake, Christina Aguilera, Kanye West, Coldplay, or any number of bestselling acts. Sometimes artists crave fame a lot more than they yearn to make the kind of music that will attract and keep fans for the long term. These musicians seem to be the ones that burn out of the business the fastest, once they realize how much work they really have to put in.

The vast majority of artists aren't like that. They love what they do and are supremely happy when they find others that love what they do too. For them, just being able to make music without having to work a job on the side is considered a success. If that describes you, I hear you and feel you. Reading this book might not get you there, but it can set you on your way. Knowledge is power—and that phrase has never been truer than in the current music stage that I call "Music 3.0." The possibilities for what can happen to your music are endless, but you've got to know how to take advantage of those possibilities before you can put them into action.

Throughout this book I'll refer to Music 3.0 as M3.0, or "M three oh." It has a nice ring and rolls off the tongue well. But you're probably wondering, "How did we get to M3.0? What were M1.0, 2.0, and so on?" While we'll go over all that in depth in chapter 1, here's how I briefly delineate the various stages of the music business.

Music 1.0: The first generation of the music business, in which the product was vinyl records, the artist had no direct contact with the record buyer, radio was the primary source of promotion, the record labels were run by record people, and records were bought from retail stores.

Music 1.5: The second generation of the music business, in which the product was primarily CDs, labels were owned and run by large conglomerates, MTV caused the labels to shift from artist development to image development, radio was still the major source of promotion, and CDs were purchased from retail stores.

Music 2.0: The third generation of the music business, which signaled the beginning of digital music and during which piracy ran rampant due to peer-to-peer networks. The industry, however, took little notice, since CD sales were still strong from radio promotion.

Music 2.5: The fourth generation of the music business, in which digital music became monetized thanks to iTunes and, later, others such as

Amazon MP3. CD sales plunged, the music industry contracted, and retail stores closed.

Music 3.0: The current generation of the music business, in which the artist can communicate, interact, market, and sell directly to the fan. Record labels, radio, and television become increasingly irrelevant, and single songs are purchased instead of albums.

This book is an aggregation of concepts about the new music business in the so-called Internet age, which I've been following for some time. It contains the guiding insights of some of the brightest minds in the music industry about where the industry has been, where it is now, and where it's going. With so much information currently available, I wanted to do what I do best—collect it, organize it, and present it in a way that everyone can understand.

As in my other books, I've sought out the help of some of the most respected voices that are on the cutting edge of different aspects of the music business, and I've included their interviews at the end of this book and incorporated selected quotes along the way. The interviews are fun and informative, and conducting them was one of the most enjoyable aspects of writing this book.

Let me briefly introduce these respected industry experts to you:

Ted Cohen: Known throughout the technology and music industries as being part ambassador and part evangelist, Ted has been on the cutting edge of digital music from its inception. Currently a managing partner of the industry consulting firm TAG Strategic, Ted is one of the most influential voices in digital music today and can be heard speaking on the subject worldwide.

Richard Feldman: A very successful songwriter, producer, and Grammy winner, with platinum and Number 1 records to his credit, Richard is the CEO of a music-library publisher called ArtistFirst Music. He comes to publishing from the point of view of a musician and songwriter, and he has a unique perspective on the changes that M3.0 brings.

Larry Gerbrandt: An expert on entertainment analytics, Larry's Media Valuation Partners advises its clients on the economics of media and content on traditional and emerging technology platforms. Formerly a senior vice president with research giant Nielsen Analytics, Larry provides a wealth of experience in entertainment market research that I'm pleased we could tap. Get ready for some interesting and insightful facts and figures regarding sponsorships, branding, and advertising—all the things necessary to monetize M3.0.

Bruce Houghton: Bruce started his highly influential Hypebot blog because he wanted to better understand the changes in the music business in order to help educate the clients of his Skyline Music talent agency. Since then, his blog has become a must-read for anyone at any level of the music industry. Bruce's keen observations come from being not only a highly prominent blogger but also a booking agent working in the industry trenches every day.

Ariel Hyatt: One of the first, if not the first, to understand that the music world was rapidly changing and move her traditional PR firm to a socially based "Cyber PR," Ariel is responsible for helping hundreds of artists navigate the social medium through her company and books.

Thom Kozik: A seasoned tech-industry executive for more than 20 years, Thom has spent considerable time on the gaming side of the tech industry, having served as president of gaming search engines Wazap and All-Seeing Eye (which he sold to Yahoo in 2004) before he became director of business development for Yahoo's media group. Thom has since served as executive vice president of online gaming for Atari and is now a much in-demand consultant to the gaming industry.

Gregory Markel: One of the pioneers of search-engine optimization and marketing, Gregory owns the search engine marketing company Infuse Creative, which touts major entertainment clients such as Gibson Musical Instruments, New Line Cinema, the National Geographic Channel, Led Zeppelin, the Rolling Stones, the television show *24*, and many more. As a recording artist (and a great singer) formerly signed to Warner Brothers, Gregory has a deep empathy for the plight of today's artists, and provides an abundance of social media advice in his interview.

Rupert Perry: One of the most respected and beloved executives in the music industry, Rupert held a variety of executive positions with EMI over 32 years—from vice president of A&R at Capitol, to president of EMI America, to managing director of EMI Australia and, later, EMI Records UK, to president and CEO of EMI Europe, to the worldwide position of vice president of EMI Recorded Music. During his time at EMI, Rupert worked with a variety of superstar artists such as The Beatles, Blur, Duran Duran, Iron Maiden, Nigel Kennedy, Robert Palmer, Pink Floyd, Queen, Radiohead, and Cliff Richard. Rupert is well up on the latest technology and trends within the music business, and shares some surprising contrasts between the old business and the one we're in right now.

Ian Rogers: Formerly the general manager of Yahoo Music, Ian is now the CEO of Topspin Media, one of the premier direct-to-fan services currently available. A frequent panelist at industry conferences worldwide, he is one of the most respected people in the music business.

Ken Rutkowski: Ken is widely considered to be one of the most informed and connected people in the media, entertainment, and technology markets today. His daily radio and Internet show, *World Tech Round-Up* at kenradio.com, is a source of inside information for listeners in more than 40 countries, often scooping the major media and giving perspective to emerging trends, developments, and industry maneuvers. Ken is also the creator and guiding force behind the Media Entertainment Technology Alliance (METal), a members-only group of alpha influencers.

Derek Sivers: Derek's life has certainly been interesting so far, from working as a musician/ringleader of a circus, to a having a stint at the publishing giant Warner/Chappell, to being on the road as a touring musician, to creating and running CD Baby, one of the most widely used music-distribution services today. Since selling CD Baby in 2008, Derek now spends his time thinking of new ways to help musicians. As you'll see, his insights are as thoughtful as they are cutting edge.

Howard Soroka: I first met Howard when he was the primary programmer for the famed GML recording-console automation system some 25 years ago. Since then, he's gone on to being more an executive than a programmer, rising to vice president of media technologies at Universal Music Group's eLabs. Always on the cutting edge of technology, he provides some great insights on the digital workings of the world's largest record label, as well as a look into the future of the music business.

Jacob Tell: Jacob's Oniracom is a new breed of company that provides a full line of digital media services to artists, labels, and management. Helping artists in the digital space before there was a YouTube, MySpace, or Facebook, Jacob has watched the development of Web 2.0 and learned how an artist can best take advantage of it along the way.

Michael Terpin: Michael is the founder of SocialRadius, a marketing and public-relations company focusing on social media outreach and strategy. Among the projects that the firm has worked on are the outreach for recording artist Will.i.am's "Yes We Can" video for the Obama campaign (which won 2008 Emmy, Global Media, and Webby Awards); social media event marketing for Live8, LiveEarth, the Green Inaugural Ball, and the David Lynch Foundation; and the social media launch of startups ranging from Software.com to Shapeways.

When reading this book, be aware that there is one basic concept that it subtly follows. It's an idea I've lived by for some time, and it helps to clarify an artist's intent (which is now more important than ever) if kept in mind.

> Art is something you do for yourself.
>
> A craft is something you do for everyone else.

You'll see as you read this book that it's really important to know whether what you're doing is really an art or if it's a craft, since that will determine your level of involvement in the many jobs required to advance your career as an artist. If you're making music for yourself (as compared to for someone else), all the rules change—as does your level of commitment to the muse itself!

As said before, the music business is changing rapidly and, although painful, will ultimately change for the better. There will be a lot of the old guard who will fall by the wayside, but it's probably time that happened anyway (perhaps it's long overdue). Consumers are more selective and sophisticated in their tastes and about technology, and that's something that everyone in the industry should not only be aware of but also cater to. It's the only way to survive in today's music world.

Keep in mind that there are many, many issues that reach out to us in M3.0, but things change so quickly that this book would be obsolete before it even got on the retail shelves if it were too specific in certain areas. I won't discuss the legal issues of copyright, I won't evaluate individual distributors and social networks beyond some generalities, and I won't discuss the relative merits of a particular website or service. Once again, things could all change so quickly that you'd get no value from the book if it were that detailed. I'll look mostly at the big picture, but drill down where it's appropriate.

This book looks at how to utilize Music 3.0 to its utmost. If you're an artist, you've got to be aware of all your options—both traditional and online. This book will tell you who controls today's music industry; who the new movers and shakers are; how to grow, market to, sell to, and interact with your fan base; how to utilize the new concepts that power M3.0; and what you need to do to harness the potential of M3.0, all without spending so much time online that you aren't left with time to make music.

It seems like a lot of information, but if you want to control your destiny in the new music industry, this book will show you how.

This second edition of Music 3.0 has five entirely new chapters, new interviews, and the latest updated info whenever possible. There's some philosophy, some how-to's, and some predictions, but it's all based on some excellent information provided by a variety of expert sources, some of whom you'll meet in this book.

Keep in mind that this book is not only for the musician but also for other members of the music industry. Everyone must understand his or her options and challenges in order to survive in this new business environment. Hopefully, you'll find this book to be an invaluable tool as you go forth into this new world.

Bobby Owsinski Bibliography

. . . .

The Mixing Engineer's Handbook, 2nd Edition (ISBN 978-1598632514—Thomson Course Technology): The premier book on audio mixing techniques provides all the information needed to take your mixing skills to the next level, along with advice from the world's best mixing engineers.

The Recording Engineer's Handbook, 2nd Edition (ISBN 978-1598638677—Course Technology PTR): In this book that reveals the microphone and recording techniques used by some of the most renowned recording engineers, you'll find everything you need to know to lay down great tracks in any recording situation, in any musical genre, and in any studio.

The Audio Mastering Handbook, 2nd Edition (ISBN 978-1598634495—Course Technology PTR): Everything you always wanted to know about mastering, from doing it yourself to using a major facility, utilizing insights from the world's top mastering engineers.

The Drum Recording Handbook, with DVD (with Dennis Moody) (ISBN 978-1423443438—Hal Leonard): Uncovers the secret of amazing drum recordings in your recording studio even with the most inexpensive gear. It's all in the technique, and this book/DVD will show you how.

How to Make Your Band Sound Great, with DVD (ISBN 978-1423441907—Hal Leonard): This band-improvement book and DVD shows your band how to play to its fullest potential. It doesn't matter what kind of music you play, what your skill level is, or if you play covers or your own music; this book will make you tight, it will make you more dynamic, it will improve your show, and it will improve your recordings.

The Studio Musician's Handbook, with DVD (with Paul ILL) (ISBN 978-1423463412—Hal Leonard): Everything you wanted to know about the world of the studio musician, including how you become a studio musician, who hires you and how much you get paid, what kind of skills you need and what gear you must have, the proper session etiquette required to make a session run smoothly, and how to apply these skills in every type of recording session, regardless of whether it's in your home studio or Abbey Road.

The Music Producer's Handbook (ISBN 978-1423474005—Hal Leonard): Reveals the inside information and secrets to becoming a music producer and producing just about any kind of project in any genre of music. Among the topics covered are the producer's responsibilities and all the elements of a typical production, including budgeting, contracts, selecting the studio and engineer, hiring session musicians, and even getting paid! The book also covers the true mechanics of production, from analyzing and fixing the format of a song, to troubleshooting a song when it just doesn't sound right, to getting the best performance and sound out of the band and vocalist.

The Musician's Video Handbook (ISBN 978-1423484448—Hal Leonard): Describes how the average musician can easily make any of the various types of videos now required by a musical artist either for promotion or final product. But just shooting a video isn't enough. The book will also demonstrate the tricks and tips used by the pros to make it look professionally done, even with inexpensive gear and not much of a budget.

Mixing and Mastering with T-RackS: The Official Guide (ISBN 978-1435457591—Course Technology PTR): T-RackS is a popular stand-alone audio mastering application that includes a suite of powerful analog-modeled and digital dynamics, and EQ processor modules that also work perfectly as plug-ins during mixing. While T-RackS is an extremely powerful tool for improving the quality of your recordings, all of that power won't do you much good if it's misused. With Mixing and Mastering with IK Multimedia T-RackS: The Official Guide, you can learn how to harness the potential of T-RackS and learn the tips and tricks of using T-Racks processor modules to help bring your mixes to life, then master them so they're competitive with any major label release.

The Touring Musician's Handbook (ISBN 978-1423492368—Hal Leonard): For a musician, touring is the brass ring. It's the thing that everyone dreams about from the first time he or she picks up an instrument. But what do you do when you finally get that chance? How do you audition? What kind of chops do you need? What equipment should you bring? How do you prepare for life on the road? Regardless of whether you're a sideman, solo performer, or member of a band, all of these questions are answered in The Touring Musician's Handbook. As a bonus, individual touring musician guides for guitar, bass, drums, vocals, keys, horns, and strings, as well as interviews with famous and influential touring players, are also included.

The Ultimate Guitar Tone Handbook (ISBN 978-739075357—Alfred Publishing): The Ultimate Guitar Tone Handbook is the definitive book for discovering that great guitar sound and making sure it records well. The book definitively outlines all the factors that make electric and acoustic guitars, and amplifiers and speaker cabinets, sound the way they do, as well as the classic and modern recording and production techniques that capture great tone. The Ultimate Guitar Tone Handbook also features a series of interviews with expert players, technicians, recording engineers, producers, and manufacturers that gives you an inside look into the business of guitar tone, and an accompanying DVD provides both an audio and visual reference point for achieving the classic sounds you hear on records.

The Studio Builder's Handbook (ISBN 978-0739077030—Alfred Publishing): No matter how good your recording gear is, chances are you're not getting the best possible sound because of the deficiencies of your room. While you might think that it costs thousands of dollars and the services of an acoustic designer to improve your studio, The Studio Builder's Handbook will strip away the mystery of what makes a great-sounding studio and show how you can make a huge difference in your room for as little as $150.

Bobby Owsinski's Social Media Connections

Bobby's website—bobbyowsinski.com
Bobby's Music Production Blog—
bobbyowsinski.blogspot.com
Bobby's Music Industry Blog—
music3point0.blogspot.com
Bobby on Facebook—facebook.com/bobby.owsinski
Bobby on Twitter—@bobbyowsinski
Bobby on YouTube—youtube.com/polymedia

music 3.0

ONE

CHAPTER

The Six Life Stages
of the Music Industry

The history of the music business can be broken down into six distinct stages. Each stage is readily apparent, although the exact beginning and ending points may not be. In order to understand the significance of the stage termed *Music 3.0* (we'll call it M3.0, pronounced "em-three-oh," from now on), it's important to look closely at the other stages to spot the changes, and the opportunities, that present themselves.

One thing to remember is that what we all think of as the "music business" is based around popular ("pop") music, meaning music that's aimed at reaching the largest number of people possible. This popularity is mostly measured by sales activity, which, for better or worse, is reflected in the charts published primarily by *Billboard* magazine, although new charts such as the Ultimate Chart (ultimatechart. com) that take all media in to account are beginning to gain traction.

Music 0.5—The Precursor Business

In the days before recorded music, the music business was a different animal indeed. This was an industry centered around sheet music, which is how music was disseminated to the public. Thus, the only way music was heard was to buy sheet music and perform it live in your home, so the original music industry promoted the song, not the artist.

Although this industry really started in the 18th century, by the late 19th century, the center of this industry was based around the music publishers of New York's "Tin Pan Alley" district. When player pianos, the first big leap in music delivery, were introduced, the publishers created the system of what we now call "promotion" to get their songs included on player rolls, the mechanism that allowed the pianos to play by themselves. Promotion soon became an essential part of the music business that exists to this day.

NEW TECHNOLOGY DRIVES THE BUSINESS

Various new music technology delivery systems were soon created, changing the focus of the industry more the artist. The first record player, the Gramophone, was introduced in 1890. In the 1920s the radio was introduced, and music delivery quickly grew as new popular songs and the artists who recorded them could now spread to a wide audience rapidly. The late 1920s then gave us motion pictures with sound ("talkies"), which soon became another source of music dissemination. In 1932, the first record store in the US came into existence ("George's Song Shop" in Johnstown, PA), and in 1941, the first store of what would become the largest chain of record stores ever, Tower Records, was opened. With the rise of the rack jobber, department stores all over the country now dedicated a portion of the store just to record sales. During this time period, entrepreneurs worldwide began to recognize the new opportunities of the music business, as nearly 200 record labels were created in the US alone and retail record stores began to pop up in every town.

The music business had been formed. There was now a delivery format (vinyl records), a delivery system (record stores), and a promotional system (radio and movies) in place. The opportunity for profits had not escaped many corporations though, and by 1930, the long, slow road to industry consolidation had begun.

In 1929, Radio Corporation of America (RCA) acquired the largest manufacturer of phonographs and records, the Victor Talking Machine Company, to become RCA-Victor. In 1931, their British affiliate, the Gramophone Company, merged with the Columbia Graphophone Company to become EMI, a music industry powerhouse for years to come. RCA went on to sell its interest in EMI in 1935, but both companies were now in position to become major industry players in the future. The business was still in its infancy however, and would have more than a decade to grow before it started to gain major traction with consumers.

Music 1.0—The Original Music Business

. . . .

The music business as we know it today really started in the stage called Music 1.0, a period that lasted from the 1950s to the early 1980s. During this time, the music business mostly experienced unprecedented yearly growth, except for a brief period around 1980 when it experienced a major recession. Year-to-year sales and profits surged upward until they caught the attention of Wall Street, which turned out to be one of the industry's defining moments (more on that later). For historical purposes and to educate younger readers about how business was conducted during those times, here's an overview of the business structure of Music 1.0.

For almost 50 years, the way the music business worked remained the same. The artist (usually after submitting his or her demo tape) was signed to a recording contract by the record label, which then assigned an A&R (Artist and Repertoire) person to be the liaison between the artist and the record company product manager for the record releases. In the beginning, the A&R person would also assign a producer, who was responsible for making the record, although how this was accomplished eventually became a mutual decision with the artist over the years. Many times the producer would be on staff, and in other cases, the A&R person also served double duty as the producer.

The structure looked like this:

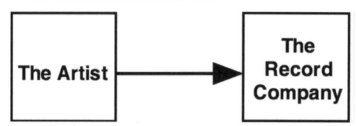

In the early days of the record business, the artist usually had minimal control over the end product, as that was the domain of the producer. As the business developed, and more and more artists demanded and received artistic control, the producer assigned to help the artist record was often an independent contractor from outside the label who was amenable to the musician's artistic wishes, as long as they fit the vision of the label. After some success (that is, hit records), many artists even bore responsibility for production as well.

After the song or album was recorded, the label pressed the vinyl record (and later, the cassette and CD) and distributed it to dedicated retail record stores either through the label's own distribution network or via an independent network of distributors, rack jobbers, one-stops, and wholesalers—which, under the right circumstances, placed the record in every record store, diner, car wash, department store, and anywhere else where floor space could be rented.

The structure now looked like this:

The record label was also responsible for the marketing of the record, which centered around radio airplay. If you could get a record a lot of airplay, you would probably sell a lot of units (as long as the record was in the stores and available to buy).

The other thing is how people consumed content in those days, which was that people mostly listened to the radio. Then the

Japanese came up with the transistor radio, which was portable. Suddenly portability meant that the consumer didn't have to sit in their living room in front of that radio. That was the start of something else from a distribution point of view. You can look at all the things that changed, but then you look at the transistor radio and think, "Gosh, the portability was so important."

—Rupert Perry

Airplay was crucial to the success of a record and resulted in large promotion departments within the record labels dedicated to getting radio airplay. Competition for airplay became so fierce that promotion departments began to resort to using gifts of cash, prostitutes, vacations, and anything that would influence a radio station's program director to place a song in rotation. This was known as "payola," a practice that eventually was outlawed and subsequently resulted in several scandals and investigations of the record and radio industries and the way they did business together.

The structure now looked like this:

In order to avoid being prosecuted for payola, record labels decreased the use of their in-house promotion departments and went instead to independent promoters, on the theory that anything a third-party promoter offered to a program director essentially eliminated the label's legal responsibility (which was eventually found by the courts to be illegal anyway). Regardless, radio airplay was the key to a hit, and promotion was the key to radio airplay.

The structure for the Music 1.0 way of doing business finally evolved into this:

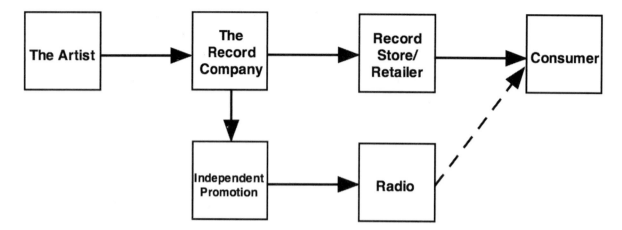

With the exception of limited exposure to the consumer via fan clubs and in-store album signings, the artist was segregated from the consumer and distribution chain. The artist might do some occasional promotion on radio, but his or her connection with the consumer was limited. Luckily, interaction and communication with the fan wasn't needed at this time, thanks to the overwhelming influence of radio, the 800-pound gorilla in the room of Music 1.0.

Music 1.0 gave into lots of record-label foibles in addition to payola. In order to exaggerate chart position, labels would fudge sales by having record stores intentionally report that a record was selling even if it wasn't. This practice was later put to rest with the implementation of SoundScan technology, which would compute sales via the scanned bar code on each album or CD. Although it seems like a fair way to determine actual sales, SoundScan used a system that would weight a sale in each territory differently, causing a sale in a large city such as Chicago to have a greater determination on the chart position than a sale in Grand Rapids—a point that caused heated debate throughout the industry.

Another interesting practice of the era was the "shipped platinum" syndrome. To exaggerate sales, labels would ship huge numbers of records, and then state that the record "shipped platinum" (meaning it sold enough to be certified as a platinum-selling record, with sales over one million units), insinuating that the demand was so great that the units shipped were presold. It usually wasn't reported, however, when the records were returned to the label in platinum numbers for not selling.

Music 1.0

The record label is all powerful.

The artist is isolated from fans.

Radio is the key to hits.

Artists were given multiple release-opportunities for long-term development.

It's a singles world.

But the album makes more money.

Music 1.5—The Suits Take Over

. . . .

The era of Music 1.5 produced the greatest level of business that the industry has seen or is ever likely to see.

When the CD was released in 1982, record companies got a boost to ever-greater profits in several ways. Because the technology was initially expensive, the labels increased the retail price on each CD while decreasing the royalty rate to the artist, supposedly because of the "technology expense." While the retail price never decreased even after the technology was amortized (it increased, in fact), artists eventually saw this royalty charge eliminated, but they never saw another contract clause from the past terminated. "Breakage," a 10 percent charge against royalties—left over from the days when vinyl records would break in transit, and irrelevant in the new CD age—was never deleted from typical recording contracts during this period.

Perhaps the biggest shot in the arm to record labels was the ability to resell their catalog to a public eager to switch to CDs and buy a copy of an album they already owned on vinyl. Catalog sales (sales of records from an artist before his or her most recent) increased profits, because production costs were minimal (just the cost of pressing the CD), as were promotional costs. Consumers bought the new and better-sounding (to some) CD to supplement their newfound CD collections, thereby providing a financial windfall for the labels deep with catalog items.

Record companies now had a cash cow that shot profits through the financial stratosphere, which immediately gained the attention of Wall Street. Always the poor stepchild of the entertainment industry, the record business was suddenly every investment banker's darling, with the remaining four of the six major labels that were still independently controlled eventually sold to multinational conglomerates during this period. Columbia Records was bought by Sony (eventually becoming Sony Music); Warner Bros. Records by Time Inc. (becoming Time-Warner); Universal Music by Matsushita (later purchased by Vivendi); and EMI by Thorn Industries. Polygram was already owned by a conglomerate (the Dutch electronics company Philips), and BMG was owned by the German giant Bertelsmann AG (although it recently merged, then unmerged, with Sony). Now all six major labels were under conglomerate control.

The other big thing that happened was the compact disc. When it came along, there was a big upsurge in the growth of the business, and a lot of large corporations began to take notice. When CBS, who was the king of the business at the time, sold their record business to Sony—that was huge! It was a momentous happening because CBS decided they wanted to exit the music business, which they had been in for years.

—Rupert Perry

With conglomerate ownership came MBAs, accountants, and attorneys running the business—a major departure from the seat-of-the-pants, street-smart music men such as Mo Ostin, Ahmet Ertegan, Jac Holtzman, Berry Gordy, and Howie Stein, who could feel a hit in their bones. Where previously a label would nurture artists or groups through three, four, even five albums until they broke through, the new corporate structure demanded instant results "this quarter." Artist development, so crucial for the stars and superstars that we know today, died—slowly at first, then faster and faster as bottom-line results became the mantra.

THE RISE OF MTV

About this time, another unexpected boost came to the music industry in the form of a small cable television network startup called MTV. Suddenly, music was on television, and a new level of exposure increased sales yet again. MTV soon had the power to "make" a hit, just like radio previously could, by the simple act of placing a music video in heavy rotation.

Although no one expected it at the time, the Buggles' song "Video Killed the Radio Star" (which was the first video ever played on MTV) actually came to pass. Image soon became much more important than musical ability. If you didn't look appealing, you weren't getting on MTV; and if you didn't get on MTV, your chances of having a hit diminished greatly. Quickly the newfound corporate culture began to shift gears to find good-looking "musicians" to fill the bill. Artistry became just one component of a new act instead of *the* component, as image became foremost in the label mindset.

To a non-record-industry executive, art doesn't make sense. Academia demands repeatable outcomes, and art is not a part of that equation. Craft was a big part of the corporate hit-making formula though. First find an artist similar to whoever is the most popular at the moment. Then get a successful songwriter to write the perfect generic (usually pop) song, add a producer with a proven track record, and record it all in a studio where big hits have been previously made, and with the musicians who have played on those hits. The actual "artist" matters little in this corporate scenario. He or she had better look great though, because the music videos (put together by directors, choreographers, and stylists with recent hits on their résumés) must project the image that Madison Avenue deems necessary to sell product, since that's ultimately who's footing the bill.

THE FARM TEAMS DISBAND

Unfortunately, the passage of the drunk-driving laws in 1983 negatively affected long-term artist development in a real way. Prior to 1972, the legal drinking age ranged from 18 to 21, depending upon the state, but the war in Vietnam brought about the "If I can fight for my country, I should be able to drink" argument (which we're seeing again today). By 1972, most states agreed that if you were old enough to vote and fight for your country, then it should be legal for you to partake in an alcoholic beverage, and the drinking age was lowered to 18 countrywide. This opened the floodgates to clubs everywhere to accommodate a whole new set of thirsty patrons, and the way to get them in the door was to provide live entertainment.

Clubs sprang up everywhere, and live music thrived. If you were a half-decent band, you could easily find somewhere to play almost every night of the week, and get paid for it too ("pay-to-play" didn't exist at the time).

This was great for the music business, because it gave neophyte musicians a place to get it together both musically and performance-wise. Just like The Beatles did in Hamburg in 1962, a band could play five sets a night for seven nights a week and really hone their chops. Do that for a year or two, and you were ready to take the next step toward doing your own thing, if that's what you wanted to do.

Unfortunately, it was also easy to fall into the trap of just playing clubs forever because the money was so good, but those with ambition took their club days for what they were and moved on up. They had learned what they needed to by constantly playing in front of crowds.

Since the drinking age was raised to 21 in 1982, the excitement and diversity in music has steadily decreased. Music has become bland and homogenized, and there hasn't been a major new trend since rap, which hit the mainstream in the early '80s, and grunge in the early 90's. This is because of the large-scale reduction of the club scene due to the higher drinking age and the tougher DUI laws. Higher drinking age and more arrests meant fewer club patrons. Fewer club patrons meant goodbye to many clubs.

This musical support infrastructure is greatly diminished these days. A band that is considered to be playing a lot today is lucky if it works once a week. That means it will take a group a lot longer, not only to get more comfortable in front of crowds, but also to become musically and vocally tight. The longer it takes a band to make progress, the more likely it is that it will break up or change its direction, which means that perhaps the next great trend in music has shriveled on the vine.

Musicians need the constant feedback and attention that only an audience can bring. The more you play live, the better you get at it, which leads to more experimenting, which means the more likely you are to find your own voice.

Music 1.5

Major labels are now owned by conglomerates.

Quarterly profits take precedence over art.

Many album songs are just filler.

MTV is created and has a significant role in record sales.

The artist's image becomes more important than the art.

DUI laws kill the farm team.

Music 2.0—Enter the Digital Age

The day that the first MP3 music file was shared was the first day of Music 2.0 (sometime around 1994). Although no one knew it at the time, this became the disruption that would someday bring the music industry to its knees.

> *If we roll forward to the start of the Internet in 1993, people in the content industry didn't get just how monumental the change was. To have any form of content available through a computer was a totally new form of distribution, but the difference was that the record label had no control over it. Up until that point, any of the media distributors (film, television, or music) were always able to control the distribution, and when you did that, you could decide where it went, who got it, and what people paid for it. With the Internet, that went out the window fast.*
> —Rupert Perry

Up until the MP3 arrived, a CD-quality digital file of a song was both large in size (a little over 5 MB for every one minute of a stereo song) and took a lot of bandwidth to play 1,411 kbps), which meant that it was just about impossible to play over the Internet given the technology at the time. The same file encoded with the MP3 format would take up about 1/10 the space, with a bandwidth of between 128 and 256 kbps, which would make the file easy to download even on the primitive dial-up network connections available during that period. Using an MP3 codec is like letting the air out of a bicycle tire: the tire becomes small enough to fit into a small box, yet it's the same tire. The MP3 codec "let the air out" of a digital file, making it a lot smaller. Although the audio quality of the MP3 wasn't as good as the CD, consumers had previously shown when they heartily adopted cassette tapes that audio quality wasn't a major issue in their purchasing and listening decisions.

P2P MAKES ITS MARK

Peer-to-peer (shortened to P2P) networking was the second new technology that changed the music business during this era. In a peer-to-peer network, each computer on the network can supply and receive files without using a central server, with bandwidth and processing distributed among all members of the network. In other words, files live on multiple interconnected users' computers, with each user able to download a file (or pieces of the same file from multiple computers) from anyone he or she is connected to (see peer-to-peer illustration).

Napster was the first of the many massively popular peer-to-peer file-distribution systems, although it was not totally peer to peer, because it used central servers to maintain lists of connected systems and their files (a factor in their later legal undoing). Although there were already networks that facilitated the distribution of files across the Internet—such as IRC, Hotline, and UseNet—Napster specialized exclusively in music and, as a result of its enormous popularity, offered a huge selection of music to download.

Shortly after its inception, the company was presented with multiple legal challenges from artists (Metallica, Dr. Dre, Madonna), record labels (A&M), and the music industry itself (the RIAA) regarding copyright infringement, and was eventually shut down in July of 2001. Napster use peaked in February 2001, with 26.4 million users worldwide.

MP3.com, started in 1999, was another similar service, although it primarily featured independent music instead of signed acts. Sued by

Universal Music Group for copyright violations, the company settled for an out-of-court payment of $200 million to UMG and was essentially put out of business. At its peak, MP3.com delivered more than 4 million MP3 audio files per day to over 800,000 unique users and had a customer base of 25 million registered users. The company was eventually purchased by Roxio and renamed Napster, which now provides legal paid downloads and a subscription streaming service.

Although the original Napster and MP3.com were shut down by court order, they paved the way for decentralized peer-to-peer file-distribution programs such as Gnutella and Limewire (now discontinued), which are much harder to control. As a result, the RIAA aggressively prosecuted users who used those services, despite the outcry from the public and the industry. It has since backed off from prosecuting when it was determined that they were spending millions in legal fees only to recover paltry amounts in damages, not to mention that harm incurred to the overall industry's reputation.

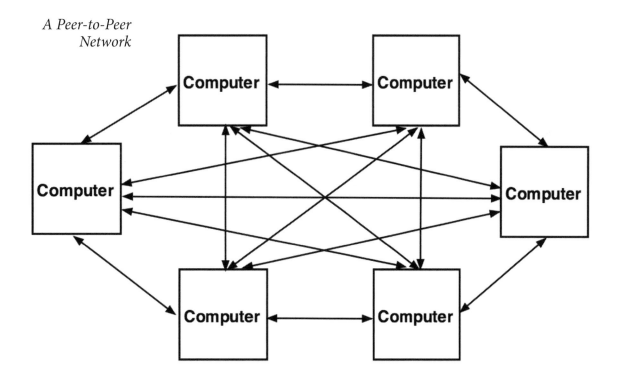

A Peer-to-Peer Network

PIRACY TAKES ANOTHER FORM

Another major disruption of the traditional music business came as a result of the inexpensive CD burner, and its impact cannot be underestimated. In the days of vinyl, unauthorized manufacturing was almost unheard of because of the economics of a pirating operation. Pressing a vinyl record required large, costly, and specialized gear that was beyond that of even the most dedicated enthusiast. When the CD was introduced, the first CD recorders were found only in professional mastering studios because of their cost (about $250,000, with blank CDs costing $200 each). Economics kept the pirates and the casual traders at bay.

Of course the audiotape cassette, from its very inception in 1964, was a thorn in the music industry's side. Using the compact, relatively inexpensive (around $1.00 for a blank tape), and easy-to-use cassettes, home tapers could record a hit song off the radio with ease. Generally providing mediocre audio quality, the cassette was the first example where quality was a minor consideration when compared with price.

When the CD burner began to appear on just about every computer, and blank CDs fell below the $1.00 level, digital music rapidly became a runaway train going down a slippery mountain: you could try everything to stop it, but once it reached terminal velocity, there was no halting it. And so began the digital age of the record industry.

Music 2.0

Digital music arrives.

Peer-to-peer music pirating arrives too.

Digital music trading begins.

CD ripping/burning takes a bite out of sales.

The record labels are complacent.

Music 2.5—Digital Music Is Monetized

Soon it became apparent that unless the music industry jumped onboard, it would be left behind in an ocean of digits. Ironically, it was the computer industry that threw the music industry a lifeline. While different digital-music services presented alternatives to the labels for paid downloads, it was Apple Computer's iTunes that proved to be the business model that worked. Basically a closed system because iTunes initially required Apple's iPod digital music player (the platform choices were later expanded), iTunes was a winner with consumers for its ease of use (a trait Apple is known for) and the iPod's newfound place as a fashion accessory. Now the industry could finally monetize its digital offerings. But at $0.99 per track, there wasn't a lot left for profit (see Fig. 1.6).

How the Money From an iTunes Song Is Distributed (in Cents)

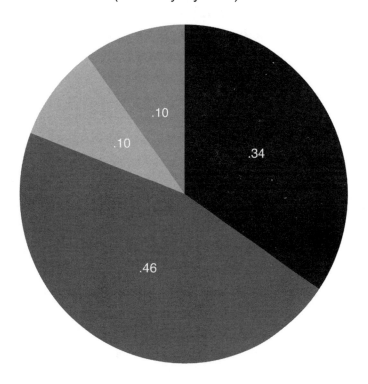

Released in January 2001, iTunes was an instant success that was followed by frequent and significant upgrades. In late 2001, iPod support was implemented, which started the snowball down the hill for the industry as digital music began to become the rage. In 2003, the iTunes store was introduced, and both the consumer and Apple have never looked back. In the years since, movies, television shows, music videos, podcasts, applications, and video games have been added to the extensive iTunes Store's catalog. In April of 2009, the iTunes store went to a tiered pricing structure after much prodding by the major labels. Songs are now available for $0.69, $0.99, or $1.29. At the time that this book was written, over 10 billion songs have been downloaded since the service first launched on April 28, 2003.

While iTunes is the monster of the digital-music industry, other worthy competitors have emerged. From Amazon MP3 to the retooled Napster to the upstart SuperPass, there are now numerous places online to buy songs. We'll go over these in more detail in chapter 9, "The New Distribution."

If there is one kind of online digital-music service that labels now endorse, it's a subscription service, which means that you pay a set monthly fee to be able to listen to as much music as you want during that time with no limitations. The music is usually streamed, so you don't actually own it, but since it's available at any time, there's really no need to keep it on your computer, phone, or mobile device anyway. While subscription services such as Rhapsody and Napster are on the rise, their numbers are still relatively small as compared with the straight download services such as iTunes.

The labels are hoping that the subscription model finally gains consumer traction, because they like the idea of a fixed monthly income stream as a result of their license agreement with the service. The artists aren't as keen, however, since much of the money collected by the labels is not passed on in what they feel is an equitable fashion (see chapter 9). Publishers are dubious as well, noting the high cost of administration versus the income generated (see chapter 11). Regardless, although the number of registered subscribers is expanding, music subscription hasn't reached anything near critical mass yet.

Monetized digital music also brought about another big change, with the return to the singles business that was similar to the '50s and early '60s. Rather than being forced to buy an album of ten songs in order to get the one he or she liked, the consumer could now buy only the songs that he or she wanted. Since the entire economics of the music industry had been centered around the album format and the money it generated, returning to the single-song purchase was a major blow to the financial model that had been in place for 40 years. Overhead had been set up for sales that were in $10.00 increments (the approximate wholesale price of an album). That was suddenly cut to sales that were in increments of less than $1.00 (the sale of a download), and the labels' financial structures were shaken to their cores.

ENTER THE 360 DEAL

To make up for the lost revenue, the major label had to have income streams that went beyond the sale of the CD, and the logical place to get that was from the artist. Since it's always been understood that 90 percent or more of an artist's income comes from touring, the record labels saw that as a potential income source and wanted a piece, and so they launched what came to be known as "360 deals." The term 360 deal means that the record label shares in the income from all income streams available to an artist beyond just the music recordings, including things such as publishing, merchandise, and touring. The label would, in effect, become an artist's manager and share in everything he or she made.

While you can see why a record label would want to share in all the income of an artist, you have to wonder why an artist would want to let them. The argument goes that if the label's expertise is in selling CDs (which aren't really selling all that well), then what kind of management experience does it have? While this may be the only way to do business with a major label these days, it's yet another reason for an artist to ignore it under most circumstances.

In the meantime, traditional artist management was becoming even more powerful, because the manager was now required to make more decisions for the artist than ever before. With the influence of the record labels waning, it was now up to the manager to find new sources of income, deal with potential sponsors, and make deals with online digital distributors, among other things. With much of the sales and marketing now in the hands of the artist, managers had incrementally larger responsibilities than in previous eras, and their guidance and impact became that much more valuable to the artist.

Music 2.5 Overview

Digital Music is monetized.

Sales go back to singles (no album filler).

Major labels impose 360 label deals on artists.

There's a rise in the importance of management.

Music 3.0—The Dawn of Artist/Fan Communication

The biggest change that came with Music 3.0 is in its structure. In M3.0 the middlemen can be cut out of the loop. The artist and the fan are now directly in touch on any and every level they choose to be, from creation to promotion to marketing to sales. But merely staying in touch with a fan can be as fleeting as it sometimes is with friends or family. True fans, just like friends and family, want regular communication, and whether artists know it or not, so do they.

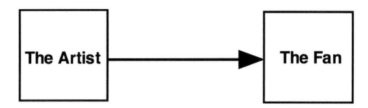

Music 3.0 allows the artists to promote and market directly to the fans. If they can reach the fans, they can make them aware of their products (music, event tickets, and merchandise). If they can reach the fans, they can sell directly to them (although "offer them a product" might be a better way of putting it). Most importantly, Music 3.0 allows the artists to have dialogs with the fans in order to help the artists with sales and marketing. What do the fans want? Just ask them. Do the fans want to be alerted when the artists come to town? Do the fans want remixed versions of songs? Would fans be interested in premium box sets? By the artists just asking, the fans will gladly let them know. And this is the essence of Web 3.0—communication between the fans and the artists.

Another factor in M3.0 is that the audience has become niche oriented. From Swahili polka to Mandarin madrigal, if an artist searches long enough, he or she will find an audience. But although stratification of the audience means more opportunities for more artists, it also means that the possibility of a huge multimillion-selling breakout hit diminishes as fewer people are exposed to a single musical genre than ever before. Nearly gone are the days that a television appearance or heavy-rotation radio or MTV airplay can propel an artist to platinum-level success.

While remnants of the old Music 1.0 structure still exist (record labels, brick-and-mortar record stores, terrestrial radio, MTV, and so on) and can even be useful to the Music 3.0 artist, they will probably never again be the primary driving factor in the success of any artist. In a roundabout way, they never really were (the music is always the defining factor), although their influence was admittedly higher in the past.

It's said that a record label never signed an act because of its music; the label signed the act for the number of fans it either already had or had the potential of developing. If you had lines around the block waiting to see you play, the music didn't matter to the label, because you had an audience that was willing to buy it. And so it is with Music 3.0, only now you can develop that audience in a more efficient way and actually make a living with a limited but rabid fan base (see the section "The 1,000 True Fans Theory" in chapter 10).

The rest of this book is about how to make use of the benefits that Music 3.0 affords an artist.

Music 3.0 Overview

The middleman can be eliminated.

Direct artist–to-fan communication pervades.

Direct sales can be made to the fan.

Direct marketing approaches can be made to the fan.

The audience is stratified.

T W O

CHAPTER

How the Music World Has Changed

J ust like everything else technological, the music business has changed considerably in the past few years, and it continues to change at a rapid pace. Although we've seen industry evolution before, never has there been one as dramatic as M3.0. Although the phrase has been overused, the paradigm has truly shifted, and many of the traditional players in the industry have new, less prominent roles. Let's look at some of them.

Who's in Control?

. . . .

Although it may not be readily apparent, Wall Street and Madison Avenue indirectly control the remaining M2.5 music industry through their tremendous influence on the financial bottom lines of record labels, record stores, concert promotion, radio, and television. If you're owned by a publicly traded conglomerate (as all major labels, major concert promoters, and radio and television stations are), then you're in the business of selling stock, not servicing the consumer. What that means is that nothing matters more than quarterly earnings. To keep those earnings as high as possible, Wall Street turns to Madison Avenue to devise the best marketing strategies for keeping the profits high. Madison Avenue (in the form of the major advertising agencies) can bring in the big ad dollars, but only under certain content conditions (such as programming that is tailored around the advertising), and the process repeats itself over and over. The advertising industry (Madison Avenue), not the music industry, therefore drives the music cycle in the United States.

In M2.5, it's all about passing focus-group tests, which have separated listeners into the distinct demographic groups that advertisers are then able to tell stock analysts they have micromarketed their products to. As a result, radio, television, and live performances are no longer about aggregating and entertaining large audiences, but rather just a group of market niches. The bright side to this fact is that there's one heck of an opportunity opening up for folks who don't get hung up on trying to sell advertising.

Wall Street and Madison Avenue have tried to redefine what music means to people, but most people are voting with their wallets by refusing to buy any new recordings. The view of the vast majority of consumers is that very few new recordings are worth buying compared to those released a couple decades ago, and this has become the dilemma of the industry. You have to sell product to survive, but it's impossible to develop that product while trying to please your corporate masters. It might work when selling soap or clothing or any other consumer product, but a creative endeavor like music just doesn't work that way. It's too personal, both to the artist and the consumer, to be a mass-market product.

Who Controls M2.5

Wall Street and Madison Avenue
control the media.

Record labels need to keep stock price
and quarterly profits high.

Radio and television only play what
appeals to advertisers.

Consumers are divided into demographic groups.

Music becomes devalued.

Where Did the Record Stores Go?

· ·

Although sales of physical product such as CDs are way down in the music business (off by more than 65 percent since 2000), a major reason is that consumers often can't find the product when they want to buy it. It used to be that almost every town had some kind of store where you could buy recorded music, but now even major shopping malls around the country are CD-barren wastelands. Since 2003, 3,500 music retailers have closed, according to the Almighty Institute of Music Retail, an industry research group. There are now fewer than 2,500 stores left.

I think that the end of music retail is in sight and it really has accelerated in the last two years. What that means is we're only a couple years away from not caring at all about getting records into stores. That's huge because it eliminates a marketing opportunity where a clerk in a record store who likes your record will tell people about it, so it's a little sad because that point of contact at the record stores is going to be gone in a few years. On the other hand, it's really exciting because that barrier where a band feels that they needed a nationally distributed release is gone.

—Bruce Houghton, owner of the Hypebot
music blog and the Skyline Music Agency

So where did the music retailers go? Just like so much else in M1.0 through M2.0, music retailing was once a thriving business that had no shortage of customers, but several factors throughout the years delivered a knockout blow from which the retail part of the industry now finds it difficult to recover. First up came the closing of the large music retail chains such as Tower (93 stores), the Wherehouse (320 stores), and Sam Goody (1,300 stores), all now defunct. While initially good for business, these chains began to put price pressure on the small independent retailers that were the backbone of the industry. If you can buy it cheaper from the chain store, that's where you'll go, and so the buying public did.

But soon the music retail chain stores got a taste of their own medicine. In the '90s, Best Buy, Target, and Wal-Mart began to stock CDs as a loss leader in order to get customers in the door to buy their pricier merchandise. This combination of the music-buying experience along with traditional shopping proved hard to beat. Soon these three megaretailers were responsible for more than half of all CD sales, and their leverage hit home with record labels and traditional record retailers alike. The music retail chains, finding it impossible to compete with CDs priced at wholesale prices and below, soon closed, leaving only a dwindling number of independent stores. Ironically, all three megaretailers have now decreased their in-store inventory to only Top 40 selections, and are looking to trim that even more in the future.

Then came the rise of M2.5, as digital music files (MP3s) penetrated the consciousness of the consumer, and soon CD sales began to drop year after year. Digital piracy, online CD sales, CD copying via CD burners, paid digital downloads, and the lack of new music trends and blockbuster product have caused the number of music retailers to fall to unprecedented low levels. Even the highest-grossing record store in the country, Virgin Records in New York's Time Square, closed in 2009—not because it was losing money, but because more money could potentially be generated from the same square footage with another business. So even when a new blockbuster music product that everyone wants exists, you can't buy it if you can't find it.

Many of the indie record stores that are left have been forced to diversify in order to keep the doors open, concentrating more on hard-to-get box sets, books (yet another industry in flux), and music accessories and merchandise. While vinyl records have been a temporary boon to indie retailers, with sales in 2010 increasing by 14 percent, they represent a minute part of the business, with a total of only 2.8 million units sold (not counting used sales). But the used vinyl market, even though it's small, continues to thrive.

What does the future hold for the record store? No less than Sir Richard Branson, whose initial fortune came from his string of Virgin Megastores in the UK, predicts that there will be no record stores left anywhere in the world by the year 2020. That assessment may be a bit radical, but we can be pretty sure the number will continue on a downward spiral.

Reasons for Record Store Decline

Online purchasing

Loss-leaders from Best Buy, Wal-Mart, and Target

Digital pirating

CD burners

Fewer blockbuster releases

The rise of the MP3

Why Traditional Radio Is No Longer a Factor

Broadcast radio was once the lifeblood of the music industry. Even moderate airplay of a song could be enough to establish an artist, while heavy rotation of enough of his or her different songs could almost guarantee the artist's long-term career success. Today, radio is just a shell of its former self, almost irrelevant in its impact on the success of an artist. In fact, airplay on some stations can even be harmful to an artist's credibility, since much of traditional broadcast radio is now so poorly regarded by consumers and true fans.

Radio used to be one of the things they trusted, but now it's transformed into something that music lovers can't even tolerate, so real music fans don't expect FM radio to turn them on to new music like it once did. Therefore, for new artists, radio is moot.

—Derek Sivers, founder
and former CEO of CD Baby

So how has radio gone from Holy Grail to dirty coffee cup? Radio has undergone its own version of technological morphing paralleling that of the music industry. Back in the early days of radio, each station was locally owned and reflected the tastes of the community and region, including the music. Much of the great music from the '50s through the '70s came about as a result of these local tastes; from Philadelphia to Detroit to Memphis to Cleveland to Chicago to Houston to Los Angeles, each region had its own distinct sound.

Another factor in radio's rise was the relative freedom that disc jockeys had, being able to play just about any record that they liked. In the late '60s and '70s, this freedom hit its apex on FM radio, as people tuned in specifically because they trusted the taste of the DJ. You could hear back to back a raga from Ravi Shanker, hard rock from Led Zeppelin, jazz from Miles Davis, and acoustic folk music from Richie Havens. With the air of discovery high and listeners flocking to the major FM stations in each region of the country, your DJ was your personal music guide, who could take you to new musical destinations if you just let him or her.

During this period, FM radio was considered a poor stepchild to AM, because the proliferation of FM radio was just beginning, and its advertising revenues were still relatively low, so large ownership groups generally overlooked the format as a potential source of revenue. But money always follows listeners, and soon FM radio was raking in big advertising dollars, which attracted major players from both Wall Street and Madison Avenue looking for a new income stream. Soon local AM and FM stations were purchased by station groups, and the station groups by conglomerates. In an effort to maximize profits, radio "consultants" were hired to review the stations' playlists and make them more listener friendly. When this happened, the DJ lost all his or her freedom of what to play as the playlists were tightened. The consultants even picked the time when the songs they chose could be played. Since the same consultant was determining the playlists for the entire station group, stations using the same formats were playing the same songs virtually everywhere in the country, regardless of the region. Radio became homogenized and stale.

Worse still was the fact that what had always been a localized media soon became anything but, with some stations turning to automated broadcasting with no live on-air personnel or even local news. Soon came the endless commercial spots from national advertisers, since few local advertisers could now afford the service.

For the listener, radio went from a point of endless music discovery, where listening all night could be considered a reasonable leisure activity, to a sonic clump of audio goo designed to be as inoffensive as possible. In an effort to grow their profits, big corporations turned radio into a supplier of background music, rather than the companion that it used to be.

Prior to the influx of big-money ownership, radio couldn't afford demographic market research, and each station decided what to play by noting the calls from listeners they received or by calling the local music stores to see what customers were buying. Although the possibility of overhyping a particular record existed, this information bore more of a relationship to what the people in the area were actually buying and listening to. Now, because focus-group results take precedence over the preferences of listeners, we have more "turntable hits" than ever before, in which a recording gets massive exposure but no one is willing to purchase it.

Advertisers want to control what's being played around their advertising dollars, and the need to please the advertiser (instead of the listener) is one of the reasons that radio is where it is today. No advertiser is willing to take the risk of being associated with new music when, for the same money, they can be associated with a known quantity. Yet listeners have proven over and over that they are more than happy to embrace something new.

Before cheap data processing came along, calling up a record store and playing what they told you people were buying was a cheap form of market research. Music flourished in that environment. The minute it became a game of attracting the right demographics in a focus group, it was the end of commercial radio playing any music that people were passionate about. I think it's mind boggling that some people are taking this idea seriously.

—Bob Ohlsson, media sage and historian
(and former Motown engineer)

Arbitron ratings between stations continue to be important, but far less so than when there used to be competition between stations as opposed to station groups.

The change has been due to what's called micromarketing. Each chain sets up stations that are each fine-tuned to a particular demographic group in the same market. Then they sell advertisers combinations of those stations that fit the precise marketing profile the advertiser is looking for.

I think this selection process is what dumbs down the music, because in the old days, it was still about selling advertising, only the music played was based largely on local record sales. The musical motivations of the audience have been taken out of the process.

—Bob Ohlsson

COLLEGE RADIO ON THE BRINK

For many years, college radio has been the beacon of hope shining brightly across the wasteland that is commercial radio. As radio has become more and more homogenized, thanks to group ownership and consultant-led playlists, the only place for many indie acts to break has been the local college radio station. But now college radio sadly faces extinction as more and more colleges either close them down or sell them off. This is due to a couple of reasons:

▶ Fewer on-campus listeners. Students just don't listen to radio much anymore, opting to discover their music online. Ironically, studies by the stations themselves have found that most of a college radio's listenership is off campus. That being said, college broadcast courses will remain in place as university radio stations move to the Web, but the traditional college broadcast radio station may soon be gone.

▶ Budgetary shortfalls. Thanks to the recession, college administrators everywhere are faced with the prospect of making cuts, and frequently the first item to get the axe is the radio station, especially if it can be sold off.

Realistically though, college radio had been infiltrated by big business more than a decade ago, after record labels discovered that it was the last bastion of open playlists. That being said, at least the consultants (who are largely responsible for homogenized radio) have been kept out of it, hence the continuing local flavor that each remaining station maintains.

Just like the music business, radio isn't what it once was and probably never will be again. In the end, it might not matter much if college radio ceases to exist, since in many ways it's been gone for while; just not many have noticed.

Broadcast Radio's Decline

Loss of local control

Local stations bought by station groups

The rise of the consultants

Market share loss to Internet and satellite radio

The slow death of college radio

Why Television Is No Longer a Factor

It used to be that an appearance on television could give an act a pretty good sales boost. During the 1970s and '80s heyday of *Saturday Night Live*, an act could count on at least 100,000 unit sales (usually more) the following week of an appearance, and of course MTV made acts into bona fide stars and superstars. For the most part, those days are over.

First of all, SNL's viewership is down. It used to be that it did a 12 rating, but now it might do a 2 or a 3. What that means is that only 2 percent of the households are viewing it, or to put it another way, it's not being viewed by 98 percent of the available households. So there's been some dramatic drops in viewership, and as a result, traditional media becomes a lot less effective.

—Larry Gerbrandt, media analyst and principle in Media Valuation Partners

Today, an appearance on a late-night talk show such as David Letterman's will probably go unnoticed, since the demographic watching is falling off to sleep. A new act might get some small amount of traction on Conan O'Brien or Jimmy Kimmel's show, but probably won't sell many units because of it. Daytime TV can help sales though. An appearance on Oprah can be sales gold, as can an appearance on Ellen DeGeneres's show, but the demographic is narrow (mostly women age 25 to 45), so this type of appearance can't be utilized by every artist.

The Disney Channel and Nickelodeon are the only major star-making venues on the television airwaves today, although they're limited by their demographic as well (kids between the ages of 6 and 14). An act appealing to prepubescents can truly move product, but the time window is small because the audience grows up, which usually makes for short careers. Disney and Nickelodeon sell cute, not art, and there's only room for a few acts.

In the end, television is much like the Internet, with so many vertical avenues that have sucked viewership from the major networks. If you have an eclectic viewing taste, there's probably a channel for you, but there's less and less space for music instead of more. MTV and its sister stations are now more about lifestyle than music, and any music show on an outlying cable network has an already limited viewership (*Live from Abbey Road* on the Sundance channel, for example). The fractured demographic and viewing habits mean that fewer and fewer eyes see music on television, which translates into fewer sales being made.

What's happening is that the numbers for traditional broadcast television are dropping dramatically. In a five hundred channel

universe, viewers simply have a lot of choices, and a lot of the
programming is simply not compelling enough.

—Larry Gerbrandt

Music on Television

Daytime television helps sales more
than nighttime.

Disney and Nickelodeon are the main
outlets for star making these days.

Disney and Nickelodeon sell cute, not talent.

Most music shows have small audiences.

TV appearance no longer ensures a sales bump.

Even Concert Attendance Declines

Regardless of the ups and downs of record sales, one part of the
industry that was always a sure thing in terms of consistent revenue
growth was the concert industry. Even as prices rose year and year,
there seemed to be an insatiable appetite for tickets that could not
seem to be quenched. While ever-rising prices, service charges, and
the general feeling of gouging was tolerated by concert goers during good economic times, when money is tight as it was during
the economic downturn of 2008 through 2010, reality soon creeps
back into the marketplace. Consider the following data collected
by Pollstar magazine, regarded by many to be almost the bible when
it comes to ticket sales:

▶ The revenue of the 50 biggest grossing tours in the world declined
12 percent in 2010. It was even worse in North America, where
sales were down 15 percent.

▶ The number of tickets sold declined 7 percent worldwide and 12
percent in North America.

▶ Yet ticket prices increased by 4 percent, despite last-minute discounting by giant concert promoter Live Nation.

▶ The top 50 acts played 8 percent fewer shows than the year before.

▶ Promoters slashed prices to as low as $10.00 for the Jonas Brothers, Maroon 5, Stevie Winwood and Santana, Creed, and the American Idol tours, among many others.

▶ Concert promoter Live Nation indicated that 10 percent of their tickets were discounted in some fashion. Among the discounting weapons used, four-packs and $10.00 lawn seats were cited as the most aggressive sales drivers.

A number of additional revelations, such as the ticket "convenience" fees actually going to the artists, and the best seats in the house being intentionally sold directly to scalpers at inflated prices, finally caught up with the industry, causing concert goers to stay at home because of the high prices. As a result, many marquee acts had to cancel some shows for lack of sales (The Eagles and Christina Aguilera to name a few), and tickets for major artists began to show up for as little as $10.00 near the day of the show. The promoters are in the business of getting people in the seats, so they'd rather give the tickets away (or at least steeply discount them) to get the parking fees and concession revenue, but that just upsets the people that paid full pop for the ticket, which will make them less likely to buy the next time around.

This was probably a healthy course-correction in the business. As a result, we may see more reasonable pricing, fewer tours by acts that were out the previous year (you can't tour the same places with the same songs every year and expect big sales), and maybe some sanity returning to a business that never had to worry about a recession before.

Concert Attendance Declines

It's the economy, stupid.

The acts get greedy.

Tours and shows are cancelled
due to lack of sales.

Tickets are discounted to fill seats.

The Trouble with Labels

The record label used to be the be-all, end-all to the music business. It was the gatekeeper, the taste maker, the banker, and the sales and publicity engine that the music world revolved around. While on the superstar level all that's still true in M3.0, even though a record label, especially a major label, holds much less influence in virtually all facets of the music industry than ever before.

WHY DIGITAL MUSIC HAS FAILED

When the music industry was at its peak, all of its revenues and projected revenues were based around the album. The retail price for a CD was anywhere from $10.00 to $18.00, which, although the margins were thin at many points of the supply chain, still provided enough of a return to drive industry revenue to new heights. With sales of physical product in double-digit decline year over year, the industry held out hope that revenues of digital product might take the place of the CDs.

According to the IFPI, although a full 50 percent of record label revenues in the US came from digital sales in 2010, total music sales were still down 2.4 percent from the year before, which illustrates the big failing of digital music. You can't take a product that sells for $10.00 to $18.00 and replace it with one that sells for $0.99 and expect the industry to remain healthy. Plus, you can't sell fewer products than you did in the past and expect everyone in the business to remain smiling either.

While digital album sales in the US climbed by 13 percent in 2010, they still weren't enough to offset the decrease in physical sales, which were down by about 65 percent from 2000 according to Nielsen SoundScan. In fact, total album sales (including physical and digital) were down 13 percent from the year before, and overall music sales were down 2.4 percent. So why have album sales failed to catch on in a big way in the digital age?

▶ **It once was a visual experience.** During the vinyl record age, the album form had the advantage of that wonderful piece of cardboard known as the album jacket. The album jacket contained the cover art (still found on CDs), and most importantly, the liner notes on the back, which we'll get to in a second. But one thing that everyone either forgets or has never experienced is the fact that millions of albums were purchased completely on impulse because of the album artwork alone!

It may be hard to believe, but it was quite common to come across an album cover that was so cool that you'd buy it without knowing a thing about the artist. Sometimes it would be a total loser, but you still had the liner notes to read, and occasionally that would still make it a worthwhile purchase.

▶ **It was an informational experience too.** Those too young to have experienced the age of vinyl don't know how much the liner notes meant to nearly everyone who bought an album. You could spend hours reading a well-written gatefold jacket, checking out every credit, wondering just where these exotic studios were, and generally soaking up any info you could about the artist. Of course, this was in a time before the Internet, so the liner notes were sometimes the only place to find any info on the artist at all. To say the least, the visuals and information along with the music made buying an album a total experience that today's album doesn't some close to.

▶ **Too much filler.** Most vinyl albums are between 35 and 45 minutes long. This was out of necessity because of the physics of a record. Make it any longer and it starts to get noisy, the frequency response suffers, and it won't play as loudly. But 40 minutes or so turns out to be the perfect amount of time for listening. There's a time commitment you have to make, but it's well within reason, especially if you like the music.

A CD is capable of containing a bit more than 73 minutes of music. Unfortunately, artists began to think that it was a really good idea to put all the secondary material that they normally would've tossed from a vinyl record, and put it all on their CD. Now instead of having 40 minutes of great music, we had 55 minutes of mediocrity. Even if the artist had some great songs, they were frequently buried under another 50 minutes of filler. Now not only was the fan paying more money, but he or she was paying more money for less quality. Something had to give.

When MP3s came on the scene, the music business was eventually pushed from an album-oriented business into the singles business that it has now become. Ironically, popular music started with as a singles business, to whence it now returns.

IT'S THE MUSIC, STUPID

Overlooked in all this is the effect that the actual music has on consumer buying habits. If consumers can't relate to or identify with the music, they won't buy it. Some industry critics feel that the release of safe music guided by the hand of Madison Avenue (like the boy bands N' Sync and Backstreet Boys) is as much a factor in the decline of music sales as anything else, and indeed, they may have a point.

Instead of making a judgment as to whether or not music is as good as "the old days," there's a better way to describe it—it's just stale. There hasn't been a major trend in about 20 years since grunge hit mainstream, so there's been no new blood to energize the overall music scene. Prior to that, we experienced a new trend every 6 to 13 years from the beginning of recorded music. We're long overdue.

THE DEATH OF ARTIST DEVELOPMENT

The industry has been slow to develop a new generation of artists, instead relying on so-called "heritage" artists such as The Eagles and Madonna for large sales numbers. Since, as mentioned above, grunge was the biggest genre trend in the past 20 years or so, it can be said that the industry is long overdue for something new. But with less artist development than ever before, when will this happen?

Artist development has always been the lifeblood of the industry, even as far back as M1.0. A good example of this is Geffen Records (now owned by the Universal Music Group). To build his label, David Geffen signed three of the biggest stars in the world at the time (1980): Donna Summer, Elton John, and John Lennon. Donna Summers's and Elton John's first albums for Geffen stiffed outright. While John Lennon's was also headed for the dumper, he was unfortunately killed, which caused his entire catalog's sales to spike. It wasn't until the label signed new acts that it truly became successful, with Whitesnake and Guns N' Roses leading the way. As always, if you want to get rich in the music business, you've got to invest in the new.

The nature of artist development has changed through the years, going from being one of patience to that of instant win or lose for the artist. In the music business's so-called glory days of the late '60s and '70s, it was not uncommon for a record label to stay with an artist for three, four, or even five albums (as was the case with megastars David Bowie, Fleetwood Mac, and Tom Petty) as the artist built an audience and eventually broke into the mainstream music consciousness. This is because the most successful labels such as Warner Bros., Atlantic, and Elektra were run by music visionaries instead of large corporations worried about their quarterly bottom lines. As the conglomerates gradually took over the major labels, that patience grew less and less until it reached today's "the first record must be a hit or you're dropped" mentality. Luckily, M3.0 finally provides an alternative to this way of thinking within the corporate music industry.

THE DEATH OF A&R

The job of A&R isn't what it used to be, and looks to be dying even faster than the major record labels. According to former Arista Records A&R man Rich Esra, one of the publishers of the *Music Business Registry,* a quarterly publication that tracks A&R people and provides their contact information, there were only 25 A&R execs hired in 2010, while 40 were let go without a single one of them being rehired. In 2009, there were 58 hired and 51 laid off, and in 2008, there were 80 hired and 60 terminated. Notice a trend?

Rich recently posted the reasons that he thought A&R was dying in the excellent *Digital Music News* newsletter. According to Esra:

1. The major labels are hiring fewer and fewer A&R executives because the volume of acts (and more importantly, the types of acts) being signed have dramatically decreased.

2. The A&R process used to be about the discovery, signing, and nurturing of the act. Today, A&R executives are not looking for talent per se. They are looking for an ongoing business.

An artist who has developed some kind of traction and awareness on his or her own is what I'm talking about. Today, acts need to be "developed," or at least be developing in a business sense, for any label to have even the slightest amount of interest. The idea that today's A&R executives will discover an unknown act/artist and develop that artist is an illusion. They have neither the desire, time, or money, for that matter.

3. This is why from an A&R perspective, only the most generic, ubiquitous type of acts get any attention from labels today. There is only a certain type of act these days that major labels are willing to sign.

We've all heard the stories about the meddling A&R guy who knows nothing, yet demands that an artist change his or her music or direction for reasons known only to him, but the fact of the matter is that there were far more good A&R people employed than bad ones. Someone has to find the next generation of talent just to keep these companies alive, and without A&R, it's more likely than ever that the major labels will die along with the position.

WHERE THE PIRACY ARGUMENT FAILS

Many consumers choose to illegally download pirated copies of legally purchased songs every day. While the industry has long claimed piracy to be a major reason for flagging sales, other factors may loom as large or larger. With iTunes Store purchases at over 10 billion since its inception in 2001, there's no doubt that consumers are choosing to buy the digital music they love. The exact amount that piracy impacts sales has always been debatable, but it certainly existed before digital downloads (especially in M1.5 and M2.0), going back as far as to when recording devices first became commercially available. While piracy's impact cannot be underestimated, it shouldn't be overestimated either:

for many years, the music industry has used piracy as a convenient excuse to cover its many other ills and shortcomings.

> *But what really people forget is that by the end of the '70s, the recorded music business was in deep, deep trouble. There was a recession and a couple of years of downward trends, and a lot of people thought, "This is the end of it." There was a lot of piracy, thanks to the cassette player and that issue of that "Record" button, and people just weren't buying vinyl records anymore. The issue of people making their own copies was a pretty big issue even in those days. People were copying music for free off the radio or from another cassette or record. We reckoned that we were losing at least 25 percent of our business to home taping. So when people talk about "free" today, there's nothing particularly new about it, it's just a different version of the same thing.*
> —Rupert Perry

While music industry sources such as the RIAA and IFPI often float claims that every 9 out of 10, to 19 out of 20, files downloaded are illegal, it's always difficult to know what to make of these statistics. As difficult as it is to get precise numbers on real sales that aren't being reported (anything outside of SoundScan, such as direct downloads or CD sales from a distributor such as Tunecore or CD Baby or off an artist's website, usually isn't taken into consideration), what makes anyone think that the piracy numbers are anything more than a number pulled out of thin air?

Now a study conducted at Carlos III University of Madrid in Spain, in collaboration with scientists at the IMDEA Networks Institute, the University of Oregon (USA), and the Technical University of Darmstadt (Germany), seems to give us a better picture of exactly what's happening in piracyland. The researchers found that illegal file sharers tended to be either organizations such as record labels that put up fake or malware-infected files to discourage piracy (called "fake publishers"), or "top publishers" that earn a profit from advertising and subscription using pirated content as bait.

In the end, the study concluded that "since BitTorrent's popularity is tied to a small group of users who engage in illegal file-sharing for 'economic benefits,' if the same users lost interest or simply disappeared, BitTorrent's traffic would be 'drastically reduced.'"

This suggests that piracy, while still a problem, isn't as bad a problem as we've been lead to believe, and certainly no worse than it's ever been. If that's true, the problems of the music industry surely must lie somewhere else.

The Trouble with Labels

Little artist development

Safe artist signings

No new music trends

Longer time period between trends

Decline in album sales

No replacement format for the CD

Fewer A&R executives, with
limited signing power

Piracy may be only a convenient excuse

THREE

CHAPTER

The New Music Industry

I f you've read the previous chapters, it's evident that the music industry is entering some uncharted waters. There are remnants of the old that will probably always survive, but what we're seeing is a reset from the old way of doing business to a new, still partially undiscovered method. This makes the new music industry both exciting and a little scary at the same time, but only if you've experienced the previous business version. Let's take a look at what the new music industry looks like.

The Music Industry Is Not Dying

. . . .

Despite the doom and gloom that you hear from the many industry pundits, anyone who thinks the music business is really dying is absolutely wrong. It's evolving, morphing, transmuting, adjusting, adapting, reconfiguring, transitioning, and progressing; but it's not in any danger of dying.

Consider these figures:

▶ While it's absolutely true that album sales are down 65 percent from 2000, that still means that 326 million were sold in 2010 in the US alone. That's a lot of music being sold.

▶ 2010 also saw nearly 1.2 billion digital downloads purchased. Again, a huge amount.

▶ Internet radio service Pandora has over 80 million registered users and 30 million active users a month, which is almost one in ten Americans.

▶ As of the beginning of 2010, more than 278,000 artists sell their music at CD Baby, and over 5 million of their CDs have been sold online to customers.

There are still a lot of people out there willing to part with their hard-earned money for the music they love.

For better or worse, more and more people make music than ever before, thanks to powerful yet inexpensive tools that go way beyond what an artist, producer, or engineer could even dream about during the Music 1.0 era. The good part is that if you'd like to make your own music, it's easier than ever. The bad part is that there is more and more mediocre music available than at any other time, mostly because the built-in filters of the A&R departments of the record labels are extremely diminished in their clout or just bypassed completely.

Although consumers' listening habits have changed dramatically, there's proof everywhere that they're still willing to pay for music they like, as evidenced by British singer Adele, who sold over a million units of her album 21 in less than a month in the UK—an accomplishment, considering that the UK's population is only 1/5 as large as that of the US. This shows that people are willing to pay for quality music; they just haven't seen or heard enough of it in a while to get really excited with their pocketbooks in the numbers they used to. And there's lots of competition for those dollars and the listener's attention than ever before. If anything, music has to be better than ever to compete.

Remember, the music industry only dies when people stop listening. See any evidence of that lately?

The Music Industry Isn't Dying

Huge numbers of CDs are still sold.

More people than ever before listen to music.

More people than ever before make music.

People are always willing to pay for quality music.

The New Radio

As outlined in chapter 2, traditional radio has gone from being a cultural juggernaut to almost a media has-been, but new flavors of radio have significantly energized the medium to the point of rebirth. Let's look at some of the ways today's radio listeners consume its product.

INTERNET RADIO

Radio is said to have gone through its own version of M3.0, with Radio 1.0 being the early, startup days of AM, R1.5 being the age of the Top 40 formats of the '60s and '70s, R2.0 being the rise of FM, R2.5 being the rise of talk radio, and R3.0 being the era of Internet Radio. You can say that we've entered into R3.1 as Internet Radio has matured and now moves into the car.

Internet radio has risen in popularity quickly as a whole new set of online-only virtual stations have appeared along with Internet counterparts of many of the terrestrial stations as well. In fact, Internet radio has radically changed our listening habits, according to Arbitron/Edison Research, a leader in media opinion and marketing research used by the radio industry. In their *Infinite Dial 2010* report, they state:

▶ Approximately 70 million people a month listen to radio online
▶ 52 percent of all radio listeners have listened to radio online
▶ 23 percent listen to Internet radio while working
▶ They listen to Internet radio because of the control and variety it provides
▶ Pandora is the clear leader in top-of-the-mind awareness at 28 percent

The report has some interesting demographic material as well:

▶ The online audience skews 55 percent male
▶ Nearly two-thirds of the audience is between the ages of 25 and 54
▶ Online radio attracts an upscale, well-educated and employed audience, with 55 percent having a college degree and 61 percent employed
▶ 30 percent of 12 to 25-year olds are interested in listening to Internet radio in their cars or on their cell phones
▶ 27 percent of all listeners are interested in listening to online radio in their cars (a point that we'll cover in depth later)

Most independent Internet radio stations differ from their terrestrial cousins in that they utilize the vertical nature of the Internet to provide very specific targeted programming to their listeners. But while terrestrial stations have a sales staff with a host of customers used to advertising, their independent Internet counterparts require a different business model to survive, as they are relegated to traditional Internet sales support, such as banner and contextual ads, paid search, and pay per click, if they don't utilize on-air advertising.

Pandora, MOG, Slacker and similar services are successful because they solve the filter problem. You program your own music channel, and your choices are analyzed and some additional recommendations given. This is the antithesis of traditional broadcasting, where the programming choice is made for you via consultants, focus groups, advertiser requirements, or in the good old days, by the DJ himself. It's also one of the reasons why these services will continue to gain support, as the various services try to outdo one another with better recommendations.

One of the biggest problems for Internet radio is the issue of performance fees, which broadcast radio does not pay (although this might change soon). Currently, an Internet radio station pays on a sliding scale, depending on the type of station and number of listeners, but the rates gradually rise each year until 2015, jeopardizing one of the truly great resources to new artists. As the cost of doing business for Internet radio rises, many stations will have to resort to the advertiser-supported model of their terrestrial cousins to survive. This also brings with it the same problems that their terrestrial counterparts now endure, meaning outside pressure on the makeup of their playlist. The bottom line remains that the fans are out of the loop in advertising-supported entertainment, other than their passing interests in something like chart statistics.

In the end, technology doesn't change the lessons of broadcast history or the fact that there is always intense competition for advertising dollars. There is very little difference between electronic distribution and broadcasting once you peel away all of the hype.

THE CONNECTED CAR

The real revolution in radio is the connected car, and that journey is only just beginning. With WiFi or 3G (and soon 4G) becoming more and more available, any Internet radio station is capable of being streamed or cached. With Pandora and MOG the current heavy hitters, new apps such as iHeartRadio and iKillRadio may change the driving experience forever. How? Until the recent introduction of satellite radio, listening to radio in a car was a geographic experience, since you were limited to the local stations around you. With the connected car, this limitation is breached for good, as you can now access any station from any spot in the world. You can access any format, music genre, or personality that you desire.

Already auto manufacturers are racing to add Internet radio capabilities into their cars. Ford, Mercedes, Toyota, and Hyundai are offering Pandora connectivity on certain models; MOG is available on the Mini Cooper; and Toyota is offering ClearChannel's iHeartRadio, which simulcasts 750 of the network's major stations. Indeed, the race is clearly on to capture this huge audience, with the prize goal of 70 to 80 percent of in-car listeners for one lucky service.

But could the advance of Internet radio be the last nail in the coffin of local radio? Already suffering from corporate homogenization, local radio has been severely criticized in recent years for not attending to the needs of its immediate community. It is not local enough. With its listener base further fractured by yet more choices for the listening consumers, Internet Radio could either be a death blow or a new beginning, as corporations decide that radio is no longer a contributor to their bottom line and sell the stations back to the locals. It could be one situation where more diversity actually leads to greater listener selection.

SATELLITE RADIO

Satellite broadcasting was once thought to be the next revolution in radio, and while providing a superior listening experience to the consumer in many ways, it has run into many more snags than expected. The two original competing services, XM and Sirius, have merged in the face of staggering startup costs and overhead, and while the subscriber base of the new company is a healthy 20 million listeners as of the writing of this book, program licensing costs with the NFL, MLB, and especially the latest $80 million per year deal with shock-jock Howard Stern continue to be a huge impediment to profitability.

But despite these large cost burdens, Sirius XM provides programming unlike any found on terrestrial radio, with more than 180 digital channels coast to coast, including 71 commercial-free music channels and original music and talk channels created by the company's XM original programming unit and by leading brand-name content providers such as Martha Stewart, Oprah, John Madden, and Bob Dylan. Sirius XM is now available in over 200 car models (cars being the main target of the service), and with car sales inching up at the time of this writing, Sirius XM projects to add 1.4 million users a year to its subscriber base.

Some wonder whether Sirius XM can survive despite its die-hard following, since the eventual replacement of its satellites will require a large influx of cash that the marketplace seemingly can't support. This calls into question the subscription model for programming versus the age-old advertising model, which, as we've seen, eventually leads to controlled playlists. And while Sirius XM has solved the problem of endless radio commercials, it still hasn't solved the problem that many of their stations sound just as much like the dreaded terrestrial ones, just without the ads.

WHAT IS RADIO'S FUTURE?

While we can easily see what radio is like today, it's much more difficult to look into a crystal ball at its future, but a study by Edison Research called "The American Youth Study 2010," which examined the media and technology habits of 12-to-24-year-olds in the US, may give us some insight as to what to expect. The first part of the study looked at the music discovery and consumption habits of this group and produced some significant findings:

▶ 12-to-24-year-old Americans use the Internet roughly 2 hours and 52 minutes per day, which is triple this age group's reported usage from 2000 (59 minutes).

▶ Surprisingly, radio continues to be the medium most often used for music discovery, with 51 percent of 12-to-24-year-olds reporting that they "frequently" find out about new music by listening to the radio. Other significant sources include friends (46 percent), YouTube (31 percent) and social networking sites (16 percent).

▶ 20 percent of 12-to-24-year-olds had listened to Pandora during the last month of the study, with 13 percent indicating usage in the last week of the survey. By comparison, 6 percent of 12 to 24s indicated they had listened to online streams from terrestrial AM/FM stations in the last week of the survey.

▶ Music tastes have shifted among 12 to 24s over the past decade. Radio listeners who indicated that Top 40/pop stations were their favorite have more than doubled, while alternative rock stations were selected by only half as many listeners in 2010 as in 2000.

▶ Today's 22 to 34s have significantly changed their media consumption habits since the first study in this series ten years ago. In 2000, 44 percent of 12 to 24s most often began their day by listening to the radio. Today, radio continues to lead, but with 29 percent of the same age group reporting that radio is the medium they use most in the morning, while television (25 percent) and the Internet (23 percent) have gained significantly.

Providing that none of this data is skewed (no guarantee there), radio is currently listened to more, and has a greater influence, than anyone thought. Not only that, the type of music being listened to by the group (Top 40) is certainly a surprise. While it may be true that local radio is on the serious decline, and Internet may be its future, good old-fashioned terrestrial radio has some life left in it yet.

The New Radio

Internet radio has energized the medium.

The connected car is the next revolution.

Local radio is on the brink as a result.

Satellite radio is holding its own, but its prospects look shaky.

People still discover music via the radio.

The New Television

As with just about all media, television is in the middle of a huge transition. Where cable television dominated for the last 30 years with one of the most desirable business models of any business, that subscription business is showing signs of deterioration as more and more video is being consumed online. Indeed, some of that content may be restricted in the future in an effort to stop the cannibalization of the broadcast audience, and to keep the connected viewers from "cutting the cord" by dropping their cable service and viewing strictly online.

THE EFFECT OF YOUTUBE

In many ways, YouTube can be considered the new television. Consider the following numbers for 2010:

▶ 2 billion videos are watched per day on YouTube.

▶ 35 hours of video are uploaded to YouTube every minute.

▶ 186 online videos are watched by the average Internet user in a month (USA).

▶ 84 percent of Internet users view videos online (USA).

▶ 14 percent of Internet users have uploaded videos online (USA).

▶ People now consume more music by watching it than any other means. 57 percent have watched music videos on computers in the last three months from sites such as YouTube.

As far as music is concerned, YouTube has become a major music discovery site. Although YouTube Music accounts for only 31 percent of the site's 1.2 billion total visits per month, at 378,900,000 visits, it's by far the largest slice of the pie. Another music-video hub, Vevo, garnered 3.8 million visits in December 2010, a 211 percent growth on the year, but not even in the same ballpark as YouTube.

Music video as a whole has become a primary means of music consumption. According to a 2011 Nielsen Music report entitled "Digital Music Consumption and Total Access", 57 percent of consumers worldwide regularly watch music videos on the computer and 23 percent on their mobile phones. Considering that former number is higher than the 48 percent that have downloaded a song from the Internet without paying for it, the music video has become a major mover and shaker in the music world.

THE BROADCAST ALTERNATIVES

Traditional over-the-air or cable television is taking a hit from alternative forms of television consumption such as NetFlix and Hulu. With DVD sales declining even more quickly than CD sales, there's now a 61 percent chance that any given legal movie stream or download comes from NetFlix, thanks to its inclusion in newer television and set-top boxes. In fact, Netflix subscribers can stream videos to practically every popular device currently available, including iOS devices, Android devices, Roku boxes, Apple TVs, Xbox 360s, and more. And with a library of over 120,000 movies and television shows, it has quickly become the service of choice of many consumers.

With 30 million monthly users that access over 260 million content streams as of the end of 2010, Hulu is already big, but it looks like it will get even bigger in the coming years. Hulu boasts 627 advertisers and 250 content partners as of the writing of this book, which represents meteoric growth over the last three years. When the site launched, it had only 2 content partners and a dozen advertisers.

What does the change in television have to do with music? Where once upon a time, a performance on television could insure a boost of sales and some new fans, that's not the case any longer, as television becomes just as fragmented and stratified as music. Indeed, a performance on a late-night television show is for fans only (if that), resulting in few new fans and a negligible sales bump. And with the new on-demand nature of television instead of the "television by appointment" of the past, a television appearance or show underscore can no longer be counted on to be fresh and up to date.

THE CONNECTED TV

With most major consumer electronics manufacturers now offering some sort of connected TV, watching videos is no longer relegated to the computer. What is a connected television? It's a TV that connects directly to the Internet like a computer, allowing the viewer to access content from YouTube, Hulu, NetFlix, Amazon or any other video distributor so you can watch it on that big 55-inch screen instead of your 15-inch laptop.

But the connected TV means much more—potentially. It now lends itself to true interactivity, allowing the viewer to discover information on the characters, actors, and back story, and even socially connect with friends and other viewers in real time. Until now, you'd need a computer or tablet to be able to do at least some of that (known in the industry as "the second screen").

The connected TV is also a new means for marketing and sales, allowing you to buy products as you see them onscreen, respond instantly to discount offers, and even browse while watching a program. The new tablet computers also open up new avenues of viewership as the screens are optimized for video. In fact, in the future the kids may prefer iPads to televisions in their rooms. They're more personal.

While sales of connected televisions to date have been primarily of customer unfamiliarity, connection confusion, and customer support, they're clearly the wave of the future. With them opens a wide range of creative, marketing, and sales opportunities to the M3.0 musician.

The New Television

The future television viewer will be increasingly connected.

YouTube is the new television in many ways.

YouTube is now a major music consumption and discovery site.

Television performances no longer add fans or sell product.

The New Players

Control of the music industry has slowly drifted from the power days of the record label executive to the new power base of today—management and the promoter. That said, a new generation of record label entrepreneurs could someday change that balance.

MANAGEMENT

Managers of talent have always been powerful (especially with a big-selling act in the stable) and have, for the most part, stayed behind the scenes. After all, it's the acts that should have the most attention. But as the music industry transitions into Music 3.0, managers are more powerful, and more needed, than ever. The reason is that the fortunes of the manager are directly tied to the act. If the act makes money, so does the manager; if the act tanks, the manager starves. As a result, the manager has to truly believe in the act and represent it with a passion. The manager's singular vision must be to make that act successful. Any other member of the artist or group's team, from producer to attorney to record label to publicist and so on, will not have his or her fortunes tied so directly to the artist's success, and, as a result, his or her passion can't be expected to ever be as high. With most service contractors that an artist employs, you can never be sure where their loyalty actually lies. Is it with the record label, distributor or promoter, or the artist? With a manager, the answer to that question should never be in doubt.

So why has the manager's role become more profound in M3.0? Because as the choices for the artist have expanded, so has the manager's influence. In M1.0 through 2.5, the manager's main focus was on dealing with the record label and getting the act booked. The label was the 800-pound gorilla in the room, and the manager was the keeper. With the record label's influence now decreased to that of a chimpanzee, the manager has ascended to become the giant in the act's life. As we'll see in later chapters, there are far more possibilities for every aspect of the act, and that means far more decisions are required.

An interesting trend is that management is now adapting to M3.0, bringing multiple talents in-house for instant access and attention by the artist. These talents include concert promotion, Internet promotion, dedicated social networking, the handling of street teams, and where it's legal, even acting as a booking agent.

Not every artist is able to connect with forward-thinking management of this type, or even any kind of organized management, but that's okay. Personal management is ineffective unless the manager is passionate about you, since passion can overcome inexperience. Passion is something that you can't buy or contract—the manager has to truly believe in you or you're wasting your time. And as the act gets bigger, it's easier for a less powerful manager to plug into a larger management company and "four-wall," or get the best of both worlds: the power of the larger management company with the attention of the smaller.

THE PROMOTER

The second most powerful entity in M3.0 is the promoter. Regardless of whether he or she is booking a coffee house on a community-college campus or a 10,000-seat arena, the promoter is needed to keep the act doing what it should do best, which is playing in front of people. Promoters have always been important, since despite what you might think, most artists have always derived the majority of their income from touring rather than from record sales. In M3.0, promoters are an even more crucial link in the chain than before. No longer do acts tour to promote their records as they once did in M1.0 to M2.5. In M3.0, the record promotes the tour and is often relegated to being an additional piece of swag for the onsite vendors to sell. In M3.0, it's more important than ever that the artist's tour be successful, and the promoter's influence has risen appreciably as a result.

It used to be that promoters relied on SoundScan numbers to determine the ticket-selling potential of the act. These days, they could care less where a record sits on the charts, because ticket sales are the only figures that matter. In the promoter's M3.0 world, success begets success. If you sell tickets in one region or venue, a promoter in another is more likely to work with you than if you have a release in the current Number 1 chart spot.

Thanks to changing tastes and leaner economic times, the promoters' general approach to talent has changed. Back in the M1.0 to M2.5 days, the promoter was willing to lose money on an act on its way up in the clubs in order to reap the rewards in the arena later. Unfortunately, there's little of that these days, since there are fewer indie and regional promoters than ever before, having been rolled up in numerous industry consolidations into what has become the Live Nation and AEG behemoths. As a result, most of the middle- and upper-tier promoters are large corporations with deep pockets (sound familiar?), which leaves the smaller indie promoter unable to roll the dice on an act in fear of losing money. While a promoter might take a chance in the past in the hopes of gaining some loyalty from the artist, this scenario has become less and less likely.

That being said, today's promoter is more willing to think outside the box. Paperless tickets (which are hated by some and declared the future by others), multitiered pricing, and coupons and promotion tie-ins to other entertainment such as restaurants are all the things that the promoter is now willing to try.

But promoters still hold the keys to a successful career for an artist. Financially successful recorded music is very much a reflection of people's experiences in enjoying live music. The more they experience it, the more they are likely to buy it. The promoter is an integral part of that success.

THE NEW RECORD LABEL

Record labels both large and small are transforming before our very eyes in order to adapt to the new music-buying audience. Where once the record label was the gatekeeper to talent and a filter that separated the worthy from the worthless for the masses, today's label is in many ways struggling to find its way in the M3.0 world.

While major labels are excellent at exposing and exploiting mainstream-oriented acts, they're no longer in the business of much else. And as outlined before, talent development and A&R have largely fallen by the wayside. The problem is that it's a numbers game, and the numbers are no longer on the side of the majors. If only one out of ten acts makes money, but only makes 1/10 of what it made during the good old days, that's not much of a value proposition.

The new record label is no different from the record label of the '50s in spirit. It's built by people who love music and are more concerned with exposing talent than making money. Their overhead is low, the execs don't draw hefty salaries (or any salary at all in many cases), and they're willing to keep putting out releases by artists they love regardless of the sales figures.

Their marketing consists of mostly social media and online promotion because that's all they can afford, and that's all their audience responds to. And they're willing to try different approaches. Labels such as Kill/Hurt, Not For Fun, Bridgetown Records, and Burger Records print limited runs of cassettes and vinyl, two formats long ago given up for dead, and they not only stay alive but manage to grow.

The major labels of tomorrow are the indie labels that are a mere blip on the radar screen of the industry today, and those labels wedded to the past will be engulfed by it.

The New Players

Managers have more power and influence than ever.

Management has brought many traditional artist services in-house.

To a promoter, only ticket sales, not chart sales, matter.

Promoters are less willing to take a chance on a new act.

Record-company influence has decreased.

The new indie labels are more concerned about music than money.

And they're willing to think outside the box.

The New Audience

Today's audience is a stratified vortex of special tastes and ultratargeted desires. Regardless of whether your taste lies in electronic Bantu music or alien space music, if it's out there you can find it. But finding the music that moves you is both the key and the dilemma.

> *I see more and more niche markets finding more coherent audiences. You can be into Hungarian Death Metal or Central Canadian Bluegrass and easily fill your iPod with songs of that particular genre, then in your spare time you can read blogs pertaining to only that subject.*
> —Bruce Houghton

One of the main attributes of the new M3.0 audience is how it likes to receive and play the music it loves. More and more of the current audience chooses to listen to its music in a streaming or downloadable digital format such as MP3 or Apple's AAC. With more than 1.1 billion digital downloads purchased in 2010, digital music has become a major distribution method, although the growth has slowed to just 1 percent year over year, and industry analysts such as Forrester Research predict sales will completely level off by 2015. Still, digital music has caused listening and buying habits to change.

> *They've changed because they can't be spoon-fed anymore and they can't really be sold or persuaded as much as before. Because they have endless selection, they only receive and act on recommendations from trusted sources, usually friends.*
>
> —Derek Sivers

The new digital demographic has become a consumer of the single song (or "single"), opting for buying only 1 or 2 known and liked songs, as compared to the 10 or 12 normally found on an album. While full-length albums were the cash cow of the industry until M2.5, the M3.0 buyer has returned to the habits of the '50s, when the single was the main point of interest. The M3.0 consumer still wants to discover new music and is willing to sample songs from any of the music distribution or discovery sites, but he or she is no longer compelled or required to purchase an album that has only 1 or 2 good songs on it. As a result, according to Nielsen SoundScan, both physical and album sales in 2010 fell 13 percent from the previous year, a trend that began in 2002.

The new audience also has many more entertainment choices than ever before, and it's only natural that music is going to suffer for it, just as network television has suffered in the face of the expanded cable universe. Facebook, videogames, YouTube, and a host of other on- and offline activities now occupy the time that used to be reserved for listening to music.

The tastes of the new audience are different from their predecessors as well. A shorter attention span and proficiency in multitasking has taken its toll on the album. While in the late '60s and the '70s (M1.0 and M1.5) an album release would be an event (usually followed by a listen front to back without a break), that rarely happens in M3.0. The M3.0 audience wants to taste a little from everywhere rather than take a long sip of just one drink.

The New Audience

Singles are more important than an album.

Album filler material is rejected.

The audience has a shorter music attention span.

Ultratargeted demographics are developed.

Stratified tastes arise.

There are more entertainment choices than ever.

Enter Music 3.0

. . . .

Music 3.0 is the natural evolution of the music business. It allows the artist to take into account the current deficiencies of the business entities of M2.5 and provides the ability to bypass them completely in the course of building an audience and career, until those entities can be used to the artist's advantage. In M3.0, there is only the artist and the fan, with no one in between. Assuming that the artist creates music that can capture an audience in the first place (however small it might be), the opportunity to build an audience is more available than ever before, providing that the artist has the skills to take advantage of M3.0. Let's take a closer look at M3.0 and the best way to develop those skills.

FOUR

CHAPTER

The New Masters
of the Domain

To understand Music 3.0, you have to understand its major influencers. M3.0 (and beyond) is shaped by the following men and the concepts they bring, so it's important to grasp the significance of their contributions. They set the guidelines for the future of music and the way the artist interacts with it.

Seth Godin's Tribes

Seth Godin has been one of the most influential voices in marketing for some time now. He has written 12 bestselling books on marketing, and his marketing blog (sethgodin.typepad.com) is one of the most read on the Internet. His most significant contribution in terms of M3.0 comes from his book *Tribes: We Need You to Lead Us. Tribes* illustrates a concept that is at the core of M3.0, which is that an artist's fan base is his "tribe," and the artist is the tribal leader.

A tribe, in the context of M3.0, is a group of people who are passionate about the music of an artist (although it could be about an entire genre or subgenre of music too). The artist is the most passionate (since she's the creator) and is therefore the leader. What the tribe craves most is communication and direction.

A tribe can have a large number of members or be very small, but it must have at least three members to exist. It's different from a typical fan base, special-interest group, or community, in terms of the intense passion it presents. A fan base usually has one thing, such as a person or product (or both when it comes to music), that draws people to the group, while a special-interest group is built around a shared interest or value, such as C++ programming or voluntourism. A community involves a special-interest group that has some form of group communication, such as a newsletter or a phone call, to keep the members informed. Thanks to email, blogs, chat, and Twitter, these groups become a tribe when its members gain the ability to interact with each another and a leader comes forward.

Some leaders create the tribe, while some tribes find their leader. The leader sets the direction and facilitates a way for tribe members to interface with each other.

How is a tribe different from a brand? A brand is a promise of quality and consistency. No matter where in the world you go for a McDonald's hamburger, you know what to expect. No matter what product you purchase from Apple, you can expect sleek high-tech design and an easy-to-understand user interface. Brand management is protecting the image of the brand and carefully selecting how to best exploit it. Tribal management looks at a brand in a different light.

Whether the tribe is a brand, a person, a service, or music, people want to interact with other people, not with a company or the "brand" itself. If someone in the Killers' Brandon Flowers's tribe hears from Island Records in company-speak rather than from Brandon directly, that satisfies no one and defeats the principle of the tribe. Now if a real person who happens to work for Island interacts with the tribe, that can work. The tribe wants a story to tell and something to discuss, but only if it comes from another tribe member. Or if Brandon's assistant communicates with the tribe on behalf of Brandon, that can work as well. The idea in M3.0 is to feed and grow the tribe and not the brand. You don't look for a customer to sell music to; you look to provide music that the tribe will want. The M3.0 artist should be aware that people will form a tribe with or without him or her (if he or she is popular enough already); the idea for the artist is to be a part of the tribe to make it better.

Here's how a tribe works in M3.0. Let's assume that you're a big fan of singer/songwriter Tori Amos. As a member of her tribe, what you want most (besides her music) is communication directly from Tori herself. If she's touring near where you live, you want an email from her asking you to come to the show. If she's planning to record a cover song on her next album, you want her to ask you for suggestions (see the two-way communication?). If she's coming out with a limited box set, you'd love to hear from her about the chance to buy it before anyone else can. Maybe Tori is trying to raise some money to record her next album and asks you to prebuy a copy. If you're a big fan, you might buy five just to make sure that the album comes out in a timely fashion.

But being the leader of a tribe takes a lot of work and some expertise. Many artists justifiably prefer to spend their time making music, or maybe they just can't get their arms around the tech portion of the job. Some artists are afraid of interaction with fans on such an electronically intimate basis. That's why an external tribal management source is so important. This is what a record company should be doing in M3.0: either helping to manage or directly managing the tribes of their artists. (A few third-party companies do this already; see the interview with Jacob Tell of Oniracom in the interviews section of the book).

There are other companies out there who offer services to the independent artist. I'm aware of at least one very good one who we like a lot. You might think that we look at a company like that and think, "Oh, my God. They're the enemy. How can we kill them," but it's not like that at all. In at least this one case, we're actually very friendly with their CEO and we look for opportunities to work together. They lean towards more of

an indie market, but we think that's just what those guys need.
There's no doubt that we can, and should, help each other.
—Howard Soroka, Vice-President of Media Technologies,
Universal Music Group

While we're illustrating a tribe in the context of music, remember that brands, products, services, and even experiences can all have tribes. For instance, Disney, Virgin, and Apple Computer are brands that have their own tribes, while services such as Greenpeace and Wikipedia do too. Products such as Kleenex, Sharpie pens, and Harry Potter have tribes, while leaders such as Al Gore, Nelson Mandela, and Barack Obama have founded tribes that have a much larger impact than the individual himself.

Perhaps the best illustration of the ultimate leader of a tribe is an example that we'll get to in a little bit—Trent Reznor of the group Nine Inch Nails.

A Tribe

A tribe is group of people passionate about the music, the artist, or both.

The artist is the leader.

Members crave interaction with the leader and each other.

Radiohead's Grand Experiment

On October 1, 2007, the highly respected British alternative-rock band Radiohead announced that its seventh album, entitled *In Rainbows*, would be released in ten days (see Fig. 4.2). Normally, an album-release announcement wouldn't be anything special; it's been happening somewhere almost every day for the past 70 years or so. But *In Rainbows* was different in that it was to be available only as a digital download, and the band would allow its customers to pay whatever amount they liked. While it's still unknown whether this strategy was part of a grand master plan or was just a simple salute to the band's fan base, the move paid off handsomely as a public-relations coup, with press from all over the world running with the story, and the album and band receiving much notice within the music industry. In the ten days running up to the album's release, Radiohead reportedly received 1.2 million pre-pays for the album (the band's management never released the official figures). Little did they know at the time that this would be a much heralded and studied test case.

Radiohead's
In Rainbows

With a Website that stated "It's up to you" in the payment box, the *In Rainbows* experiment yielded some interesting statistics. According to the Internet marketing-research company comScore, 62 percent of the album's buyers in their focus group did not pay a single cent for the album. In other words, they downloaded it for nothing! Four percent of the band's fans paid between $12.00 and $20.00 (about the retail cost of a CD), while 12 percent paid between $8.00 and $12.00, which comScore determined to make up 52 percent of the band's profits.

In the end, those that paid forked over an average of $6.00, with the buyers from the United States paying about $8.05 per purchase and those from the United Kingdom paying about $4.64. According to comScore senior analyst Andrew Lipsman, Radiohead was estimated to have made a profit regardless of whether they intended to or not. "If [Radiohead] is getting $6.00 on average, and it's basically going straight into their pockets and their costs are minimal, it could be economically viable," Lipsman told *E! Online.* The band needed to make about $1.50 per download to break even, he estimated, so at $6.00 per buyer, the group seems to have made out pretty well.

But having the fans decide the amount they wished to pay accomplished something else that was perhaps more important. By giving In Rainbows away, Radiohead actually strengthened the sales of the CD when it was released later that year. Going directly to Number One on both the US's Billboard 200 and the UK Album Chart, the disc box set (including a second disc and a hardcover book of artwork) went on to sell more than 3 million units worldwide.

By allowing the customer to set the price, Radiohead exercised what was then a new business theory called "The Economics of Free" (or EoF). In M3.0, EoF encourages content owners to give some of their products away for free, because if done correctly, you can increase your market size greatly, as seen in the case of *In Rainbows.* Both Franz Ferdinand and Arctic Monkeys are rumored to have unofficially leaked their initial releases for just the same reason, with great results.

You can't just start giving away your precious content without thought though. It has to be the center of a larger marketing plan. In terms of M3.0, an EoF campaign means the following:

▶ You, the artist, have two types of products: infinite products and scarce products. Infinite products would be your music, especially in digital form. Physical products such as CDs don't fit in here, because it actually costs you money to produce them (the CDs, not the music on them). Digital music is easy to copy and steal, and just as easy to give away.

▶ Scarce products are tickets to live shows, access to musicians, signed merchandise, backstage passes, private concerts, custom CDs, CD box sets, time spent with you, writing a song for a fan willing to pay for it, and anything else that has a limited supply.

So to take advantage of the Economics of Free, the artist must do the following:

1. Set the infinite products (or just some of them) free. Put them on a Torrent site, Facebook, YouTube, and anywhere you can. The more you get it out there, the greater the publicity and the wider the visibility. This makes the scarce products more valuable.

2. Because of the free infinite products, you can now charge more for the scarce products. Before number 1 is implemented, access to the artist or backstage passes might not be worth anything, but now they are. Before number 1, maybe no one wanted your CDs or vinyl albums, but now they're valuable as a collector's item, as are the box sets.

Setting your infinite products (your music) free expands your tribe. As your tribe expands, the demand for your scarce products grows. In M3.0, an artist that sticks to the ways of M1.0 through 2.5 will be relegated to a small audience forever.

The EoF theory is perfectly illustrated by Trent Reznor and NIN, the next example in this chapter. Radiohead and *In Rainbows* took the concept one step further by giving it away for free but asking their fans if they'd like to pay for it, and many did. It's interesting to note that the band did not return to the pay-what-you-want method on the next album, *King of Limbs*, instead employing a multitiered pay product offering like we'll look at next.

The Economics of Free

Give away infinite products (digital music).

Sell scarce products (CDs, merch, tickets, and so on).

Giving a product away can increase market size.

Giving away infinite products makes scarce products more valuable.

You can now charge more for scarce products.

The Wisdom of Trent

· ·

Taking the Radiohead pay-what-you-want experiment one step further, and totally taking advantage of his relationship with his tribe, was Trent Reznor and his Nine Inch Nails project *Ghosts I--IV* (see Fig. 4.4). After splitting from Universal Records' Interscope imprint in 2007, Trent decided to take advantage of his passionate fan base and the new online consumerism with his first release that was post-major label.

Having an innate feel for dealing with his tribe even before the theory was articulated in Seth Godin's book, Reznor modeled his first release after the Radiohead experiment, with two important exceptions: he would give away some of the new album *Ghosts I--IV* for free, and he would provide products of the same release at different price points ranging from $5.00 to $2,500.

Ghosts I—IV Cover

FREE DOWNLOAD includes the following:
The first nine tracks of the album.
DRM-free MP3s encoded at 320 kbps.
A 40-page PDF book covering the album.
A digital extras pack with wallpapers, icons, and other graphics.

$5 DOWNLOAD includes the following:
320 kbps encoded MP3 files.
FLAC lossless files.
Apple lossless files.
A 40-page PDF book covering the album.
A digital extras pack with wallpapers, icons, and other graphics.

$10 2-CD SET includes the following:
2 CDs in a six-panel digipak with a 16-page booklet.
320 kbps encoded MP3 files.
FLAC lossless files.
Apple lossless files.
A 40-page PDF book covering the album.
A digital extras pack with wallpapers, icons, and other graphics.

$75 DELUXE EDITION includes the following:
A large fabric slipcase containing two embossed, fabric-bound hardcover books.

Book 1 contains
Ghosts I—IV on two audio CDs.
A data DVD that can be read by Mac and Windows computers containing multitrack sessions for all 36 tracks in WAV-file format allowing easy remix.
A Blu-ray disc containing the stereo mixes of *Ghosts* in 96 kHz, 24-bit audio, plus an exclusive slide show that plays with the music.

Book 2 contains
48 pages of photographs by Philip Graybill and Rob Sheridan.
320 kpbs encoded MP3 files.
FLAC lossless files.
Apple lossless files.
A 40-page PDF book covering the album.
A digital extras pack with wallpapers, icons, and other graphics.

$300 LIMITED EDITION includes the following:
A 4-LP set of *Ghosts I—IV* on 180-gram vinyl in a fabric slipcase. Only available in the Limited Edition Package.
A large fabric slipcase containing three embossed, fabric-bound hardcover books:

Book 1 contains
Ghosts I—IV on two audio CDs.
A data DVD that can be read by Mac and Windows computers containing multitrack sessions for all
    36 tracks in WAV-file format allowing easy remix.
A Blu-ray disc containing the stereo mixes of *Ghosts* in 96 kHz, 24-bit audio, plus an exclusive slide
    show that plays with the music.

Book 2 contains
48 pages of photographs by Philip Graybill and Rob Sheridan.
320 kpbs encoded MP3 files.
FLAC lossless files.
Apple lossless files.
A 40-page PDF book covering the album.
A digital extras pack with wallpapers, icons, and other graphics.

Book 3 contains
Two exclusive Giclee art prints of imagery from *Ghosts I—IV*.
These can be displayed in the book or removed for framing.
Only available in the Limited Edition package.

Each Limited Edition package is numbered and personally signed by Trent Reznor.

The release was a smashing success, as the NIN servers were knocked offline with the massive interest in the project. The $300.00 limited-edition package completely sold out of its 2,500 unit run as Reznor transacted nearly 800,000 total units within the first week. A grand total of $0 was spent on the marketing of the record, since Reznor announced it only on his blog. Even more impressive was the fact that *Ghosts* was an instrumental album!

By year end, *Ghosts* became the best-selling album on Amazon's MP3 Store and was nominated for two Grammy Awards.

In an attempt to move beyond the industry's old pricing model of one product, one price, this is a perfect example of giving something of value for free (in this case, a free nine-song download) in order to make the music easily accessible to fans and as a sample for potential fans. The massive publicity generated, plus the multiple price points, meant that there was something for every economic and interest level.

It also proved that fans are willing to support artists they really care about even if their music is offered at no cost.

Ghosts was licensed under a Creative Commons Attribution Non-Commercial Share Alike license that allows noncommercial redistribution. Creative Commons provides easy and effective ways to publish your content without abandoning all rights to its use—free distribution might be allowed, for instance, but only as long as the author is attributed and the distribution is noncommercial. For more information go to creativecommons.net.

Besides the sales, Reznor gained something else equally valuable with each transaction: email addresses. This allowed him to expand his tribe by simply reaching out to them personally, an act seen as unusually generous by most casual fans.

Another artist who has used the multitiered product offerings with great success is Josh Freese, who uses the tactic with an interesting and amusing twist. Freese, a Los Angeles-based drummer for Devo, Perfect Circle, and others (including Guns N' Roses), doesn't have the high visibility of an artist like Reznor, but makes up for it with a huge dose of humor, which becomes a marketing tool in itself.

Here are some of the package offerings for his *My New Friends* EP (taken from his website at joshfreese.com).

$5
Digital Download

$12
CD of *My New Friends*
$50
CD of *My New Friends*, CD/DVD of Since 1972 CD
A thank you call from Josh for purchasing his record.

$125—Limited Edition Box Set
1 of 100 Box sets of all 3 of Josh's CDs
Thank you phone call
Set of Signed Drumsticks
Copy of Josh's 5th grade report card
1 of Josh's boarding passes from a past flight
Bumper Sticker "I ♥ Josh Freese's New Friends"

$350—The Lunch Date
Take Josh to lunch at P. F. Chang's in Long Beach
5 copies of both "My New Friends" and "Since 1972" (Pass 'em out to friends. A perfect way to tell someone "I love you" or "You are very special to me")

Copy of Josh's 5th grade report card
Bumper Sticker "I ♥ Josh Freese's New Friends"
Signed drumhead
Signed sticks
Signed photo (can't promise what the photo will be . . . but it will be signed)

$7,500 (limited to 1)—Evoke Spirits with Tommy Lee, Danny Lohner and Josh
Engage in light "80's hair metal/pinup girl gossip" w/ Tommy, Josh and Lohner while a 'C List Porn Star' applies 'corpse paint' to your astonished face. Next you'll be escorted to the opulent gardens of Castle Renhold'r, where the four of you will be Throwing Bones under the midnight moon in a blasphemous attempt to evoke the spirit/entity of YOUR CHOICE! (BYOB)
10 Copies of "My New Friends"
Get a diddy written about you for next record (not necessarily a full on song but definitely a "diddy")
$50 gift certificate to P. F. Chang's
"Since 1972" CD
"The Notorious One Man Orgy" CD
Copy of Josh's 5th grade report card
Bumper Sticker "I ♥ Josh Freese's New Friends"
Signed drumhead
Signed sticks

$10,000 Limited To 1
100 Copies of *My New Friends*
Take home Josh's now infamous Volvo 940 Station Wagon (Perfect for hauling drums, plenty of room for getting busy in spacious back-seating area. Good for trips to Good Will or disposing bodies.)
Make Josh's next record for him
Josh joins your band for 2 days (quick book some studio time!)
"Motorboat" Sarah for a minute or so (Josh's wife's friend...couples welcome, discreet parking available)
Oh yeah...$100 gift certificate to PF Changs and a bumper sticker that says something funny on it.

$75,000 Same As It Ever Was
Josh joins your band for a month (or becomes your personal assistant)
Take home one of Josh's drumsets
Josh writes and records a 5 song EP entirely about YOU.
Take Shrooms and cruise Hollywood in Danny from TOOL's Lamborgini.
500 copies of "My New Friends" (start your own online CD store...specializing in just this one CD)
Go get matching outfits at Tommy Bahama's and make everybody very sad.

It should be noted that for his previous release *Since 1972,* Freese sold 1 $20,000 package, 3 at $5,000, 4 at $2,500, 5 at $1,000, 5 at $500, and 25 at $250. Total revenue just for the major packages was $58,750.

The bottom line is that multi-tiered offerings work, and the more exclusive they are, the more you can charge for them. Sometimes the offering itself (especially if it involves being in close proximity to the artist) is more interesting than the music itself.

The Wisdom of Multitiered Offerings

Offer multi-tiered products, from free to very expensive.

Make the music easily accessible to fans and potential fans.

Harvest email addresses from free offerings.

Fans find exclusive offerings interesting.

Sometimes an offering that involves close proximity to the artist is more interesting than the music itself.

Have the leader directly communicate with the tribe.

Expand the tribe by personally reaching out.

Chris Anderson's Long Tail

The "Long Tail" is a concept first put forward in an article by Chris Anderson in the October 2004 issue of *Wired* magazine. The Long Tail basically puts the old 80:20 rule on its ear. For those of you who aren't into sales, the longstanding 80:20 rule refers to the fact that you usually get 80 percent of your business from 20 percent of your customers, or in the case of the music industry, 80 percent of the sales came from 20 percent of available albums (in other words, the current and recent hits). Because of limited shelf space, most retail stores would carry only the current hits and a limited number of catalog albums, since the hits are the products that quickly sell. This becomes a self-fulfilling prophecy, since if only the hits (the 20 percent) are available, there's hardly a possibility that much of the other 80 percent will sell, because they're not available.

The Long Tail turns the 80:20 rule around by stating that most of your sales will come from that other 80 percent of products if they're made available and *are easy to purchase* (the key phrase). A customer may buy the hit, but then buy another two pieces from the artist's catalog (or even another artist's catalog) while he or she is at it. But except for a few brick-and-mortar megastores, such as Amoeba Music in Los Angeles; San Francisco; and Berkeley, California; and the now-defunct Tower and Virgin chains, the Long Tail would not arrive until the Internet online stores such as Amazon and iTunes, and the movie site Netflix. Now an artist's entire catalog can be available online, and the Long Tail potentially rules.

As Chris Anderson points out in his book called "The Long Tail" (derived from the original *Wired* magazine article), half of the products that Netflix rents are ones that a retailer would never have the space to carry. Over half of Amazon's book sales are unavailable at the retailer Barnes and Noble. Most of what you can buy on iTunes is not available in any record store. It turns out that when customers are given a huge number of choices in every genre possible, they start looking down the "tail" to find what else might be interesting to them, and sales increase accordingly. As a result, where the attention used to be focused on the Top 40, now there's much more attention given to other titles in the catalog (the Long Tail), and because they're immediately available, consumption goes up.

As Anderson states in his December 2004 article in *Wired*:

To get a sense of our true taste, unfiltered by the economics of scarcity, look at Rhapsody, a subscription-based streaming music service (owned by RealNetworks) that currently offers more than 735,000 tracks.

Chart Rhapsody's monthly statistics and you get a "power law" demand curve that looks much like any record store's, with huge appeal for the top tracks, tailing off quickly for less popular ones. But a really interesting thing happens once you dig below the top 40,000 tracks, which is about the amount of the fluid inventory (the albums carried that will eventually be sold) of the average real-world record store. Here, the Wal-Marts of the world go to zero—either they don't

> carry any more CDs, or the few potential local takers for such fringy fare never find it or never even enter the store.
>
> The Rhapsody demand, however, keeps going. Not only is every one of Rhapsody's top 100,000 tracks streamed at least once each month, the same is true for its top 200,000, top 300,000, and top 400,000. As fast as Rhapsody adds tracks to its library, those songs find an audience, even if it's just a few people a month, somewhere in the country.

Anderson goes on in the same article:

> The same is true for all other aspects of the entertainment business, to one degree or another. Just compare online and offline businesses: The average Blockbuster carries fewer than 3,000 DVDs. Yet a fifth of Netflix rentals are outside its top 3,000 titles. Rhapsody streams more songs each month beyond its top 10,000 than it does its top 10,000. In each case, the market that lies outside the reach of the physical retailer is big and getting bigger.

A word of caution: the Long Tail doesn't work if all of your products are considered "Long Tail." You must have the hits as well to offset the catalog. Likewise, it doesn't work if only hits are available. The Long Tail needs the balance to operate effectively.

So how does this affect the music in M3.0? Anderson has the following three Long Tail rules that aptly apply:

Rule 1: Make Everything Available
Members of a tribe want as much of the artist's music as they can get. Rehearsals, outtakes, different versions—they want it all and they want it now. While it was impractical to make everything available in the past, that's no longer the case online. Put it on every music site or limit it to your personal website; just make it available to your tribe.

Rule 2: Cut the Price in Half, Then Lower It
Many of the items that a tribe most adores are the ones that an artist spends the least time and money on, such as rough mixes, rehearsal and live recordings and videos, and original song demos. If it doesn't

oppose the artist's artistic integrity, make it available to the tribe. Since the production costs are low, the prices can be low too. For older catalog items (especially those in a digital format), prices can be lowered if a service such as Kunaki (kunaki.com) is used for CD pressing. Kunaki will press and drop-ship CDs on demand for a fixed price of $1.75 each, regardless of whether you purchase 1 or 100,000.

Rule 3: Help Me Find It

It does no one any good if you can't easily find the product to buy. The Long Tail works only when the catalog items are easy to find. You must do everything in your power to make the experience of finding your catalog products as easy as possible.

While there is ample evidence that the Long Tail theory is working (according to the RIAA, in 2008, 450,000 physical albums sold at least one copy, compared with 390,000 the previous year), there have been many rebuttals from economists and bloggers claiming that the Long Tail theory is full of holes. While it might not be as effective as originally outlined by Anderson in terms of back-end sales, I believe that the premise is basically sound. Customers will buy your older products if they are available and easy to find, and they'll buy more of these products if they're less expensive than the newer products. That is the essence of the Long Tail and should be kept in mind at all times when doing business in M3.0.

The Long Tail

More of your sales come from older products (catalog) than newer.

It doesn't work unless you have hits to balance the catalog.

Customers can't buy older products if they're not available.

They'll buy more of these products if they're cheaper than newer products.

Make everything available.

Sometimes the most valuable products are the ones that the artist spends the least to produce.

Make it easy to find.

Irving Azoff's Steel Fist

The most powerful man currently in the music business is Irving Azoff. Actually, he's been one of the most powerful men for in the business for decades, but what he currently represents is a model for M3.0 and beyond, because of the large scale he operates on.

With the innate ability to drive a hard bargain, Azoff rose to prominence in the early '80s as the head of Frontline Management, which represented musical heavyweights The Eagles, Steely Dan, Heart, Stevie Nicks, and Jackson Browne, among others. Azoff soon became the head of then-major label MCA Records (which later became what we now know as Universal Music Group), then later owned his own Giant Records (a Warner Bros. imprint) before selling out and returning to managing a few selected clients such as The Eagles and Christina Aguilera. In 2005, his reconstituted Frontline became the most powerful management company in the history of the music industry as a result of Azoff's buying some 60 smaller management companies.

As a former label head, Azoff understood the dilemma of the record labels, and realizing that he could do business without them, he went directly to the most powerful retailer on the planet, Wal-Mart, to distribute the Eagle's first album since 1979, the double CD *Long Road Out of Eden*, released in 2007. Azoff understood the power of the chain's 6,500 stores, their ability to reach their 140 million visitors a week, and the promotional value of Wal-Mart's weekly circular seen by 85 million potential customers. Even priced at only $11.88 (extremely low for a double-CD set), the set would reportedly net the band far more than it ever could have had the band been signed to a record label (reportedly near $50 million). Thus Azoff sent the first warning shot across the bow of the old industry guard.

Then, realizing how the concert-promotion business was tightly controlled and that artists make most of their money from touring, he merged with the giant Ticketmaster, and then again with their major competitor Live Nation, becoming executive chairman in the process. This means that Live Nation under Azoff is now able to manage talent, book concerts, issue tickets, and sell artist-related merchandise under one roof.

Now this is great if you're already a legacy artist, because now presumably you'll get a larger part of each ticket sale, but what does it have to do with an up-and-coming artist in M3.0? It shows that the new music industry is a business of talent (as compared with distribution in the old model), and he who controls the talent wins. As for the talent, the most essential part of an artist's team is the manager.

The major labels have less and less to offer an M3.0 artist. They sell records (recorded music—CDs, MP3s, and so on), but that's not where the business is today. The real business lies with everything else that an artist brings to the table. The labels now offer 360 deals to new acts, but that benefits only them and not the artist. If they can't do the one thing that they're supposed to do well, which is sell records (as the sales figures show), how can you expect them to sell your merch, or get you gigs?

M3.0 is the music business without the record labels of the past. Irving Azoff sees it, and so should you.

The New M3.0 Reality

A record label is no longer necessary for success.

Management is more important than ever.

Talent, not distribution, is king.

Distribution is easily available for any artist.

Sanctuary's Blueprint

In 1979, Rod Smallwood and Andy Taylor discovered and then managed the legendary metal band Iron Maiden. They subsequently named their management company after the band's song "Sanctuary" and expanded their roster to include similar bands of the genre.

Soon afterward, Sanctuary Management had a brilliant idea. As managers of "heritage acts," which had long-term appeal and large fan bases but no record deals, the company decided to independently finance CD releases for the bands themselves. After all, the audience was built in and rabid. They'd buy anything the bands would put out, so why not release it themselves if a major label wouldn't? The bands were going to tour anyway, so they might as well have a product to sell. Little did they know at the time, but this was the beginning of the new business model where the tour sells the record instead of the record selling the tour, as it did in M1.0 to 2.0.

In the past, if an act would get hot as a result of local radio play, they would then tour in that location to take advantage of the energized interest. The record sold the tour by virtue of the airplay it received. The record was selling the tour. If the record flopped, there would be no tour.

But in the new Sanctuary model, since the act had a strong enough fan base to support a tour anyway, why not have some product to back it up? With these new economics of self-financing the release, the act could now make more money than ever on fewer units sold. And since it was cheaper than ever to create a release (since by then most musicians had studios at home that were more powerful than The Beatles ever had during their heyday), the stage was set for taking advantage of both the technology and the consumer environment.

For a time, Sanctuary Records and its artists succeeded wildly, to the point that the company expanded into a full-fledged record label (and a subsidiary of Universal Music) with traditional M2.0 staff and infrastructure. Soon afterward, however, it collapsed under the weight of that traditional infrastructure. The company had ventured beyond its original concept and comfort level, and eventually paid for it. Sanctuary ceased to exist as a record label at the end of 2007. Today Sanctuary Management represents Fleetwood Mac, ZZ Top, Tommy Lee, and Velvet Revolver, among others, but has drifted somewhat from its initial intentions and goals.

Sanctuary started the trend of an artist self-releasing a record during M2.0, way ahead of the curve and way ahead of what's commonplace today. Without knowing it at the time, the company paved the way for artists living in M3.0, where self-production, promotion, and distribution are not only commonplace but becoming the norm.

The Sanctuary Model

The tour sells the record, not the other way around.

The CD becomes another piece of merchandise.

The artist is marketing and selling directly to his or her tribe.

Self-releasing can be more profitable than having a label.

The artist can make more money on fewer sales.

Justin Bieber—The Socially Made Star

To many Justin Bieber is just another example of a short-on-substance teen idol, but if you forget about the artist and look at how he was discovered and how his career was built, you'll find the perfect example of how social media can work in a big way in M3.0.

Justin Bieber was the first artist made by YouTube. He was discovered there, and has prospered there almost more than any artist other than Lady Gaga. In fact, Bieber's song "Baby" had more than 500 million views alone, and all of his videos together equal more than 1.5 billion total views (which is number 1 of all musical artists) as of the writing of this book.

His career began when he was captured on a cell-phone video as he was busking outside the Avon Theatre in Stratford, Ontario (population 32,000) hoping to get noticed, a moment that has since been shared some 3.2 million times on YouTube. In just a little over 9 months, Bieber went from playing to 40 people at an outdoor water park in Poughkeepsie to headlining 86 sold-out arena shows in 2010, all this while moving over 10 million albums worldwide over 14 months, opening his first movie on 3,000-plus screens with box-office earnings that topped $20 million, and inspiring hundreds of licensed merchandise items.

More than that, Bieber is one of the first artists to use social media to achieve superstardom, utilizing all forms of social media to capitalize on his success with over 9 million Twitter followers and 25 million Facebook fans. In fact, he is number 1 in the top 100 Twitters and accounts for about 3 percent of all Twitter traffic as of the writing of this book in spring 2011.

Bieber is not the only M3.0 superstar to fully utilize social media though; Lady Gaga, Eminem, Rhianna, Shikira, Katy Perry, Linken Park, Lil Wayne, Taylor Swift, and Akon all have 20-plus million Facebook fans, according to Famecount.com. Lady Gaga, Shakira, Katy Perry, Britney Spears, Taylor Swift, and Selena Gomez all have more than 5 million Twitter followers. All of these stars have more than 100 million YouTube views, with several near or over a billion.

It's a fact that the superstar of today cannot reach that level of success without a large social media presence. While Twitter and Facebook strengthen the connection with the fan, YouTube acts not only as the major music delivery system, but now plays a huge part in music discovery as well. Even though superstars have the resources to better craft a message and media campaign than a new act just starting out, social media is essential to artists at all levels in order to prosper.

Social Media: The Crucial Component

Facebook and Twitter strengthen the connection with the fan.

YouTube is now the major music delivery system.

YouTube is a major music and artist discovery portal.

FIVE

CHAPTER

The New Marketing—Part 1
Your Music Is Your Marketing

An artist in M3.0 requires an entirely new marketing plan than in prior periods because the techniques commonly used for M1.0 through 2.5 certainly won't work anymore, at least with the degree of success that they once had. Traditional media such as radio are no longer a major music-marketing factor, nor is television, unless you're an artist whose image counts more than your music.

Your Music Is Your Marketing

· ·

The major marketing tool for the M3.0 artist is your music itself. It's no longer the major product that the artist has to sell, although it still is a product, so it has to be used differently and thought of differently as a result.

Perhaps recorded music was never the product we were led to believe it was. In the M1.0 and M1.5 days of vinyl records and CDs, the round plastic piece (the container that held the music) was the product. While the songwriter always made money when a song was played on the radio, the artist never did (although artists might soon get their due, depending on the status of impending Performance Rights Act legislation), and even when it was sold, the artist made only a small percentage of CD and vinyl sales (10 to 15 percent of whole-sale, on average). In order for the artist to make any money from the recording, the costs involved in the production of the music product and the manufacturing of the container that transported the music (physical material costs, artwork, and so on) first had to be recouped. The fact of the matter was that the artist made most of his or her money on concert tickets and merchandise sales while touring, not in record sales.

While this has been the system that artists and labels have worked under for years, if you look at music in terms of the advertising world, you see it in a different light.

If you're selling a soap product, for instance, the production cost for a commercial to broadcast on television or the radio is trivial. It's the total ad buy (the agency purchasing the radio or television time for the sponsor) where most of the money is spent. Even then, it's considered part of the marketing budget of the product, which might be about 3 percent of total sales.

In M3.0, if you consider the music-production costs as part of the marketing budget in the same way as a national product, it takes on a whole new meaning.

Since the music is considered the major marketing tool for an artist, it could be considered a free product, a giveaway, an enticement. Give it away on your website, place it on the torrents for P2P, let your fans freely distribute it. It's all okay. Since most millennials already feel that music should be free and have lived in a culture where that's mostly so, don't fight it. Go with the flow! Just as it was during the past 60 years, the real money in the music business is made elsewhere anyway.

Further, just because you're giving it away doesn't mean that you can't charge for it, either at the same time or at sometime in the future. There are numerous cases in which sales have actually decreased for an artist's iTunes tracks when the free tracks have been eliminated.

One such musician is Corey Smith. After six years, Corey has built his gross revenue to about $7.5 million, and free music has been the basic building block of his ever-increasing fan base. You can buy his tracks on iTunes (he's sold more than 800,000 so far), but when his management experimented by taking the free tracks down from his website, his iTunes sales went down as well. The free music Corey offers allows potential fans to try him out. If they email and ask for a song that's not available for free, he just emails it back to them. He's tending his tribe!

Another example of reaping the rewards for giving it away for free is the electronic artist Moby, who's "Shot in the Back of the Head" became the bestselling iTunes track after giving it away for free on his website for two months.

Of course, you can charge for your music with enhanced products such as box sets, compilations, special editions, and other value-added offerings. But to build a buzz, the initial releases for an artist on any level (except for the already-established star) must be free.

Your Music Is Your Marketing

Music is a your main marketing tool.

Give it away for free, but charge for it too.

Most of your income comes from elsewhere anyway.

Value-added products are your best revenue source.

The New Release Schedule

. . . .

M3.0 requires new thinking regarding song releases. If we go back to the '50s, vinyl singles had a notoriously fast manufacturing turn-around time, despite the labor-intensive process required to make a vinyl record. At that time, it was not uncommon to have a single (the small 7-inch "45" with a song on each side) on the streets within days of recording (and sometimes even writing) the song! Of course, the quick turnaround was helped by the fact that the song was usually recorded in a few hours, since there was little or no overdubbing, so it was possible to record a song on Monday and have it on the radio on Wednesday of the same week. Perhaps the last time a hit record turnaround happened this quickly was with the 1970 release of Crosby, Stills, Nash and Young's "Ohio," documenting the Kent State shootings within a few weeks of the event.

When the emphasis on releases turned from singles to albums, the length of time between releases increased accordingly, which was natural considering that more songs were being recorded. During the M1.0 days, there was a limitation on how many songs could be recorded for an album because there was the limitation of the vinyl itself. Twenty-three minutes per side was the goal to get the loudest and highest-fidelity record. Any longer and the noise floor of the record increased as the volume decreased. As a result, artists were confined to about 45 to 50 minutes per album, but consumers didn't seem to mind, since they still felt they were getting value if they liked the songs.

The time limitation lifted with the introduction of the CD in M1.5. When first released, the CD had a maximum playing time of 74 minutes (the number rumored to be chosen because it could fit the entire Beethoven's Ninth Symphony), which was later increased to a full 80 minutes. No longer saddled with the vinyl album's built-in time limitation, artists were able to stretch out and add more and longer songs to each album release. This soon proved to be a double-edged sword, since it now took longer to finish recording each release because of the inclusion of all those extra songs.

But having more songs doesn't necessarily make a better record, and even backfired regarding the artist's popularity. While 40 to 45 minutes was a time bite easily digestible for a listener, 60 to 70 was not. The extra songs were not only little appreciated but, even worse, thought of as mere filler. The consumer began to think (sometimes rightfully so) that the songs were there just for the sake of being there, and they began to feel ripped off. Why pay for songs that you'll never listen to? Because you had to!

Over the years, the time between record releases gradually lengthened to the point that a superstar act might take several years. While this might have worked in M1.5 and 2.0, that strategy would never work in M3.0, as the tribe has an insatiable appetite for product. What's worse, the tribe can actually dissipate if the product does not come at regular intervals—the shorter the better.

And with CD sales way down, the album format itself seems to be going the way of the vinyl single of the '50s and '60s. Consumers in M3.0 buy only the songs they want, and therefore, they buy singles. Which brings about a new philosophy regarding recordings and how they are released.

In M3.0, artists record fewer songs but have more frequent releases. It's better to release two songs every 6, 8, or 12 weeks than to wait a year for one release of ten songs. This benefits the artist in the following ways:

▶ The artist keeps his or her tribe happy with a constant supply of new music. New music keeps the tribe interested and keeps the buzz and dialog going.

▶ The artist gains increased exposure for every song. In a ten-song album release, it's easy for a fan, reviewer, or radio programmer to focus on just one or two songs while the others fall in priority. When releases are in twos, each song gets equal attention and has the ability to live and die on its own merits.

▶ All the songs can still be compiled into an album after having been individually released. At the end of the year, or at the end of the artist's creative cycle, the songs are then put into an album that can be released in any format. The advantage is that the album has much advanced exposure and publicity thanks to numerous single releases. Plus it can be treated as a marketing event, which is also to the artist's advantage.

Make no mistake, the album format is not dead in M3.0 (although sales are decreasing), but the emphasis has shifted to the individual song.

The New Release Schedule

Single or two-song releases every 6 to 12 weeks.

Frequent new music keeps the tribe happy.

Exposure for all songs is increased.

Singles can be compiled into an album later.

Singles act as advanced publicity for the album.

Each can be treated as a marketing event.

Ten Music Marketing Ideas

It's easier to sell your music if you add extra value to it. Here are ten ways to think outside the box when it comes to distributing your music. Thanks to Bruce Houghton for numbers 7 through 10.

1. Develop a package: This could mean anything from a CD and a vinyl album, to a digital download and album with all alternative mixes, to a boxed set of CDs, or anything in between (see Trent Reznor's *Ghosts I--IV* or Josh Freese's offerings in chapter 4 for ideas). The idea is to go beyond just the typical CD and digital offerings.

2. Sequential numbering: Limiting the availability of physical products and numbering them (for example; number 7 of 500) gives it the feeling of exclusivity. The product becomes a special edition and a must-have for the true fan.

3. Tie it to merchandise: Offer a physical product that contains the code for a free download of your album. Mos Def was so successful with the T-shirt release of *The Ecstatic* that *Billboard* magazine even began counting it as a music release on their charts. Prince did the same with an inclusion of his *20Ten* in the UK's *Daily Mirror* newspaper. Other artists have sold their music via codes on such items as golf balls, bandanas, and even canned food! You can use QR Codes on just about anything physical.

4. Release a "double-sided" digital single: Rhino Records' digital releases celebrating 60 years of the 45 RPM single set a fine example for this format. For between $1.49 and $1.99, Rhino provided the original hit song, its B side (the flip side of the vinyl record), and the original artwork. You can do the same by providing two songs for price of one—an A and a B side.

5. Release on an old alternative format: Some artists (The Decemberists' *Hazards of Love* comes to mind) have released a vinyl-only physical product to great success. Cheap Trick did it on the old 8-track format from the '60s, and some bands have even recently released on cassette tape. Releasing on an older format can be good as a publicity tool (as long as everyone else isn't doing it), and who knows, maybe you can start a trend?

6. Release on a new alternative format: A new alternative format that's getting some traction is flash memory, or the common USB memory stick. Once again, Trent Reznor met with great viral success by planting unmarked memory sticks in bathrooms at NIN's concerts, and Sony even released the 25th anniversary of Michael Jackson's *Thriller* on the format. Everybody uses these things so you're bound to get at least a look, which you can't always say about other formats.

7. Three sides: Offer a song in an early studio version, the final mix, and then captured live.

8. Radical mixes: Offer two or three very different mixes of the same song, perhaps even done by the fans.

9. Two sides of [your city]: Two different bands each contribute a track to a series chronicling your local scene.

10. "Artist X" introduces _____: Add a track by your favorite new artist/band along with one of yours. This is similar to a gig trade-out with another band that many bands use as a way to play in new venues. The idea is that the band you feature will feature you on their release as well.

The New Marketing—Part 2
The Rise of Social Media Marketing

here once an artist's major marketing thrust was directed at the traditional mediums of radio, television, and print, today it focuses more online to reach current and potential fans. While social networks tend to wax and wane in popularity, there are other aspects of an artist's online presence that can't be ignored. That said, it's not the social network or the online presence that's important. Those are only mechanisms to reach the most crucial element in an artist's success—the fan him- or herself.

The New Importance of the Fan

As pointed out elsewhere in the book, prior to M3.0 the fan was treated differently. The artist wasn't able to easily come in contact with fans and, for the most part, didn't want to. Except for special releases and perks to the fan club, the fan was treated mostly as a consumer and kept at arm's length.

M3.0 has changed all that with Seth Godin's tribal concept, and now fan communication is a direct and integral part of an act's success. It's possible for an act to become hot for a while, but if the tribe of fans is not created and constantly enriched, any success will only be short term. Not only can the artist directly interact with the fan, but he or she also must interact in order to maintain the tribe!

That being said, fans know when they're being hyped, exploited, or taken lightly, and receiving anything less than total respect can prove disastrous to the fan base/tribe. Fans don't want to be marketed to, but they want to be informed of things that might interest them.

Fans want to know that the artist is listening to them. They don't need direct communication (although that's the best), but they want acknowledgement that they're being heard. Fans don't want to be talked at, but they want to be spoken to. They want to hear from the artist but not hyped or sold to, as that cheapens the experience. They don't want ad copy; they want it from the heart.

Going back to the email that Trent Reznor sent his tribe:

Hello everyone.

I'd like to thank everyone for a very successful year so far in the world of Nine Inch Nails. I'm enjoying my couple of weeks off between legs of our Lights In The Sky tour and got to thinking . . . "wouldn't it be fun to send out a survey to everyone that's shown interest in NIN?" Well, that's not exactly how it went, but regardless—here it is. As we've moved from the familiar world of record labels and BS into the unknown world of doing everything yourself, we've realized it would benefit us and our ability to interact with you if we knew more about what you want, what you like, what you look like naked, etc. I know it's a pain in the ass but we'd truly appreciate it if you'd take a minute and help us out. As an incentive, everyone who completes the survey will be able to download a video of live performance from this most recent tour (and I know what's going through your little minds right now: "I'll just grab this off a torrent site and not have to fill out the survey!!!" and guess what? You will be able to do just that and BEAT THE SYSTEM!!!! NIN=pwn3d!!!)

BUT

What if we were to select some of those that DO complete the survey and provide them with something really cool? I'm not saying we'll ever get around to it, but if we did maybe something like signed stuff, flying someone to a show somewhere in the world, a magic amulet that makes you invisible, a date with Jeordie White (condoms supplied of course), you know—something cool. See, you'd miss that opportunity AND be a cheater.

Do the right thing—help us out. You'll feel better.

Thank you and I've had too much caffeine this morning,

—Trent

Reznor treats his tribe with respect, bidding them "hello everyone" and thanking them at the end. He tells you a little bit about himself with, "I've had too much caffeine this morning." He engages his fans to interact and help him, but most of all, you get the feeling that he's talking directly to you.

A fan that's treated well might not always stay a fan (though he or she probably will), but while a fan, he or she will remain loyal and an uberconsumer of anything the artist has to offer.

The New Importance of the Fan

Communication with the artist is now integral to an artist's success.

Fans know when they're being hyped, exploited, or taken lightly.

Fans want to know the artist is listening.

Fans want to be treated with respect.

Fans want to be informed, not marketed to.

Your Email List

By far one of the most, if not *the* most, important marketing tools that an artist has is his or her email list. It's the direct link to the artist's most rabid fans and one of the primary drivers of commerce in the artist's online arsenal.

Your email list is a major component for marketing to your fan base. It's widely overlooked, since most artists believe that their Facebook friends and Twitter followers are enough, but your email list allows you to reach out and personally connect with the fans and control your message while you're doing it.

A well thought-out email blast allows you to do the following:

1. Engage your fan on a one-to-one basis

2. Design the communication without the constraints of a social network

3. Add a call-to-action

Your email list makes it easier to inform, market to, and sell to your fans in a manner true fans (superfans, uberfans, tribal members—whatever you want to call them) enjoy, if you do it well. But execution is always key in the success of any venture, so here are some aspects of your email list to be aware of.

MAIL LIST SERVICES

Having an easy way to sign up for the list is essential, but having a way for the artist to maintain and control the list is just as important. Most artists just starting out rely on their own email client such as Outlook or Mac Mail to manage their lists, but these have built-in limitations that you'll soon outgrow. For one thing, you must manually clean the list of bounces and drop-offs, which is time consuming.

Another major problem is that ISPs limit the number of emails that can be sent in a batch in order to eliminate spamming. This can mean that if your email list exceeds as few as 100 people, the email blast will get rejected by your ISP and you'll have to divide it into many smaller email groups.

A way around that is to use an email service such as iContact, Constant Contact, Mail Chimp, or any of the other similar services to maintain your list. For a small monthly fee (as little as $10.00 depending upon the mailing-list size), your email list can undergo a significant change for the better in the following ways:

▶ No limit on the number of subscribers in the email blast
▶ The list is automatically cleaned of bounces or invalid addresses
▶ Easily handles subscribers and opt-outs
▶ Extensive statistics as to who opens the email, how many click through, and how long they view
▶ Many professional email templates to choose from

Right now it's that combination of having a great email list and a great website that's constantly updated and gives the fans a reason to come back. In terms of growing an email list, I'm a big fan of the tools that Topspin and Bandcamp have, where it's something like, "Give us your email address and we'll give you this MP3," or "Here's an easy way to send this MP3 to your friends." I'm a big fan of anything that encourages viral growth.
—Bruce Houghton

Most email services have essentially the same feature set and prices, so the main difference between them is a user interface that suits the list owner—you. Most services offer a free try-out period, although some may limit the number of emails or addresses during this period.

6 KEYS TO BUILDING YOUR MAILING LIST

Building an email list seems like an easy thing to do, but it's a lot more difficult than you'd think. Here are the six keys to building a successful list:

1. Offer a high comfort level. People don't like to give their email addresses out unless they're getting something in return. In other words, they use their email information as a form of currency. If they don't have trust in your site or they're unsure what you'll do with their address, it's really difficult to get them to register. If the site is unprofessional and feels like it may disappear any day, chances are they won't sign up.

2. Make the sign-up easy to find. Make the registration prominent on not only your website but every marketing piece that you have. Most email services provide html widgets that both look good and work seamlessly without any programming on your part.

3. Make it easy to register. That means don't ask for too much information. It's easy to get their first name and their email address and maybe their city, but beyond that, many potential users begin to feel uncomfortable. Remember, you can always ask them for more information later after they sign up.

4. They need an incentive. They need a contest, a free download, or a promise of receiving something later as a reason to register. Remember, they're buying something with their email currency. They're thinking, "What's in it for me?"

5. Cross-promote. Promote your list through your social networks such as Twitter and Facebook, your blog, and even something as simple as on gig flyers or business cards. Every address is valuable, so don't let any opportunities for another registration go by the wayside.

6. Use reminders. Remind people in your videos, blog posts, podcasts, CD covers, and any other kind of content that you're producing about your email list. You don't have to be blatant about it; just make sure that the info is always present.

DESIGNING YOUR MAIL BLAST

There's no doubt that email is an important part of an artist's social strategy, but sometimes a poorly thought-out mail blast can be worse than none at all. Here are some important questions to ask yourself that will guide you in designing your email. These are questions you should know the answers to way before it's time to hit the send button.

▶ What is this email about? What's the purpose?
▶ Why should my subscribers care about what I'm sending?

- ▶ Why did the subscriber sign up to receive my emails in the first place?
- ▶ What is my call to action?
- ▶ Is my most important message above the fold (the point before the reader has to scroll down)?
- ▶ Have I run a test send?

While the first four points involve the conceptual part of the email, the last two are important design considerations. Keeping your most important message above the fold gives you the best chance of capturing readers' attention before they delete the mail and move on. Doing a test send or two to yourself is the best way to prevent an embarrassing oversight or glitch from happening. Do it even if you're 100 percent sure you're ready to go. It's surprising how often you find that you're not.

BEST EMAIL PRACTICES

When it comes to emailing, there are good and bad ways to do it. Here are what you might consider "best practices" as revealed by Jed Carlson, founder and CEO of ReverbNation in his "Email 101 for Artists, Labels, and Venues" article on Music Think Tank.

1. Always respect a person's desire to unsubscribe to your list. *Immediately unsubscribe them* if your mailing list doesn't do it for you.

2. Always talk to them without swearing. It may be part of your "persona" as a band, but some people don't like that language. The Internet Service Providers (ISPs) such as Yahoo mail, Hotmail, AOL, and so forth don't like it either, and your message will go directly to the junk box. You wouldn't talk to your grandma that way, would you?

3. Always avoid "scam" words in the subject line. Words such as "free" and "help" will land your message in the junk box 100 percent of the time.

4. Always target them with messages that are relevant to them. If you have a show in Seattle, don't message your fans in Miami. Keep your powder dry for a message to them later about something else.

5. Always give them the basics about the information you are conveying. Reporters call this the "who, what, why, when, where, how" model. If you have a show coming up, do your fans (and yourself) the service of providing dates, times, locations, ticket links, and lineup of the show. Over 75 percent of artists miss this essential piece when they email. If you want someone to respond and come to your show, for goodness sake, go so far as to give them driving directions if you can. Each ticket sold is money in your pocket.

6. Always link them to some place to find out more info about the band: This could be ReverbNation or a homepage or blog, but *always* give them a way to find out more.

So don't overlook the obvious. Your email list is your most important tool in M3.0 for reaching your fans, but you need a specialized application to use it to its utmost.

MORE IS LESS

In M3.0, "more is less" should be one of your main mantras. There's a limit to what fans can absorb, and exceeding that limit can alienate them. Too much communication can be counterproductive. Once a week is about the limit, although once a month can work too. More is okay if there's a real purpose.

> *Mailing list blasts have a definite point where it's too much. We like to limit those to a couple of times a month, or once a week at most if you're really doing something special or have unique content. If it's just announcing tour dates or trying to sell something, you shouldn't do it more than once a week, but we find once or twice a month works best. If it's unique content, that could be cool to blast weekly. On the other hand, if you're Twittering, the more the merrier because that's the kind of minutia that people are into. That platform is great for 3, to 10, to even 20 times a day.*
>
> —Jacob Tell of Oniracom

Just as 15 songs on a release are not necessarily better than 8 even if they're all great, there is a tipping point for email blasts at which fans go from feeling informed to being intruded upon. The leader of the tribe must have a feel for where that point is and be sure to never cross it. It's just overload at that point and actually dilutes the effectiveness of your message and your marketing. The leader of the tribe must have a feel for where that point is and be sure to never cross it.

Your Email List

It's the most important tool you have.

To utilize properly requires a special application.

There are significant extra benefits from using professional list-management services.

Make your list sign-up easy to find and easy to do.

Think through your email before you send it.

Observe best practices.

Fewer emails is always better.

1. Talk to your fans, not at them. Don't try to sell them, but keep them informed. Anything that reads like ad copy might be counter-productive. Always treat them with respect, and never talk down to them.

2. Engage in communication. Communication is a two-way street. Fans want to know that they're being listened to. You don't have to answer every email, but you have to acknowledge that you heard it. The more questions you ask, polls you supply, and advice you seek, the more your fans will feel connected to you.

3. Keep your promises. If you say you're going to do something, do it in a timely fashion. Don't let your fans wait. If you promise you're going to email a link and post a song, sooner is always better.

4. Stay engaged. Even if you're only sending something simple such as a link, take the time to engage the fan. Tell him or her about upcoming gigs, events, or releases. Take a poll. Ask for advice. This is a great opportunity for communication, so take advantage of it. Some of the things that you ask might be:

► Where do you live?
► Are there any venues nearby where you'd like to see us play?
► Do you prefer studio recordings or live performances?
► Would you like to obtain copies of our live performances?
► If we offered high-quality recordings of our shows, would you purchase them?
► Would you prefer personal updates or free music from our newsletter?
► Would you be interested in purchasing merch from us, and if so, what kind?
► Are you interested in seeing behind-the-scenes footage of our tour or recording sessions?

5. Utilize preorders. If you have a release coming out soon, take preorders as soon as you announce it, even if it's free. It's best to get people to act while their interests are high, and it gives the fans something to look forward to. To motivate fans for a preorder, it sometimes helps to include exclusive content or merchandise.

6. Appearance means a lot. Style counts when talking to fans. Make sure everything looks good and is readable. Spelling or grammar mistakes reflect badly on you. Try to keep it simple but stylish, but if you or your team don't have the design chops to make it look good, then it's better to just keep things simple and readable.

7. Cater to uberfans. All of the members of your tribe are passionate, but some are more passionate than others. Fans have different needs and wants, and it's to everyone's benefit if you can cater to them all. Try always to include a premium or deluxe tier for every offering, such as a free T-shirt or backstage pass as a reward for posting, a free ticket to an upcoming show, some signed artwork, some extra songs—anything to satiate the uberfan's interest.

8. Give them a choice. Give fans numerous ways to opt in, since not everyone wants to receive information in the same way. Ask if they would rather receive info by email, SMS, or even snail mail. Ask if they'd like to receive info on upcoming shows, song releases, video content, or contests. And ask how often they'd like be contacted.

Your Blog

A blog is essential to have for both communicating with your fans and having them communicate with you and each other. It's easier than ever to create a blog these days with either Blogger, Wordpress or Tumblr (which is less sophisticated and in a slightly different category), which are priced the way most artists like—free.

You can design a fancy blog site if you want, but it's really not necessary. A generic one will do just fine as long as the look is somewhat consistent with your Website and marketing materials. If you can't do that or it will take too long to design, just make it plain vanilla. Since a blog is such a valuable tool, simply having one far outweighs how it looks.

Make sure that you update it regularly with photos, videos, and journal entries of your band's latest antics. Daily updates are best, but any interval can work as long as you stick to it. For instance, it's best if your fans always know that you post at 11 a.m. every Wednesday.

You can also link with other musician's blogs and sites, have fans subscribe, add a list of blogs that you like or suggest, and add widgets from other promotion sources. If you add keywords to your posts, they will be searchable through Google, and you can even set up Google Adsense to generate some additional revenue through adds on your blog or RSS feed.

A blog can do wonders for your communication with fans and general visibility, and all it takes is a little time on a regular basis.

OTHER MUSIC BLOGS

By using the general music blogs and the blogs relating to both your genre of music and similar-sounding artists, you can develop a very effective marketing strategy. Especially when you're first starting out, any revue or mention that you get on a popular blog is an important step to spreading virally across the web.

> *Everybody knows to set up a MySpace page and a Facebook page. Beyond that, regardless if you're offering your music for free or not, you want to utilize the rest of the Web that doesn't cost you anything, meaning all the Web 2.0 and social media stuff like personal profile pages, bookmarking and tagging, and an official Twitter channel. It's figuring out a way to broadcast to your fans and affinity groups, which are groups of people that like the type of music that you play. For example, if I sound a lot like John Meyer, then I want to reach out to John Meyer fans. You can do all that simply at no cost by simply putting the time in.*
>
> —Gregory Markel

So how do you get attention from a blog? Unlike the traditional media, where the attention of a magazine or newspaper editor is difficult to get, blogs are relatively easy, since they're typically not inundated with press releases and attention. Even the larger ones are pretty much open to stories or communication because of how difficult it is to fill blog space every day.

The best way to establish a relationship with influential music blogs that discuss music similar to your own is to post frequently so the blogger gets to know you, begin a relationship with the blogger via email, then send your music and ask for a review.

Here's some great info on finding the right blogs from the DIY (Do It Yourself) section of Bruce Houghton's ever-informative music blog, Hypbot.com:

Most bloggers are true music fans who want to discover great new music and share it with the world . . . or at least their 37 friends who read them faithfully. If 10 percent of those 37 readers come to one of your shows, that's 37 fans that you didn't have yesterday telling their own 37 friends about you.

Bloggers are also more approachable then most print journalists, who often can only write about what editors assign them. And bloggers have influence. Fans respect writers that are passionate about music and prove it by writing for love instead of a paycheck. One study from NYC's Stern School of Business even showed that blogs more than some social networks helped to sell new music.

How to know which blogs to target? Two words: niche and location. Using a blog-specific search engine such as Google Blog Search or Technorati, type in "music + Chicago," or better yet a use specific genre, such as "heavy metal + Chicago." Think fans of Arcade Fire would like your band too? Try "Arcade Fire + [your city]." Try all kinds of combinations, including that obscure band that you think copied your style. If they wrote about them; why wouldn't they write about you? You can do the same thing nationally by simply searching under genres or similar artists.

Michael Terpin's Social Radius specializes in PR via blogs, and he suggests:

Quite frankly, if you're trying to "court" a blogger who covers your space, the best thing to do is to first start reading them. The nice things about blogs is they all have RSS feeds, and most of them link their most important posts to their Twitter account, which is mobile and a lot easier to deal with than a large RSS aggregator. You can follow all these bloggers on Twitter, and it'll be on your iPhone, Blackberry or anything that has a Twitter client, and they'll sort of recognize you as you become a Twitter follower and are watching what they say. You can comment on some of their posts, and all of a sudden, you have a bit of a relationship, so that when you come out, you don't come across as a salesman who's trying to spam 50 sites with the same information. It's better to come out and say, "Hey, I read your site frequently and here's what I'm doing."

Blogs

Great for direct communication with fans.

A fancy design isn't necessary.

Update it on a regular schedule.

Marketing through existing music blogs is an effective strategy.

Establish a relationship with the blogger before asking for a review.

SEVEN

CHAPTER

Marketing with Social Media

One of the most powerful methods of marketing in M3.0 is by the use of social media, which means social networks such as Facebook, microblogs such as Twitter, and video portals such as YouTube. While Facebook and Twitter are primarily used for communicating with fans, their importance as marketing platforms should not be underestimated, and as noted several times before in this book, YouTube has become the primary means of music discovery and distribution today. Before we look at these networks more closely, let's look at a former online giant that's quickly moving toward irrelevancy.

One hundred percent of my music discovery today comes from social networks, meaning that I watch what everyone that I connect to via Facebook, Skype, Twitter, and other social networks is listening to or watching, and discover from that. Now it's completely community-driven for me. I think that's a radical change, in that I used to discover only what the labels controlled, but now it's what the community proliferates among their networks.
—Ken Rutkowski, entertainment and technology insider and host of World Tech Round-Up

The Death of MySpace

MySpace has been on a downward spiral since being purchased by media giant NewsCorp in 2005, mostly for not acknowledging what it was and focusing on what it wasn't instead.

At its core, MySpace was an entertainment site centered around music. It didn't perform that function well enough to maintain its audience though, and instead of improving its core value, it chose to try to be more of a general social network. That failed miserably, with Facebook coming from nowhere to dwarf its huge initial lead in both visitors and revenue.

While Facebook has become the dominant network of the social world, it's still not an obvious successor for music, since it still lacks many of the core assets that MySpace offers, despite some of the available music apps such as RootMusic. The fact is that mixing a social network with a music network hasn't worked so far (e.g., iTunes Ping), and it remains to be seen if it will work in the future. That said, MySpace still has more than 80 million visitors per month as of the writing of this book, although that looks to be declining by between 5 and 10 percent a month. After several years of rumors regarding its imminent closure, MySpace was sold at a fire-sale price to Specific Media in July of 2011. Although singer Justin Timberlake has taken an ownership stake in the company and supposedly will play a role in its future, there's little to indicate that the network will be able to reconstitute its once formidable user base.

MySpace held such promise, and delivered little of it. It's another example of a multinational company getting involved in the music business only to slowly run it into the ground. History repeats itself again.

Marketing with Facebook

In a few short years, Facebook has transplanted MySpace, not only as the most formidable social network, but also as an indispensable one for musical artists. According to Facebook's own stats (as of the time of this writing), the social network has more than 500 million active users that spend more than 700 *billion* minutes per month on the network. The average user is connected to 80 community pages, groups, and events, and creates 90 pieces of the more than 30 *billion* pieces of content (Web links, news stories, blog posts, notes, photo albums, etc.) shared each month. Plus it's truly international with 70 percent of Facebook users outside the United States, and entrepreneurs and developers from over 190 countries build for the platform. And it's still growing!

With such a huge influence on almost any social happening, every artist should have his or her own page for promotional purposes. With numerous artist apps such as Root Music (rootmusic.com), Damn the Radio (damntheradio.com), My Band (facebook.com/rn.mybandapp), and utilities from artist platforms such as ReverbNation, it's easier than ever to design a custom page that perfectly fits the artist's needs. That said, it still comes down to regular posts for effective promotion, and many of the same rules that apply to Twitter also apply to Facebook.

EIGHT RULES OF FACEBOOK ENGAGEMENT

A white paper about Facebook engagement from the research site Buddy Media Platform provided a number of interesting points gathered in a report called *Strategies for Effective Facebook Wallposts: A Statistical Review.*

In the study they determined the Five Rules of Facebook engagement, which are:

1. Keep your posts short and sweet. Posts of 80 characters or less have 27 percent higher engagement rates.

2. Think twice before using URL shorteners. Engagement rates are three times higher using full-length URLs.

3. Post when people are listening. Posts outside of business hours (10 a.m. to 4 p.m. EST) have a 20 percent higher engagement rate.

4. Some days are better than others. Engagement rates are 18 percent higher on Thursday and Friday than the other days of the week, but Saturday and especially Sunday are good too. This can vary by industry though.

5. Avoid the noise of Monday. There's too much going on after the weekend.

You can add a few more to this list that exactly parallel the email and Twitter advice:

6. Keep your posts relevant. You're trying to promote your brand, so stay on topic.

7. Don't post unnecessarily. Too many posts can cause your fans to tune you out.

8. Keep the interaction high. Ask your fans for their opinions and advice. It will not only keep them involved, but you'll immediately feel the pulse of
the tribe.

If you're posting to keep in touch with your friends or to let them know what you're doing, then this data is of no consequence to you. But if you're posting strategically to promote your brand, then follow the above for better fan engagement.

BEST TIME OF DAY FOR FACEBOOK POSTS

While you might be writing the best, most engaging posts, they do you no good if there's no one reading, so the question then becomes, "When is the best time of day to post to Facebook so my readership will be high?"

A study from the social-media company Vitrue called *Managing Your Facebook Community: Findings on Conversation Volume by Day of Week, Hour and Minute,* which looked closely at the viewing habits of Facebook channels of selected companies and brands, found:

▶ The best times to post are at 11 a.m., 3 p.m., and 8 p.m. ET.
▶ Of those times, the absolute best is at 3 p.m. ET on weekdays.
▶ Wednesday at 3 p.m. is the best time of the week to post.
▶ Fans are less active on Sunday.
▶ Posts on the weekend can be more effective than during the week.
▶ Posts that occur in the morning tend to perform almost 40 percent better in terms of user engagement than those in the afternoon.
▶ The top of the hour (:00 to :15 minutes) get more comments than other parts of the hour, with posts at the bottom of the hour (:30) getting the least.
▶ 65 percent of users only access Facebook in the evening.

UNDERSTANDING THE "LIKE" BUTTON

It's important to understand just what a "Like" means and not make too much or little of it. First of all, a Like is an endorsement by the fan. It has touched a nerve or a similar opinion or emotion, and it's an expression of that. It doesn't necessarily mean that you're especially clever, only that your post refers to something he or she wants to associate with. It's important to step back and look for a pattern of Likes or comments, then analyze them to see if there's a common thread. It's the best way to take the pulse of your tribe.

It's also important not to get too hung up with Likes, especially if you feel that you're not getting enough. An article by Robin Davey called "Only 10% Of Your Friends See Your Facebook Posts, And Only 1% Like It" on the Hypebot blog used the empirical evidence he received by a post on his personal wall asking his friends to Like it, and received about a 10 percent response. He determined the 1 percent portion of the article by looking at the following (an excerpt from the post):

The Black Keys have 800,000 fans and they get around 800 likes per post, although they did reach 7,000 when they said "Lotsa Grammys."

Justin Bieber has 22,000,000 fans and gets between 25,000 and 50,000 likes per post.

Mumford and Sons have 1,300,000 fans and have recently pulled an impressive 17,000 likes on one post that simply said, "TOUR!!!"

But how impressive exactly is that?

The Black Keys, at 800 for the less popular posts, works out significantly below 1% of their fans choosing to like it, and just under 1% for their most popular post. Bieber's rampant fans achieve similar numbers. Mumford's impressive number is actually only just above 1%.

The flaw in this thinking is that if someone doesn't register a Like, then they're not actually reading the post, which is not the case at all. In fact many of us see and react to posts without ever registering a Like.

The reason an artist should continue to post without worrying about getting Likes is the same reason advertising works—it's all about the impressions. The more impressions, or views, the more likely the viewer will take some action, such as download some music, go to a show, or buy a T-shirt.

As long as the information you post is valuable to the reader in some way, it's worth doing, because you're reaching him or her in some way. In other words, it's nice to be "Liked," but it's not necessarily a sign of a successful post.

Marketing with Facebook

Design a custom artist page using
one of the many tools.

Keep your posts short.

Make sure to include a link back to
your website or blog.

The best times to post are at 11 a.m.,
3 p.m., and 8 p.m. EST.

A "Like" is a look at the pulse of the tribe.

A post can be effective without
receiving a Like.

Google+

Google recently introduced their new social network called "Google+," and it has a number of interesting features that could be enough to make users of other social networks seriously consider it. These features promise to change the way we interact, socialize, and connect to others, and given the huge existing user footprint that Google already has, it could spell trouble for Facebook et al. Here's a look at them:

1. Circles: The idea of Circles is to closely follow the way you organize your contacts in real life. Circles offers a simple means of organizing your social network by combining contacts into small groups such as family, friends, coworkers, and so forth.

2. Stream: Stream allows you to receive instant updates from your friends and contacts in your Circles list, and lets you decide and choose which Circles and individuals you want to share your information with.

3. Sparks: Sparks pulls in stories, videos, and other cool content relating to your specific interest that are different from the results you'd get if you put the same term into the search engine that hopefully is relevant to you and your friends. After you enter your interests, Google+ goes out and searches for completely on-topic content, something that it does very well already.

4. Hangouts: Hangouts is a video chat feature that allows up to ten people in a group to come together and video chat.

5. Huddle: Huddle is a group SMS conversation feature where mobile phone numbers of members are visible to all.

6. Instant Upload: Instant Upload allows the user to upload pictures and videos directly from the phone.

Google+ also has privacy features that go beyond what Facebook offers. This allows you to choose which Circles you want to share that content with, which can be a useful tool for communicating with your tribe.

Another big advantage Google+ has over Facebook is its "data liberation," which allows you to pack up and take your data away from Google+ should you decide to leave the service.

Experience tells us that marketing on Google+ should be similar to that of Facebook, but its new features may cause change in strategy that can only be known after some experience with the network.

Marketing with Twitter

. . . .

As for Twitter, if you're not using it, you should be. It's amazing how much you can say in 140 characters, and unlike email blasts, even with ten or more tweets a day, your fans never feel intruded upon.

The secret to successful Twittering is to only tweet about relevant topics of interest to your tribe. Keep the tweets informative and not too personal. Here's an example:

> "Playing at the Lone Star in Memphis tonite. 9:30 p.m. sharp. Meet and greet afterwards in the bar. Great place. Come and join us."

This is an effective tweet because it provides some real information for the fans, although only on a local basis. A tweet that's a bit more global yet informative might be something like this:

> "Great gig at the Lone Star tonite. You people ROK! Two girls jumped on stage and Jimmy boogied with them. Video at http://bit.ly/7GFjDq."

See how much info can be communicated in just 140 characters? Notice how it made people interested to go to the website to check out the video?

Here's an example of a tweet that doesn't work because it's a bit too personal to be effective unless your name is Prince or Bono:

> "Just had bacon and eggs and potatoes for breakfast. The bacon was greasy and the potatoes were burnt. The coffee was good though."

This isn't a compelling use of the medium because it's mostly irrelevant information. A way to take that same idea and make it work might be:

> "Just had breakfast after a great gig at the Lone Star last night. Met Sally B and Adrian there and they were at the gig. Thanks a lot guys!"

This gives a shout out to some fans and talks about the gig. The fans love it because they were acknowledged, and it makes other fans hope that you'll acknowledge them as well, all in exactly 140 characters.

The beauty of Twitter is that you don't have be "Friended" by somebody. You can follow anybody you want (thousands of people if you want) and they can follow you unless you're blocking your profile. And if you're following each other, that constitutes a friend relationship and that means you can direct message them. It becomes a very sophisticated way to search and have conversations with a wide array of thought leaders. It's a very sophisticated crowd now, but it's starting to expand to the masses. It's not real big in music promotion yet, but it will be.

—Michael Terpin

THE SECRET OF THE HASHTAG

One of the most egregious errors for an artist using Twitter is overlooking the use of hashtags (the "#" symbol before a keyword).

Using a hashtag is like including a keyword in your tweet. It's an unofficial feature of Twitter but now widely accepted and supported, and is an easy way for people to search for and find a particular topic.

Here's how it works, using some of my own tweets:

> "The Secret To The Merch Table. Want to sell more merch at gigs? Here's how. http://bit.ly/7GFjDq #merch #gig #bands"

This is a simple tweet regarding a post from my Music 3.0 blog (music3point0.blogspot.com), complete with a shortened URL link. At the end are the hashtags #merch, #gig, and #bands. How were they selected? First of all, both "merch" and "gig" appear in the tweet, but both were researched first to see if there were any searches for each by going to "search.twitter.com." On the site I searched for both "merch" and "#merch" and determined that there was enough search traffic to make it worth using, as was "gig." Since the post was aimed at bands and was a topic that they'd be most interested in, another search found that "bands" was also sizable, so that term was used as well.

Here's another way the hashtags could have been used in this tweet.

> "The Secret to The #Merch Table. Want to sell more merch at #gigs? Here's how. http://bit.ly/7GFjDq"

In this case the hashtags are embedded directly into the tweet text. This method works, but it's sometimes too difficult to read, so the practice can quickly turn into a negative for less sophisticated users. Leaving room at the end of the tweet, especially for the hashtags, usually gets a better response.

Here's another example of a tweet from my Big Picture production blog (bobbyowsinski.blogspot.com).

> "The Magic High-Pass Filter. Some tips for using the mixer's secret weapon. http://bit.ly/dpL9bv #highpass #filter #mixing"

As in the previous example, a quick search discovered that #highpass had a lot more searches than #high-pass, and #mixing had more traffic than #mixer (there was also some confusion with a food processor as well).

Using hashtags is the key way to help people find you, but don't forget to include a link to take them to your blog or website as well, since that's the real goal.

THE BEST TIME TO TWEET

If you're using Twitter for promotion, then the timing of when you tweet is critical. If you do it when most people are busy and not paying attention, then you have no hope of engaging them, since tweets generally have little shelf life.

According to a new study by Dan Zarrella, a researcher at Hubspot who looked at millions of tweets and showed their results in a webinar entitled "The Science of Timing," the later you tweet in the day, the better. The reason is that from 2 p.m. to 5 p.m. EST, your followers are more likely to see your tweet because there are fewer things demanding their attention. In fact, 4 p.m. was deemed to be the best tweet time of the day.

Zarrella also found that the weekends are great for tweet attention as people are more relaxed and aren't conflicted by work. He also found that tweeting the same link multiple times a day is an effective strategy, and unlike excessive emails, followers don't seem to mind.

It was also found that 92 percent of all retweets and 97 percent of all replies happen within the first hour of the tweet lifetime. After that, it's as good as gone.

TWITTER TOOLS

There are a number of websites that can provide keyword search, trending, and measurement information that are useful in maximizing Twitter as a promotional tool. Keep in mind that these were accurate as of the writing of this book, but websites frequently disappear, change names, or change focus without much warning.

1. Search.twitter.com is more of an all-purpose Twitter search site. If you're looking for any keywords related to hashtags, be sure to place one in front of your search term (such as #keyword). If you select "advanced search," you can make your search even more granular.

2. Twellow (twellow.com) is a Twitter yellow pages directory. It's interesting in that if you search for a keyword, you'll get the profiles of users with that keyword in their profiles based on who has the most tweets.

3. Tweetstats (tweetstats.com) and Tweetstats Trends (tweetstats.com/trends) are a good way to look at not only what your personal stats are, but also the latest trends on Twitter.

4. Trendistic (trendistic.com) is another Twitter tool that will show you the hottest trends of the day, week, or month, as well as how any particular keywords are trending.

5. Klout (klout.com) is unique in that it measures your online influence in terms of likes, retweets, mentions, and comments. The idea is to measure the size of your true Twitter audience, instead of just by followers alone.

6. Blast Follow (blastfollow.com) is indispensable for finding people in your niche (and beyond) and mass-following them with a single click. Good for research.

7. Tweepi (tweepi.com) allows you to Unfollow those who do not reciprocate. If you use this, you're using Twitter wrong.

8. twAitter (twaitter.com) allows you to schedule your tweets in advance. Good app if you're using Twitter to broadcast blog postings. Not so good if used mostly for personal tweets.

9. Tweetdeck (tweetdeck.com) allows you to organize your followers and keep an eye on the really interesting ones in separate groups. It also allows you to post to Facebook and Linkedin at the same time, and to schedule your posts as well. I use this one all the time.

10. Tweetchat (tweetchat.com) allows you to isolate the conversation based on the hashtag.

11. TweetWhen (tweetwhen.com) analyzes your last 100 tweets and retweets and determines your best times to tweet.

Remember that you need to insert the hashtag (#) before your keyword when doing a keyword search. Also, a quick look at both the searches and trends before you select a keyword can make a difference in your Twitter traffic and ultimate attraction to new followers.

Marketing with Twitter

Start Twittering, but make sure you have something to say.

Always use hashtags to reach a greater audience.

Research the traffic before using a hashtag.

Make sure to include a link back to your website or blog.

2 to 5 p.m. are the best times to tweet during the day.

A tweet's lifetime is short, with most retweets or replies happening in the first hour.

Check multiple measurement tools to evaluate your progress.

Marketing with YouTube

· ·

YouTube has become much more than a site where you can watch amusing videos. It's now a major distribution point for music, and its value as a taste maker is now unparalleled. Why is the service so influential? Here are some staggering facts from YouTube's press section:

▶ Over 2 billion videos are viewed every day
▶ In 2010, there were over 700 billion video playbacks
▶ 35 hours of video footage is uploaded to the site every minute
▶ Over 13 million hours of footage was uploaded in 2010
▶ More video is uploaded every 60 days than the three major US television networks produced in 60 years
▶ 2 billion video views per week are monetized, and that number is rapidly increasing
▶ YouTube is localized in 25 countries across 43 languages
▶ 70 percent of YouTube traffic comes from outside the US
▶ More than half the videos on YouTube have been rated or commented on by users

When it comes to music, YouTube has now become a major platform for music discovery. In fact, it's now the single most widely used website for music discovery and distribution, according to a September 2010 survey by Nielsen Music and Midem. According to the study:

▶ People now consume more music by watching it than by any other means.
▶ Age makes a bigger difference in consumers' music-video watching preferences than gender. The younger the consumer, the more likely he or she is to have consumed music videos via either of the media.

That's why it's so important to an artist's development to create a YouTube channel and start uploading videos. If you want someone to discover you, you have more of a chance here than almost anywhere else online.

YOUTUBE SEO

YouTube can be used as an effective marketing tool, but you must observe the SEO (Search Engine Optimization) techniques outlined later in this book (see Gregory Markel's interview). Before you go live on a video, make sure that you do the following:

1. Name your video something descriptive. "Emerald at the Lone Star Club video 1/9/09" is good. "Untitled_bandvideo12.mov" is not descriptive at all, so your video will never get added by the search engines, and your fans won't find it.

2. Choose your keywords based on your title. In the above case, the keyword phrases would be "Emerald" (you might want to say "Emerald band" to be more descriptive) and "Lone Star Club." Keep your number of keyword phrases to four or five, since anything more could be construed as "keyword stuffing" (that means using every keyword you can think of in hopes of getting ranked by a search engine), and you might get penalized with a lower search-engine rank as a result.

3. Make sure that your description contains the same phrase as your title. For example, "This video features Emerald at the Lone Star Club on January 9, 2011." Something like "Here's our band at the Lone Star Club" wouldn't be as effective, because it omits the keyword "Emerald."

There are other ways of using YouTube promotionally. You can:

▶ Find people making creative videos on YouTube and offer them some original music to pair with their videos.

▶ Run a contest to see who comes up with the best
music video for one of your songs.

▶ Run a contest to see who can do the best mash-up
of your existing videos.

Also, the more text the body of your description has, the more likely
it will be found by a search engine. A hundred words works well but so
could 500.

These are just other ways to get not only your current fans involved,
but also potential new fans.

THE HALF-LIFE OF A VIRAL VIDEO

Video distributor TubeMogul's Insider's Report states that a typical
YouTube video gets 50 percent of its total views in the first 6 days.
After 20 days, it's already received 75 percent of the total views that it
will ever see.

You may think that if your video doesn't receive many plays in the
first week, it may never get any, but that's just not true. This study
obviously applies to the DIY "novelty" videos, and not ones that are
meant to extend your brand. Many videos gradually gain an audience
and continue to build over time, especially after a mention on a blog
or social network. If you maintain a good video SEO practice and
your video is aimed at building your brand, you'll quickly prove this
study wrong.

STREAMING VIDEO

While YouTube has been a force in the music community for
quite some time now, streaming video from services such
as UStream and LiveStream is a trend that is just starting to explode.
Artists can use real-time streaming to offer live performances, jam
sessions, studio sessions, or acoustic "unplugged"-style performances
from the comfort of their own homes. It's also possible to directly
engage fans through a real-time question-and-answer session, or even
allow fans to request songs during a performance. To be sure, live
streaming will become much more important to the artist of the future
as the services become more widespread.

YOUTUBE MEASUREMENT TOOLS

YouTube has a couple of great analysis tools that can provide a wealth of data. One is called the Trends Dashboard, which lets you see exactly what people are viewing and sharing. The Dashboard also gives you a picture of some of the gender and age demographics of the views. Here's what it shows:

► Selection by gender
► Views or sharing
► Selection by age group
► Selection by city, country, or globally
► Comparison of any of the above

The trend information only portrays viewer habits over the last 24 hours and videos uploaded over the last 28 days.

The Trends Dashboard can be a great informational tool if approached from the right perspective. If you want to learn what's working in a particular area, you can dial it up to take a look. Even better is that you can then analyze the Top 10 videos to gain an overview of the production techniques that worked in those particular cases.

Because the timeline is only over the last 24 hours, it's best if you watch the trends for at least a week, just to be sure that you're not getting a false impression. Keep in mind that many videos go viral because of their cuteness (cats and babies), weirdness, or just plain outrageousness, which is difficult to duplicate, but this tool can definitely give you a better idea of the types of things that are working or not.

Another excellent tool is the Insight tool built into every video and YouTube channel. It features a variety of demographic details, as well as methods of discovery and audience attention.

Marketing with YouTube

People now consume more music by watching it than by any other means.

Create a dedicated YouTube channel.

Keep the video title descriptive.

Use SEO where possible.

The more text in the description, the better.

Make sure to include a link back to your website or blog in the description.

Live streaming will become more important in the future.

Keep track of your video progress through YouTube Insights and Trends.

EIGHT

CHAPTER

Social Media Management

o many areas of social media require attention that it can get a bit overwhelming at times, and that's when you need a social media management strategy.

A common mistake that artists who manage their own social media assets make is to have too many focal points (such as YouTube, their Website, their blog, Twitter, and ReverbNation, for example) all residing in different places and requiring separate updates. You can imagine how tough it is to keep every one of those sites updated regularly! Worse is the fact that it's confusing for the fan, who just wants a single place to visit. Yet another problem is that you may be collecting email addresses from each site, and they may all be going on different mailing lists.

The solution is to use one site (usually your website) as your main focal site and use that to feed daily updates and info to all the others via RSS or social media broadcast tools such as Dijit (dijit.com) or Ping (ping.fm). This means that you only need to do the work of updating a single site, with all the others getting updated at the same time.

The second component of this management strategy would be to have all of your satellite sites (blog, Facebook, and so on) designed in such a way as to feed your social media viewers into your website (see illustration below). At a bare minimum, the email registration of each satellite site should feed into the same list as your main site.

At some point social media management gets too complex for the artist to maintain, and third-party help is needed. This is usually a good thing, since you've progressed to a point that things are so massive that you need help. Furthermore, a company that specializes in social media management can keep you current with new tools and techniques that you might not be aware of. Even when outside help arrives, remember that you are still the one that drives the bus. Be sure to take part in all strategy discussions, but leave the actual facilitation to the company you've hired.

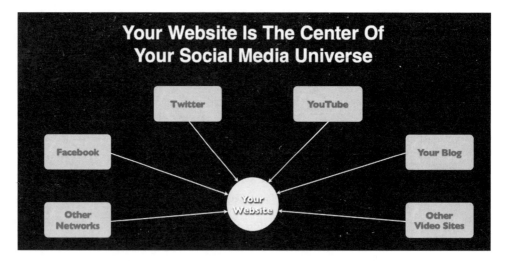

Social Media Management

Keep a single site as your main focal point.

Feed all your updates from your main site
via RSS or social media broadcast apps.

Develop your satellite sites so they all feed
viewers into your main site.

Email-list subscribers from all sites should
go to same master list.

Get third-party help when you
get overwhelmed.

Keep driving the bus!

Measuring Your Social Media Exposure

How many people have you reached with your message? How many could you have reached? In social media, there are some measurements about as reliable as a print magazine's circulation, but knowing your potential audience does have value because it represents your potential sales lead pool.

Unfortunately, as of the writing of this book, some of these metrics have to be accounted for manually, so you'll have to balance the level of effort to track the metrics versus the value you'll receive from them to determine their importance to your overall strategy.

A good example of where there can be unreliability in social measurement is when isolating unique users for each of your metrics. You want to avoid counting the same person twice in the list below, but realistically it's difficult to do.

These measurements highlight the number of people you've attracted to your brand through social media. To mitigate the potential for duplication of users, track growth rate as a percentage of the aggregate totals. This is where you will find the real diamonds.

- **Twitter:** Look at your number of followers and the number of followers for those who retweeted your message to determine the monthly potential reach. You should track these separately and then compare the month-over-month growth rate of each of these metrics so you can determine where you're seeing the most growth. A great free tool to use for Twitter measurement is TweetReach.

- **Facebook:** Track the total number of fans for your brand page. In addition, review the number of friends from those who became fans during a specified period of time or during a promotion and those who commented on or liked your posts to identify the potential monthly Facebook reach. Facebook Insights provides value here, as does Klout.

- **YouTube:** Measure the number of views for videos tied to a promotion or specific period of time, such as monthly, and the total number of subscribers.

- **Blog:** Measure the number of visitors who viewed the posts tied to the promotion for a specific period of time.

- **Email:** Take a look at how many people are on the distribution list and how many actually received the email.

SOCIAL MEDIA MEASUREMENT TOOLS

Measuring just how successful an artist's promotional campaign is (the artist's buzz) and all the data that surrounds an artist is a top issue for M3.0. This was impossible in M1.0 and 1.5, somewhat available in M2.0, but now much more widely available and easier than ever to use in M3.0. With so many new avenues available for music discovery and promotion, knowing where the buzz is coming from and how to utilize it is more an issue than ever.

Here are ten tools to help track your buzz:

Band Metrics (bandmetrics.com)—
band and song tracking.
Google Alerts (google.com/alerts)—sweeps
the Web and delivers buzz to your inbox.

Twitter Search (search.twitter.com)—track your buzz on this popular microblogging service.

Who's Talkin (whostalkin.com)—
social media search.

Stat Counter (statcounter.com)—
statistics about who visits your site and blog.

Tynt Tracer (tcr1.tynt.com)—traces images and text that have been copied off your site.

Next Big Sound (nextbigsound.com)—shows the number of new fans, plays, views, and comments.

Music Metric (musicmetric.com)—provides social network tracking, P2P network analysis, radio and sales data, and fan demographics.

RockDex (rockdex.com)—collects data from blog posts, fan connections, page views, tweets, and song plays, and spots viral trends and tracks progress over time.

Klout (klout.com)—measures your mentions, likes, comments, and followers to determine your reach and influence.

ADVANCED SOCIAL MEDIA ANALYTICAL TOOLS

As social media becomes more sophisticated, so do the measurement-tool requirements to determine both your impact and branding possibilities. Three new methods of analyzing social media data have shown a lot of promise, but it might be a bit too early in the learning curve to completely trust the data. Still, it's good to know about what's on the horizon.

▶ **Sentiment analysis** is a process that tries to determine the attitude of a speaker or a writer with respect to the topic he or she is writing about. If you actually read a blog or posting, you can tell the writer's sentiment immediately, but this analysis method tries to define and measure it as a point of data.

▶ **Cluster analysis** tries to analyze how certain words are gathering (or "clustering") relative to a search topic. It finds the words that are mostly likely to be associated with your search word, which may provide unexpected insight into what's being said about you and even predict sales before they happen.

▶ **Semantic analysis** is another measurement tool that strives to understand what words mean in context to one another. Once again, it's something that we do for ourselves as we read, but this tool puts a number to it.

All of these tools are trying to measure what we can immediately see for ourselves empirically by just wading into the social media pool. They put a number to something that we can feel.

New measurement platforms such as Sysomos and Radian6 are said to be using these tools to provide a more precise look at how you or your brand integrate with the social world.

If you need data for a meeting, to sway an investor, or appease a boss, these tools are important. If you're a marketer on a very high level, you might find the data immediately useful. If you're a band or artist just trying to make the next sale, the next gig, or make it through the next day of social media management, you'll find them interesting as best and parlor tricks at worst. But while these tools may be cutting edge today, you never know if they'll be an essential part of your marketing toolbox tomorrow. Stay tuned.

The Importance of Measurement

Know where the buzz is coming from.

Know what's working or what's not.

Know who your fans are.

Know where your fans are from.

Know what your fans like.

What Is a Brand?

For an artist, a brand means a consistency of persona, and usually a consistency of sound. Regardless of what genre of music the artist delves into, the feel is the same, and you can tell it's the artist. Madonna has changed directions many times during her career, but her brand remained consistent. Her persona remained the same even as she changed to and from the "material girl." The Beatles tried a wide variety of directions, but you never once questioned who you were listening to. It was always fresh and exciting, but distinctly them.

On the other hand, Neil Young almost killed his career with an electronic album called *Trans* that alienated all but his hardiest fans, and the well-respected Chris Cornell may have done irreparable harm to his long-term career thanks to his recent album with Timbaland (*Scream*), even though it was the highest-charting record of his career. Why did this happen? For both artists, the album no longer "felt" like them. Both Young and Cornell built their careers on organic music played with a band, and as soon as their music became regimented and mechanical, they lost their brands. After *Trans*, Young returned to his roots and slowly built his brand back to superstar level, but it's too soon to know what will happen with Cornell.

How do you determine what your brand is? It's easier said than done.

In order for you as an artist to successfully promote your brand, you must have a great sense of self-knowing. You must know who you are, where you came from, and where you're going. You must know what you like and don't like, and what you stand for and why. And you must have an inherent feel for your sound and what works for you.

And that differentiates a superstar from a star, and a star from someone who wants it really badly but never seems to get that big break.

I'M WITH THE BRAND

It seems that as a music star becomes more popular, so too does his or her desire to cash in on his or her fame through nonmusical business moves. This is so opposed to the spirit of what a popular musician used to be that it leaves those of us from that era more and more incredulous. Here are some examples of artists extending their brands into nonmusical ventures.

- ▶ Rap star Kanye West has his own Internet search engine (it's called *Search with Kanye West*).
- ▶ Aerosmith guitarist Joe Perry has his own line of hot sauce.
- ▶ The R&B singer Usher teamed up with Mastercard to launch a range of credit cards.
- ▶ Justin Bieber has, curiously for a sixteen-year-old boy, his own line of nail polish called *One Less Lonely Girl.*
- ▶ Madonna opened the *Hard Candy Fitness* centre in Mexico City, the first of what she hopes will be a worldwide chain of "first class" gyms.
- ▶ Lady Gaga has released her own range of "Heartbeat" headphones.
- ▶ Jennifer Lopez sold the first pictures of her twins Emme and Max to People magazine for a reported $6 million.
- ▶ Beyoncé is now focusing on her clothing ranges, House of Dereon and I Am Sasha Fierce.
- ▶ Jay-Z has nonmusical business opportunities, including the clothing label Rocawear and the New York nightclub 40/40.
- ▶ 50 Cent, Eminem and P. Diddy all have their own clothing ranges, while P. Diddy has also carved out an extra source of income for himself in promoting the vodka brand Cîroc.

Once again, celebrity can mean more to some people than being an artist, but the problem is that the brand soon becomes diluted. Do you know Diddy for his vodka or his music? Do you think of clothing or music when you think of Beyoncé? Many marketers might call this "brand extension," but when you lose touch with your core audience, product, or persona, you've diluted your brand.

SPONSORSHIP

Sponsorship is better thought of as "cobranding," since both the artist and the sponsor's brand image are tied together (a point many times overlooked by the artist). This can frequently put the artist at odds with his or her tribe, with cries of "sellout" in the air and on the blogs.

For that reason, sponsorship is another double-edged sword for the M3.0 artist. While it might be a source of tour support, the artist runs the risk of losing credibility with his or her fans. This credibility gap can come if the sponsor is a large, faceless conglomerate that's difficult to relate to or is at odds with the sensibilities of either the artist or, worse, the fan.

> *For instance, if an artist is sponsored by a beer company but everyone in the band is in Alcoholics Anonymous, that can be a problem sponsorship. If sponsorship by a beer company goes with the band's hard-driving, partying image but goes against the mores of its fans, that too can be a problem. However, a biker band that's sponsored by the local Harley dealer, or by Harley Davidson itself, or by the biker bar they play at, could be an effective cobranding.*
>
> —Larry Gerbrandt

Ultimately, an artist almost always risks his or her credibility in a sponsorship deal of any magnitude. Consider the risks carefully before entering into such a deal.

Branding

An artist's brand is consistency in persona and sound.

Many artists extend their brands beyond music.

Sponsorship cobrands the artist with the sponsor.

Sponsorship runs the risk of losing fan credibility if at odds with the artist's image or fan sensibilities.

Any sponsorship must have perfect image symmetry between artist and brand to be successful.

Other Avenues for Social Media

· ·

Many music discovery sites such as Bandcamp, Nimbit, or ReverbNation help your marketing by allowing you to set up a widget with upcoming concert dates, press releases, photos, videos, and stores to buy your music. They also allow you to set up a virtual "street team," where your fans can go out and promote your music for you. Most of these promotional features are provided for paying members of the particular site, but many of the free promotion features are great for someone needing to promote music but who has little money.

Don't Depend on Your Social Network

· ·

It's too easy for today's artist who only dabbles in social networking to get complacent and comfortable with the abilities of a single social network, but that can spell disaster for maintaining your fan base if you're not careful. As those artists who formerly depended upon MySpace now know, what's hot today can become ice cold tomorrow. But other negative scenarios also exist that can be far worse than the network falling out of favor.

Scenario #1: Let's say that you've cultivated a huge following on Facebook. What would happen if Facebook was purchased by Google, which decides that all it wants is the underlying technology of the network and shuts the rest down? If you didn't capture the email addresses of all your followers, you'd lose them to the nothingness of cyberspace. Don't laugh—it could happen.

Scenario #2: What would happen if Facebook (I'm picking on them because they're currently the big dog on the social block) changes its terms of service, and now charges you $0.25 for every fan past 100? If you've built an audience of 80,000 fans, it's going to cost you $20 grand to continue. What if they decided to limit everyone's fan connections to 100? Both are unlikely, but something similar could happen, where suddenly you were unable to access that large fan base that you've worked so hard to develop.

That's why it's imperative that you harvest as many email addresses as you can for your own mailing list so you can keep your social communication under your control. If you rely on an external network, sooner or later you're going to get burnt. It's the nature of the Internet to constantly change, and it's too early to get a feel for the life span of even of the largest sites and networks. So play it safe—develop that mailing list.

THERE'S MORE TO SOCIAL NETWORKING THAN FACEBOOK

When it comes to social networking, the first network we think of is Facebook, closely followed by Twitter. But even though Facebook is still the social giant that dwarfs everything else, there are 28 other social networks worldwide that have at least 1 million daily views, according to Pingdom. Here they are:

1. Facebook: 310 M
2. Orkut: 51 M
3. Qzone: 37 M
4. Twitter: 22 M
5. Odnoklassniki: 9.3 M
6. LinkedIn: 8.0 M
7. vKontakte: 8.0 M
8. Badoo: 8.0 M
9. Mixi: 7.0 M
10. Flickr: 4.9 M
11. Hi5: 4.2 M
12. MySpace: 4.0 M
13. Nasza Klasa: 4.0 M
14. Tuenti: 3.9 M
15. Hyves: 3.0 M
16. Renren: 3.0 M
17. Tagged: 2.6 M
18. Taringa! 2.5 M
19. Cyworld: 2.2 M

20. Netlog: 2.1 M
21. LiveJournal: 2.0 M
22. Kaixin001: 2.0 M
23. Wer-kennt-wen: 2.0 M
24. Sonico: 1.5 M
25. Douban: 1.5 M
26. MeinVZ: .5 M
27. Skyrock: 1.4 M
28. deviantART: 1.3 M
29. iWiW: 1.1 M

As you can see, there are plenty that aren't well known, mostly because they're popular in areas of the world other than North America, but that doesn't mean they're any less powerful in getting your message across. Ask your fans if there's another network that they visit often, and be prepared to jump in if the answer is yes.

Other Social Networks

Don't depend on a single social network.

Own as much data as you can away from any social network.

Explore other social networks to expand your social reach.

Ten Low-Cost, Hi-Tech Promotion Ideas

Never leave promotion to someone else. You must always be actively involved on at least an oversight level to be sure that not only are you getting promoted, but the promotion is something that's beneficial to your image as an artist. This even includes having a publicist, since he or she takes the cues from you. Especially don't depend on a record label, particularly in these days when so few staff people do so many jobs. It's up to you to develop the strategy, or it might not get developed at all.

That being said, here are a number of low-cost M3.0 ideas that you can do to get your promotion started:

1. Set up a Facebook page, then be sure to stay active. It won't do you much good if you just set it up and never update it. The only way it's worth your fans visiting is if you keep the updates coming as often as possible.

2. Every time a Friend request is exchanged between yourself and other Facebook users, send them a note back thanking them, and ask if you can include them in your group of friends outside of Facebook. Ask them to "Please reply with your email address if that's okay." This is a great way to build your tribe, but make sure they can easily opt out if it's not their cup of tea. It's not too beneficial to have all those Facebook Friends if you can't contact them outside of those sites.

3. Always have a "Press" section on your Website that contains the following:

► High- and low-resolution color and black-and-white photos
► Logos
► Biographical information
► Quotes from the media
► Links to any interviews
► Links to music
► Links to videos
► Social media addresses and links to Facebook, your blog, ReverbNation, and so forth
► Scans of three or four of your best press clippings
► A press-release section
► A discography
► A list of upcoming gigs
► A fact sheet with bullet points about interesting artist facts
► Scans of a promo flyer and poster
► Web-ready graphics and banners
► Publicist or artist contact info

Having these tools easily available will increase the chances of getting media coverage. It's a fact that the easier you can make it for a blogger, writer, or editor, the more likely you'll get covered.

4. Backlinks are important. Anytime you are mentioned in a club listing, on the site of a band you're playing with, or anywhere else, make sure that it links back to your site. People won't do this automatically, so make it standard operating procedure to ask.

5. Encourage fans to tag you and your content on sites such as Flickr, blogs, Digg, and StumbleUpon, then make that data available on your site.

6. Even though you may have a presence on Facebook, you still need a website. It's still the best place to gather your tribe and communicate with them. Make sure that you follow Keys to a Successful Website for creating the best website experience for your fans.

7. Engage your fans. Ask them questions. Polls and surveys are free (that magic word again) and easy to set up with sites such as PollDaddy and Surveymonkey.

8. Develop a press-release mailing list of music writers and editors from all local and regional newspapers, magazines, specialty papers, radio stations, online radio stations, and music blogs (especially) that cover the type of music that you play (you can do national and international later, when you grow into it). Remember that it doesn't do you much good to send something to a blog or magazine that specializes in metal if you're a folk singer, so don't even think about anything out of your genre. Once your list is complete, send out a short email for any major gig, event, or song release, but don't make it too frequent or you won't be covered—ever. Include links to your website and an offer for a free press pass to a show. About once a month is a good frequency. If you get a mention, be sure to send an email or even a handwritten note to say thank you.

9. Create your own YouTube channel. Make sure to post new videos frequently, and encourage fans to post as well.

10. Create a special insider email list for a few fans, key media, taste-makers, and bloggers for sending preannouncements to those people who love to know things first . . . and like to tell others.

Keys to a Successful Website

Make sure your band's name is in every one of the following: the URL, title, website description, and first paragraph of text.

Keep your keywords to a maximum of five and *be sure that they relate to the content on the page.*

Keep the flash to a minimum. Yes, it looks great, but search engines can't read it. You want fans to find you, right?

Make sure there's an easy way for people to give you their email addresses. Make sure they know what to expect from signing up.

Keep your content relevant to your keywords. Don't use Katy Perry as a keyword unless you actually have something about Katy Perry in the body text of your page, otherwise Google will penalize you.

A blog tied to your site is a great way for easy updates and a great way for your tribe to interact.

Keep the copy of each page to between 200 and 600 words.

Make sure there are no page errors (broken links). It frustrates your visitors and you'll get penalized by Google as well.

But You Still Must Hit the Streets

The Internet provides ways to interact with fans that were unthinkable even back in the M2.0 days, but they're still no substitute for the hard work that goes with being a musician. If you want to succeed, you've got to build and maintain your audience over a period of years, and for that you've still got to hit the streets. This means that you've got to play live, you have to be ready to promote traditionally as well as online, and you still have to sell yourself, your music, and your merchandise one fan at a time. Getting reviews and doing press and interviews will never go away.

All the attributes of M3.0 must be seen as an adjunct to the traditional work that is the business part of the music business. Sure, it's quite powerful and more necessary than ever, but so far, no one has made it as a result of M3.0 only. It's possible to have great visibility, a lot of "Friends" and downloads, and still not have anything other than a brief career (remember the turntable hits we spoke of before?) So even as traditional street-marketing decreases in importance, it's still vital for long-term success.

TEN LOW-COST, LOW-TECH PROMOTION IDEAS

Promotion doesn't have to cost money to be effective. Here are some ideas that can be powerful tools that don't even involve a computer.

1. Don't underestimate the value of something free. Fans love free items, either as part of a package (for example, buy a CD, and get a T-shirt free), part of a contest, or just being one of the first ten fans to email. Sometimes items of seemingly little value have a wide appeal. Backstage passes, seat upgrades, seats on stage, tickets to the sound check, invites to a meet and greet, and downloads of live songs are all prized by a real fan.

2. It's surprising that this isn't done more since it works so well: **Park a van or truck that has a banner on it across from a show by a similar act.** Every fan entering or exiting the venue will be aware of you.

3. Free or low-cost entry to show "after parties" extends the show experience and rewards the true fan. These can be promoted along with the show, and even offered as a part of the ticket package.

4. Instead of sending a "thank you" email to a promoter, writer, interviewer, or just someone who's done you a good turn, send a handwritten thank-you note by snail mail. You'll be shocked how well this works. It's unusual, it's sincere, and it's remembered. It's also very likely to be seen, since we're all getting fewer and fewer snail-mail items these days.

5. Consider asking your tribe to help you with promo. Ask them to put up flyers or send out emails. Put a PDF of a poster or flyer online for fans to download.

6. Fans always want a chance to meet the musicians. **Consider having a "meet and greet" after every show.** But make sure that the fans know about it in advance.

7. Find your niche and market to it. It makes no sense to market to Amy Winehouse's tribe if your music isn't like hers, so don't waste your energy marketing in that direction.

8. Make everything you do an event. What holiday is coming up? Is it a band member's birthday? Is an anniversary near? Try a tribute to "Fans that just got laid off" or "Fans that just got hired."

9. Use the power of your niche to widen your fan base. Flyer someone else's show in a related genre. Sponsor somebody else's event. Consider trading sponsorships and gigs with another band.

10. Align yourself with a cause you believe in. Causes often have a large PR mechanism behind them that can expose your music, but it has to be something you really believe in or it may hurt you in the long run.

> ## Hit the Streets
>
> Traditional marketing is as important as viral.
>
> Sell yourself one fan and one gig at a time.
>
> No one's broken huge yet from online
> sales and marketing alone.

NINE

CHAPTER

>off premises
backup system

internet

>Data loss

>fatal bug

The New
Distribution

For the musician, distribution has never been easier or more diverse as in the M3.0 world. There are now numerous ways in multiple areas to get product into the hands of the consumer, but these additional choices also require a new distribution strategy.

In the time prior to M2.5 (before iTunes), distribution was strictly a retail process in which the customer purchased directly from a brick–and-mortar retail store (yes, there were things like record clubs and, later, online CD retailers such as Amazon, but the bulk of the sales were made through retail stores). In M3.0 however, the artist is presented with new possibilities that go beyond the traditional brick–and-mortar retail. These include online digital distribution sites such as iTunes and Amazon MP3, digital and CD sales made directly to the customer online, and a hybrid of the above, such as CD Baby or

Tunecore. Let's take a look at some of the current available options, as well as a new way to think about distribution.

Digital, Vinyl, or Bright, Shiny Disc?

In the recent past, there have always been multiple containers (a container is the way the music is packaged for distribution) of music that an artist had available for sale. First there were vinyl singles and vinyl albums, then vinyl albums and cassettes, then CDs and cassettes, then digital downloads and CDs. With the recent resurgence of vinyl, an artist has three container options for distribution of his or her work. Let's take a look at the pros and cons of each.

MUSIC CONTAINER	PROS	CONS
Digital	No container manufacturing cost Minimal distribution cost No costs for graphics/liner notes High promotional value Large and growing market Fast release to the marketplace	No collectible value No resale value High rate of piracy Intangible worth Difficult to get reviewed Difficult to get traditional airplay Vulnerable to obsolescence as digital formats evolve
CD	Tangible worth Potential revenue stream Collectible value Opportunity for added value More likely to get reviewed	Cost of container manufacturing Cost of container distribution Decreasing market size Limited sales outlets Slow into the marketplace due to manufacturing time Difficulty getting paid from distributors

MUSIC CONTAINER	PROS	CONS
Vinyl	Tangible worth Potential revenue stream Collectible value Opportunity for added value	Cost of container manufacturing Cost of container distribution Hidden costs such as breakage Small market size Limited sales outlets Unlikely to get reviewed Slow into the marketplace due to manufacturing Difficulty getting paid from distributors

As you can see from the chart above, each of the current music containers has an assortment of pros and cons. This is not to say that one container is better than another in M3.0 (although that's clearly true), but it helps to be aware of the benefits and disadvantages of each.

DIGITAL DOWNLOADS

A digital container has no manufacturing costs, so there are few additional expenses after the initial production of the music. Since there is no physical container, there's no need for disc and album artwork or liner notes, so there is no additional expense or time required for manufacturing other than typing in the metadata.

Downloadable music makes it easy for numerous services to distribute a digital song for anywhere from having a nominal charge (either a yearly or a submission fee, all well under $100) to being free. And it's relatively fast to distribute a digital container, making it instantly available on your website (although it may take two to six weeks to go live for some online distributors such as iTunes). If you want to use a digital song (or songs) as a promotional track, again the cost is minimal, since there are no manufacturing costs to recoup. Finally, the market for digital music is huge and it's growing, a claim that cannot be made about the other containers.

While the digital container will always be the container of choice in M3.0, it has some downsides to be aware of. The fact that any attempt to monetize digital downloads is hampered by the ease of piracy has been discussed ad infinitum, so I won't go beyond simply making it a bullet point. Perhaps a larger issue is that digital's worth is intangible; it's not something that you can physically hold in your hand. This fact has given a whole generation of consumers the notion that music is free, which is difficult to overcome. Indeed, a digital song has no collectible value. It won't be traded or prized, and you can't resell it, which is why the perception remains that it should be free.

Another serious consideration is that digital formats such as MP3 and AAC are subject to obsolescence as new formats are introduced and evolve. While today that doesn't seem to be much of an issue in the consumer world, it's become a serious problem in the professional audio world, with early digital masters becoming unplayable as formats progress. Digital file-compression formats such as MP3 and AAC were initially used for distribution because bandwidth was both expensive and in short supply. With bandwidth becoming less of an issue every day, we're already seeing that files are getting larger because listeners are demanding higher quality. As a result, bit rates have gradually increased from a norm of 128 kbps to one of 320 kbps and higher. Lossless formats such as FLAC and AAC+ are also gaining momentum, which can mean that releases done in the current MP3 format and bit rate will have to eventually be rereleased in a lossless, higher-bit-rate format. In fact, there may soon come a day when bandwidth is high enough that the music doesn't have to be compressed at all, maintaining its original 44.1k or 48kHz AIFF or Wav format used during production (musicians, engineers and producers everywhere will rejoice).

Finally and most overlooked, it's still difficult to get digital files reviewed by traditional or even some online reviewers, or to get airplay from a traditional broadcaster. At the time of this writing, you are just not considered legit in the eyes of reviewers unless you present them with a CD.

CD–THE BRIGHT AND SHINY DISC

Getting reviews isn't the only reason to consider having CDs in your distribution strategy, since there are still clear advantages for replicating CDs, even in M3.0. Even though CD sales have fallen off the cliff (CD sales are less than 65 percent of what they were in 2000, and they're declining steadily), they will remain a viable music container for at least a few years to come. Indeed, some music lovers still prefer buying a CD to any other format.

CDs are still viewed as an item of tangible worth by buyers because of their physical nature and the fact that they include graphics and liner notes. For many, there is an added collectible value if the CD is numbered or in short supply, and there is the ability to add value to the unit by including in the packaging something additional such as show tickets or any number of premium items (see the section called "The Wisdom of Trent" in chapter 4). All this adds up to a clear revenue stream for the artist that can surpass anything that a digital download can provide. Of course, that's assuming your music is something the fan wants to buy in the first place, but we're assuming a bare minimum of popularity of the artist throughout this book.

We may never get to the point where we don't want to press physical product. In fact, I'm a believer that physical product acts like a souvenir of the band. If bands think of a CD that way and package it as such, they might find some increased success with it.

—Bruce Houghton

Even with costs ranging as low as $.060 for a basic CD package (in large quantities, of course), manufacturing still represents a substantial up-front cost that the artist must bear, which is a clear disadvantage. Add the costs of graphic design for the disc artwork and jewel-case trays, with the time the design, manufacturing, and shipping takes before the product gets to market (two weeks minimum but likely much more), along with the difficulty one can have getting paid by distributors, CDs soon become a music container that many artists prefer not to deal with.

THE VINYL RECORD

After the CD was unleashed on the public in 1982, it seemed as though the vinyl disc would soon be headed the way of the horse and carriage, but it never totally went away, and has had a revival of sorts in recent years. In fact, the remaining vinyl mastering houses and pressing plants are busier than ever, running 24/7 pumping out product.

Why has vinyl realized a resurgence despite the technological breakthroughs of M3.0? Many claim that the audio quality is still superior to CDs (although that greatly depends upon the stylus and turntable involved), in spite of the fact that a record loses fidelity with every play. Others still love the cardboard album covers for their artwork and easily readable liner notes. Vinyl has a substantial collectible value and can be priced as such, giving the artist an additional revenue stream. In fact, a record is often an integral piece of the premium package offered by an artist.

But pressing a record does have its downsides as well. Aside from the obvious graphic design and manufacturing costs, and the manufacturing delay to market, there's the additional issue of breakage, or the fact that some records break or warp during shipping. Breakage was normally calculated at 10 percent and deducted off the top of the gross income in a typical recording contract during M1.0. While breakage might have been that high at the time (which is debatable), the actual amount is closer to 2 percent and must be accounted for when budgeting. And finally, a record-only strategy is probably a loser in M3.0 because the market is so small to begin with and because of the unlikelihood of the record getting reviewed due to the fact that most reviewers don't own a turntable.

Music Containers

Digital is convenient but easy to pirate
and has little aftermarket value.

Digital has the cheapest distribution.

Many buyers still only buy CDs.

Vinyl is undergoing a resurgence in popularity.

Vinyl is subject to breakage during transit.

Collectibles

....

We've spoken about the CD and the vinyl record as being collect-ibles, but just what does that mean? A collectible is an item (usually a nonessential one) that has particular value to its owner because of its rarity and desirability. Antiques, paintings, and coins are collectibles because of their rarity, which makes them highly desirable. Do you see the conundrum with a digital song? Because a digital song is so easily transportable and transferable, there's no rarity involved. And it isn't something that you can display, show your friends, or resell, so there's virtually no collectability factor either.

Vinyl records and CDs, on the other hand, are collectible in their very basic form. In a premium package consisting of CDs, vinyl, downloads, DVDs, and so on, everything but the digital download becomes a collectible, especially if it's signed by the artist. With the market for CDs rapidly diminishing, the discs may eventually become as rare as vinyl. With added value content such as concept graphics and liner notes, they become still retain a must-have to true fans.

There are certain music genres (country and metal, for instance) in which fans still prefer CDs to digital downloads. While this might be caused by fans either lagging behind in terms of technical sophis-tication or being part of an older demographic, it might also be an indication that the fans of these genres have a greater affinity for col-lectibles, which should not be underestimated.

Collectibles

The rarer it is, the more valuable it becomes.

CDs or vinyl can be collectible.

Digital music is not collectible because it's not physical product.

Digital Music Distribution

· ·

Digital distribution is, of course, the backbone of M3.0, whether it's paid or for free, and there seem to be more and more options every day. Since most of these services rise and fall in popularity weekly, I'll mention only the largest and most stable, and how as a genre they might contribute to an artist's success.

PAID DOWNLOADS

With the number of digital downloads increasing every year, paid downloads (meaning a downloadable song that you buy and own) are a primary revenue stream for an artist in M3.0. In fact, in 2010, just slightly under 1.2 *billion* digital downloads were purchased, according to Nielsen SoundScan, a sales-tracking system that tracks sales of music and music video products throughout the United States and Canada.

Although the payment for a download varies from site to site, the average is around $.060 per song downloaded, $6.50 per full-album download, and $0.25 per listen or stream (when people listen to your song as if it were on a radio station, but don't actually download or buy it). This is the amount paid by the service to either you or your record label.

ITUNES

If ever there were a leviathan in the entertainment room of the music industry, it's the Apple iTunes store. Thanks to Apple iPods, iPhones, and iPads dominating 71 percent of the digital-music-player market share, iTunes holds a commanding 63 percent of the digital marketplace. From its ambitious start in 2003, iTunes has gradually risen to become the largest music retailer in the United States, even topping retail giant Walmart (according to the NPD research group). And even though newcomer Amazon MP3 has garnered its share of users, NPD also states that most of them are new digital users, with only 10 percent of them ever having used iTunes before.

Until April of 2009, all iTunes songs had the same price: $0.99. After much prodding by the major record labels, Apple expanded its offerings and went to a multitiered pricing system, with a limited number of songs available at as low a price as $0.69, and some of the current hits available without DRM (Digital Rights Management) and with higher-quality encoding for $1.29. Most of iTunes's more than 14 million songs still remain priced at $0.99. iTunes is now also offering a pseudosubscription service called the iTunes Pass, which provides an album along with extra content such as videos, remixes, and exclusive singles for $18.99.

> *I recently wrote a blog about how the industry was making a horrible mistake if they increase their prices at this really critical time. The idea of variable pricing, when I was promoting it at EMI, was to put new artists on sale, to create special bundles, to create value, to create differentiation, and to get a premium out of certain artists only where it was appropriate. If Coldplay came out with a new track a month before the new album, sure, charge $1.49 for it. But the buyer might get $0.50 or even $1.00 off the new album when it comes out.*
>
> —Ted Cohen, industry sage and
> principal in TAG Strategic

OTHER DIGITAL DISTRIBUTORS

Although iTunes is the largest digital distributor, there are numerous other choices available. Here are just a few of the online stores that offer paid downloads (limited to services that have a catalog of 1 million or more songs):

- ▶Amazon MP3
- ▶7Digital
- ▶GoMusic
- ▶PlayNow
- ▶Puretracks
- ▶Sky Songs (UK only)
- ▶Walmart Music
- ▶Zune Marketplace
- ▶FairShare Music (UK only)
- ▶iMesh (including 15 million free songs)
- ▶Moozone
- ▶eMusic
- ▶Napster (also offers paid streams, see below)

►Rhapsody (also offers paid streams, see below)
►ShockHound

AMAZON MP3

Although second to iTunes in market share, Amazon MP3 hasn't made much of a dent in iTunes's dominance, having only risen to 13 percent of the market (compared to iTunes's 63 percent) in 2010, according to the NPD Group. Digital music executives at record labels say the disparity between the two may be even greater, with Amazon commanding just 6 to 10 percent of the market in any given week, and Apple closer to 90 percent.

But what Amazon MP3 does have going for it is pricing, with a "daily deal" album at $3.99, a monthly promotion of 100 albums priced at $5.00 each, and most of the rest of the more than 14 million song catalog typically at $8. The price levels are broken down like this:

► **Front Line:** The highest retail price in the store (good for new releases)
► **Midline:** Slightly lower than front line (good for new releases and other current releases)
► **Catalog:** Slightly lower than midline (good for older or lower-selling releases)
► **Special:** The lowest retail price in the store (good for promotions, old releases, and low-selling catalog songs)

Like iTunes, Amazon MP3 sells digital songs and albums via different stores, depending upon the territory, and also does not use DRM on music they sell. All music is sold as unprotected MP3s.

RINGTONES

It wasn't that long ago that ringtones were being hailed as the savior of the music business, but like so many things in the our fast-churning society, the craze flashed out quickly. This was partially because of the prices (standard pricing was $2.49 for a mere ten seconds of the song), and new apps that enabled the user to create his or her own ringtones. The short-lived fad was ahead of its time when it came to purchasing though.

GroupieTunes (now defunct) was the first company to offer independent and unsigned artists the ability to sell their music as ringtones and bill the buyer's cell phone service directly without the need for credit cards or micropayments, a practice only now become widespread. The company partnered with AT&T, T-Mobile, and Sprint/NEXTEL.

Considering that the ringtones sold at the standard price of $2.49 (US dollars), the royalty was no great shakes for the artist though. For instance, if a ringtone was purchased by a fan with an AT&T cell phone, the artist would receive $0.71, but that royalty rate would drop $0.54 if the service provider was T-Mobile or Sprint/NEXTEL, a small amount when compared with a digital download.

Even though the Ringtone market declined by 28 percent in 2010, it still represents a $526 million market based on sales of 220.5 million units, according to the RIAA. There's still some life left, but it does not seem to have much of a future.

SUBSCRIPTION IS THE NEW DOWNLOAD

Music subscription has been talked about to death, but the bottom line is still true—consumers are beginning to see the value in subscription music, and their interest will only grow. There's both a lot of hope and a lot of record label resistance to subscription music. On the one hand, everyone likes the idea of a steady monthly income that $10.00 a customer (the reported target price) might bring. On the other hand, how that money gets split up has labels, publishers, and artists all wringing their hands in simultaneous anxious hope and fear.

But consumers are seeing the value of not condemning 20-plus gigs of hard-drive real estate to a library that provides you no discovery options, and where you only listen to a few hundred songs anyway. An all-you-can-listen-to, anytime, anywhere option that subscription promises is beginning to make more and more sense to more and more people. Someone will get music subscription right, and the world will beat a path to his or her door.

SUBSCRIPTION SERVICES

With a subscription, you pay a set monthly fee to be able to listen to as much music as you want during that time without limitation. The music is usually streamed, so you don't actually own it, but since it's available at any time, there's really no need to keep it on your computer, phone, or mobile device anyway. There are some subscription services in which the music you choose is downloaded and stored on your playback device, but if you discontinue the service or are late paying, the files will no longer play. In many ways, it's as though your fans joined a service that lets them rent your music. As soon as they stop paying their monthly rental fee, they no longer have access to listen to your music. Every time that more than 30 seconds of your music is listened to, you get paid a fee called a streaming pay rate.

There are typically two types of streams: tethered and nontethered.

▶ A tethered stream means the media player (usually a computer) must be connected (or "tethered") to the Internet at all times in order to listen to the music.

▶ A nontethered stream means the media player (either a computer or, more often, a portable iPod or iPod-like device such as a Creative Zen Vision, Toshiba Gigabeat, and so on) needs to be connected to the Internet only once a month for the service to confirm that the user has paid his or her monthly subscription fee. After one month, if the person either stops paying the fee or doesn't connect the device to the Internet to verify that he or she has paid, the songs will stop playing on his or her computer or portable player.

Many brilliant business minds both within and outside of the music industry have predicted that all online music business will eventually move to the subscription model. Perhaps that's because a widespread acceptance of subscription services is wishful thinking on the part of the major record labels, as it would solve many of their current problems, thanks to a steady monthly income. That's a nice thought, but consumers have been slow to embrace the idea, although the momentum is beginning to pick up. Most artists signed to a record label are also not convinced that subscription is the way to go, since it's more than likely that the label will get the majority of the income because many of the royalty splits haven't been worked out yet.

I think what we'll see eventually is the prevalence of a model where people will say, "I own this much music. Give me access to it everywhere," or "I don't need to own any music. I'm just going to rent it and have access to it whenever I want." Those two things might blur into one.

I have a slide in my deck for the last three years that says, "For $10.00 a month, you can get 10 songs on iTunes or 10 million songs on Napster." Access trumps ownership. I totally believe that in a 360-degree connected world where I have pervasive connectivity (we're still not there yet but we're getting there), I don't need to own music. As long as I have my music whenever I want it, I would always pay for access over ownership. There's a point where we get past that fear of "It's music rental."

—Ted Cohen, industry sage and
principle in TAG Strategic

Rhapsody and the reborn Napster (the service that record labels used to love to hate) lead the charge for the subscription services, with Rhapsody at about 750,000 subscribers and Napster hovering a bit over 500,000 as of the writing of this book. Now owned by giant retailer Best Buy, the current Napster is derived from the original peer-to-peer file-trading service that was shut down because of actions taken by the RIAA (Recording Industry Association of America) after it was discovered that copyrighted content (artist's songs) was being freely traded (a better word might be "pirated") without the record labels, songwriters, or artists being paid.

In what seems to be a capitulation to the tastes of the digital market, Rhapsody no longer provides a streaming-only plan. Instead, for $10.00 a month you get Web and device streaming plus the ability to stream and download to one iOS device, although Napster also has a version of a download service. For $15.00 a month you can stream to up to three iOS devices.

eMusic is another subscription service, but it's different from others in that it offers exclusively independent artists to its listeners. The service tries harder to gain customers by providing 50 free downloads for a paid subscription, and 25 for a trial subscription.

A new service to the US is Spotify, which claims to have 250,000 users in the United Kingdom and a million worldwide (it's now integrated inside of Facebook). While it's unknown just how many users are in the premium $9.95-per-month tier, a free ad-supported tier uses smart viral-marketing tactics in which each user is provided a large number of invites. Spotify also utilizes a simple interface and is being heralded as extremely easy to use, a feature that not all subscription services can claim. Because of its connection to Facebook, it's predicted that it will reach 50 million subscribers quickly, so look to them to become a force in the subscription space in the near future. Other subscription services include Rdio, MOG, Thumbplay, and mSpot.

GETTING PAID

Each time your music streams, you get paid the streaming pay rate for that store. The exception is that some stores let potential customers stream for promotional purposes or as a "free trial." In those cases, even though your music may stream, you don't get paid.

The following stores/services offer streaming pay rates:

MusicNet (all stores)
Napster
Rhapsody

Stores that send statements and payments by 45 days after the end of each month are the following:

Amazon MP3
iTunes Australia
iTunes Canada
iTunes European Union
iTunes Japan
iTunes New Zealand
iTunes UK
iTunes US
iTunes Video (all territories)
MusicNet
Napster (digital downloads only)
Rhapsody
ShockHound

Stores that send statements and payments by 45 days after the end of every three months:

eMusic

Napster (digital downloads for that month and streams for the full three months)

THE DIGITAL STORAGE LOCKER (CLOUD MUSIC)

Digital storage lockers work on the principle that instead of storing all of your music on one desktop, laptop, phone, or tablet, you probably want the same music available on all of those devices. Currently the big pain is having to copy and transfer all of your music files over to each one, and in many cases, you just won't have the storage space to do so anyway. A cloud music locker such as Amazon's Cloud Player, Google's Music, or Apple's iCloud allows you to store all of your music on their online servers ("The Cloud"), which you can then access from any of your playback devices, such as your phone, MP3 player, or iPod. This saves you the time it takes to transfer your files to each device, as well as any storage space that might be required.

There are some significant differences between the services though. You have to manually upload your music to both Google Music Beta and Amazon Cloud Drive, which could take a tremendous amount of time depending upon how large your library is and the speed of your Internet connection. That won't be necessary with Apple's iCloud however, since the company entered into a licensing deal with the major and indie labels to enable it to use a feature called iTunes Match. If Match sees that you've already paid for a song or sees a song that you ripped on your hard drive, it automatically loads a copy into your storage locker without you having to upload it. That means that your upload time can theoretically take only a few minutes instead of potentially weeks.

What's important to an artist is that iTunes Match costs a user $24.99 a year, of which 58 percent goes to the record labels and 12 percent to the publishers. Apple also reportedly paid the four major labels a $150 million advance. Whether artists signed to record labels will see much of that remains to be seen, since the language of current and past contracts may not cover this technology, but indie artists could see an immediate new revenue stream, however small. It should be noted that these agreements apply to the US only, for the moment.

If and when Amazon and/or Google decide that they really should have these same licensing deals in place, it's going to cost them a lot more to get it done. Apple has already set the precedent with its label agreements, which probably won't get better for the other two as a result. Any additional costs will get passed on to the consumer, so the Apple service may end up being cheaper to the user than the other two in the long run.

Amazon's digital music locker service starts all US Amazon customers with 5GB free, which they can upgrade to 20GB for $20.00 per year, which should be plenty of storage for the vast majority of music libraries. One downside is that the service only works on any device that uses the Android operating system, which eliminates iPhones or iPads for now, but an even larger issue is that the labels and artists don't see a penny of that income.

The bottom line is that if music consumers get used to streaming their music from the cloud as predicted, it can become another revenue stream for the artist, at least from iCloud.

Digital Distribution

Paid download means the customer owns the music.

Subscription means the customer rents but has access to the service's entire catalog anytime.

Subscription may become the new download.

The digital storage locker allows streaming of your own music to any device that you own.

Ringtones are a digital fad that's quickly fading.

Submission Services

There are so many digital music sites that it's become a lot of work to submit a release to all of them. Not only is the sheer number of submissions daunting, but the different file-format requirements take a great deal of time to prepare. For instance, Napster requires WMA files at 192 kbps, iTunes requires AAC files at 256 kbps, and Amazon MP3 wants MP3 files at 256 kbps. For that reason, a number of submission services have been created to save you not only the hassle of submission, but also the file preparation. In addition, the companies will collect the royalties from the various services and forward them to you.

In exchange for these services, the companies (Tunecore, ReverbNation, and CD Baby are the most popular) usually charge a small initial fee or take a small percentage of the royalties. These companies can also provide bar codes and ISRC codes that identify the song, the album, and the CD that makes it easy for the CD to be digitally tracked. TubeMogul is a similar service for music videos.

Submission Services

Saves the hassle of individual submission

Submits to different digital distributors

Submits in different formats and bandwidths

License or Distribution?

If you're not involved with a record label, this doesn't apply to you, but if you are, listen up. A battle is currently raging as to whether a digital download is subject to a license fee or a distribution royalty, and it could eventually mean a lot more money in your pocket from digital download sales.

Traditionally, a license agreement means that you give a company the right to make copies and sell your product (this could mean music or merchandise). A distribution deal, on the other hand, gives a company the right to resell the product that you make. This was pretty cut and dried in M1.0 through 2.0, when physical product was the normal sales container. If a distributor sold records or CDs that the record company made, then it was a distribution deal. If the record company gave a copy of the master to a distributor so that the distributor could make the records or CDs themselves, it was a license deal. In M3.0, where digital products are the norm, the line between distribution and license deals becomes blurry.

In a test case, rapper Eminem's F.B.T. Productions sued his record label, Universal Music Group (UMG), over what amounts to the definition of ownership of a digital file. F.B.T. claimed that UMG owed the company more money because a digital file sold by either iTunes or Amazon MP3 is actually a license. UMG insisted that regardless of whether it's a CD, a vinyl record, or a digital file, Eminem's music is part of UMG's distribution deal. So the question became, "Is this licensing or is it distribution?"

F.B.T. claimed that since there were no manufacturing or packaging costs (which are covered by the record label), and only a single copy was delivered to the digital download companies, then it should be considered a license, because that's what occurs with other licensing deals. UMG argued that a sale is a sale regardless of how it happens, and that it was therefore a distribution deal, and the terms of the recording agreement should still apply.

A lot of money was at stake here. If the court decided that selling a digital file on iTunes amounted to a licensing deal, then the record label and the artist would split the proceeds 50/50 and the artist would be entitled to about $0.30 per download. But if the court decided it amounted to distribution, then the original recording agreement would be in force, and the artist would make about 15 percent, or about $0.10 on every download instead.

In a very closely watched case, the court initially ruled in favor of UMG, but FBT appealed and had the ruling overturned. Then UMG essentially appealed the appeal and took the case to the US Supreme Court for a ruling. The Supremes refused to hear the case though, and sent it back to the 9th Circuit Court of Appeals to determine the damages.

There's some speculation that this is at least a $50 million decision for Eminem and FBT, and all other major artists will now go back to their record labels with their palms open wide. Lady Gaga and newer artists will not have this ability, however, as labels have since tightened up their contract language regarding downloads, but anyone with an older agreement can probably expect some dough. Regardless, its ultimate outcome will have an enormous impact on the music business.

Games—Hip or Hype?

Having a song included in a game has become a new source of revenue for mostly "heritage" artists, but it's doubtful that the trend will extend to artists who haven't yet achieved that stature. Is this a fad that has run its course? Bands such as Aerosmith and Metallica (among many others) have recently reaped rewards for long careers filled with classic songs by having their material included in games like Rock Band and Guitar Hero. But it's unlikely that this trend will continue, since sales have already dropped for subsequent versions of the games as their popularity wanes.

While record labels feel that they licensed the material too cheaply, game manufacturers are also pushing for better deals in the wake of lower sales. That being said, a new generation of smaller, cheaper games may offer some opportunities to acts that have not reached superstar status.

According to game-industry expert Thom Kozik:

This whole genre of games, which is a multibillion-dollar industry within gaming, has not yet embraced music, and I think that's where the next major wave is. The Asian imports have a lot of monotonous synthesized loops and background tracks that aren't designed to invoke any imagery or really provide anything except a background.

Now that you have some Western sensibilities impacting these games, I think we'll start to see a different creative process and more music being brought into it. The indie developers in this space are going to look for differentiation, and a lot of it will come from music, so you'll see music play much more of a role. The question is, how do the music industry and the artists participate in that? I don't know yet, but I do know that the appetite is there on the gaming side.

For a while music games such as Guitar Hero and Rock Band were hot, and mostly legacy artists made a fair amount of money. With that fad basically dead, another opportunity has emerged for the M3.0 artist instead.

With much of the game business turning to online rather than console games, there's more need for music than ever before. The difference is that the soundtrack to a game no longer has to be baked into the code, and can in fact be dynamic. That means it can easily change or even be selectable by the player, which means that the game now becomes more of a distribution platform for a new artist. The gamer is given a number of selections to choose from, and can even purchase music by his or her favorite artist to be used as the soundtrack. The opportunity for the artist is that he or she can now collect a royalty based on sales rather than a one-time licensing fee as with console games.

If this model is adopted, gaming may soon turn into a significant source of income for many artists, with more opportunity for new artists than ever before. For more about music in games, read the Thom Kozik interview that appears in the second part of this book.

Games

Music games will live on, but don't enjoy the popularity as before.

Console games pay a license fee for music.

Online games can pay a royalty based on sales.

Games may become a new music distribution platform.

The New Brick-and-Mortar

It's been noted in the press and various industry blogs (including my own, which is at music3point0.blogspot.com) that sales of as few as 40,000 units can now get you a Number 1 position on the Billboard charts. In M1.0 to 2.0, a Number 1 slot on the album charts would've had at least an additional zero on the end. So why are CD sales so bad today? As stated in chapter 2, contraction and the demise of the major record retail chains, along with the demise of half of the independent music stores, have left a gap in music retail. An enterprising individual or company could take advantage of this gap, but the chances are slim that would happen in the current economy.

That being said, there is still a network of about 2,500 independent retail music stores to service a release. New M3.0 companies like CD Baby and RouteNote make independent CDs available to most of the remaining brick-and-mortar retail stores and distributors, as well as provide additional mastering, packaging, and graphics services, and bar and
ISRC codes.

The Many Ways to Ask for the Sale

It's one thing if you're selling through one of the many online distributors, since their prices are set, as are their sales methods. It's another thing entirely if you're trying to sell your music on your website. There, the way you ask for the sale directly affects how many sales you'll actually make.

Amp Music Marketing ran a study regarding "call to action" buy buttons where they decided to test a number of buttons to see which was most effective when it came to selling music. The choices were:

"Get The Music"
"Download The Music"
"Buy The Music"

It turns out that the most effective was the most direct "Buy The Music" (album, CD, etc.), while "Get The Music" was the least. It seems that consumers relate "Get The Music" to a bait and switch in which they're lured into clicking, only to find that there's something additionally asked of them.

When it comes to sales, sometimes the very best technique is the most direct. Ask plainly for the sale. If your fan or customer really wants to buy from you, you're doing him or her a favor by making the process streamlined and easy. If your fan or customer is unsure, you're not helping the cause by being ambiguous.

And another thing. Keep the choices to a maximum of three (two works best). If given too many choices, the customer is likely to throw his or her hands up in the air in frustration and not buy anything!

TEN SALES TIPS

Here are ten sales tips to always keep in mind:

1. Ask for the purchase. Never forget that even though you're selling yourself, you're still in sales.

2. Sell a package. With a ticket you get a CD, with a CD you get a T-shirt, with a T-shirt you get a ticket. The idea is to make each purchase something with added value.

3. Sell merchandise at as an affordable price as possible. Until you're a star, you should be more concerned about visibility and branding than revenue. If you want to spread the word, price it cheaper.

4. There are other things to sell besides CDs and T-shirts. Hats, a song book, a tour picture book, beach towels—get creative, but choose well. Too many choices may actually reduce sales as a result of buyer confusion. You can now sell a variety of branded merchandise with no up-front costs using CafePress.com or Zazzle.com.

5. Begin promoting as soon as possible. That allows time for the viral buzz (a.k.a. free promotion) to build and ensures that you'll get a larger share of your fan's discretionary spending.

6. Capture the name, email address, and zip code from anyone who makes a purchase, particularly ticket buyers.

7. Always give your customers more than they expect. By giving them something for free that they did not expect, you keep them coming back for more.

8. Give it away and sell it at the same time. In the M1.0 to 2.5 days, you used to give away a free track to sell other merchandise such as the album. Now if you give away a track, that track will help you to sell more.

9. The best items to sell are the ones that are the scarcest. Autographed items, special boxed sets, limited-edition vinyl that's numbered—all these items are more valuable because of their scarcity. If the items are abundant, price them cheaper. If the items are scarce, don't be afraid to price them higher.

10. Sell your brand. You, the artist, are your own brand. Remember that everything you do sells that brand, even if it doesn't result in a sale. Just the fact that people are paying attention can result in a sale and more revenue down the road.

T E N

CHAPTER

The M3.0 Rules for Survival

L ike just about everything else, the rules to survive and flourish in M3.0 have changed from those rules that worked in the past. In M1.0, the success path might have looked like the following:

The path in M3.0 is much different; it's shorter than before but at the same time more complex for artists because they must do so much of the work themselves.

While it might seem simple, since the path to the consumer is so direct, each step is much more complicated. Assuming that you've already created your music (if not, check out a few of my other books for tips), let's take a closer look.

Developing Your Audience

M3.0 is totally dependent upon the development, care, and feeding of your tribe. Your tribe is only a piece of your total audience though. Your audience can be broken down into the following two categories: your *fans* and your *tribe*.

Your total audience, or your fans, are fervent about a particular small niche of music that's usually a subcategory of a larger genre, which means that they love speed metal (as opposed to the much larger metal or hard-rock genres), bluegrass (as compared to the larger country-music genre), or alien marching bands (as opposed to either of the larger alien-music or marching-band genres). If you're an artist in that particular niche, your audience will automatically gravitate toward you, but still might not be your fans. This includes casual fans, occasional listeners, and people who like what you're doing yet aren't particularly passionate about it. Although this part of your audience can't be ignored, it's probably not a good idea to expend all your energy on it. They're aware of you and will probably give you a try with every release, unless they're disappointed too many times in a row. They can be turned into passionate fans though. One "hit" song or album, a change in image, or a change in general perception, and they become the passionate critical mass needed for the breakout that turns a respected artist into a true star.

In a post on the blog *Digital Noise* from March 3, 2009, Matt Rosoff states:

> In the case of music, there's a core audience—I'll be generous and say it's around 1 percent—who understand and care deeply about music, who use their ears more than their other senses, and who couldn't live without it. The other 99 percent attend shows and buy CDs for other reasons--to fit into a peer group, to stave off the boredom of another evening at home watching TV, to attract a mate, and so on. This isn't conjecture—a Columbia University study I've cited several times strongly suggests that a particular song's popularity is influenced primarily by the opinions of others, and has no relationship to its objective quality (as measured by a control group where listeners voted without being able to see how their peers were voting).

Matt Rosoff is an analyst with Directions on Microsoft, where he covers Microsoft's consumer products and corporate news.

In M3.0, your most important core audience contains your most passionate fans, or your "tribe," as described in chapter 4. They'll buy whatever you have to sell, work for free, recruit other fans, and basically do anything you ask. All they want is access to and communication with the artist, which is the basis of M3.0. But how do you develop your tribe?

Developing Your Audience

Your audience consists of your fans and your tribe.

Fans may like an artist but may not be particularly passionate.

Your tribe (true fans, uberfans, superfans) is very passionate about everything you do.

Most of your energy should be directed toward your tribe.

Establishing Your Tribe

According to Seth Godin, the originator of the tribal concept, a tribe is a group of people connected to one another, connected to a leader, and connected to an idea. In M3.0, tribe members are connected to each other and to the artist via their passion for the artist's music, but the leader is the integral part of the tribe. In fact, without a leader, the tribe is only a self-organized group. As an example, a blog may have thousands of readers who never add a comment, so this makes it a group. The blogger could be the leader, but if she's the only one that posts, there's still no tribe.

Now we're assuming that there are more than three people that are passionately connected to the artist, since this is obviously essential to the creation of a tribe. The music is what connects them to the artist and to each other.

THE LEADER

The most important thing that the tribe needs is a leader. Although the artist is the most logical leader, a representative that speaks for the artist works in that capacity as well. In the old fan-club days, the fan-club president acted as leader, and today he or she still could be the leader of the tribe. But unless he or she directly represents the artist, the tribe isn't as powerful or as dynamic as it could be.

So how does one become the leader of the tribe? The leader initiates contact with the tribe and leads the conversations. For instance, the artist/leader might send or post a tour schedule with a list of "meet and greets" especially for tribe members. He or she makes it easy for everyone to participate and rewards the members that do so. Before the artist makes a new recording, she might ask the tribe what direction they'd like her to go in, then reward the ones that respond by sending them a link to download a special mix of the song. And most importantly, the leader gives projects to tribal members to work on. The artist might ask for people to send suggestions on venues in a certain area or to pass out flyers before an upcoming gig. Remember that tribal members are passionate and truly want to be part of something. Active participation fulfills that longing.

However the leader reaches out, it must be authentic and show true caring for the tribal members. Tribal members can feel in an instant if you're just going through the motions, and the tribe will begin to dissolve. If you're posting just as an exercise because "That's the way M3.0 works, dude," then you're better off finding a surrogate leader.

The next thing that a tribe needs is a place to meet. This is pretty easy in M3.0, as there are a variety of alternatives that range from blogs to Facebook and Twitter to a custom social network on Ning. Whatever the online technology used, the tribe has to be able to communicate with one another easily, or the glue that holds the tribe together will be weak. That being said, having just a simple mailing list can be enough to connect the tribe.

Establishing Your Tribe

You don't have a tribe without a leader.

The leader doesn't have to be the artist.

The leader initiates contact, leads conversations, and makes it easy to participate.

The tribe needs a place to meet and communicate.

GROWING YOUR TRIBE

Now that your tribe is established, it must be carefully expanded (we'll get into some of the reasons besides the obvious in a minute). While not seemingly a method for expanding the tribe, the way the leader treats the tribe is as integral to expansion as any external methods. Tribes flourish from within. Word of mouth is perhaps the most powerful marketing method, and your tribe will champion you to anyone that will listen if you give them the slightest reason. Therefore, the first and most important way of developing the tribe is by nurturing it.

The easiest way to nurture the tribe is to transfer some of the social standing that the artist has onto them. To you, the artist, it might not seem like much if you have only 10 dedicated members in your tribe, tally a dozen downloads a week, and get only 15 people to your shows. But your tribe feels that you're the greatest thing since Christina

Aguilera or Coldplay and that they've discovered you before anyone else. In their eyes, you have a degree of prestige and status that comes with the uniqueness of your music. You must transfer some of it to them in ways such as the following:

▶ If a certain fan has seen you 15 times, call him out at a show. Bring him backstage for a meet and greet or invite him to an after-show party.

▶ If a member consistently posts in a helpful manner for the betterment of the tribe, develop a personal off-list dialog with the fan, offer her a free ticket to the next show, or post a picture of her on the meeting space.

Any small action, such as the ones listed above, that transfers a bit of status will make the member more loyal and vocal, and will encourage other fans to take more action in hopes of reaping the same rewards.

The leader must constantly check the pulse of the tribe to hear what the members are feeling and thinking. This can be helpful in determining just what the tribe likes and dislikes about you and your music. Maybe there's a direction that you briefly touched upon on your last record that drove the tribe wild, or maybe one that they hated? You might choose to follow your musical instincts instead of listening to tribal feedback, but at least you won't be surprised by the resulting reaction.

Taking the tribe's pulse also lifts the mood of its members, since interaction with the leader is always appreciated and results in more participation. Showing your appreciation for their participation fosters even greater loyalty and participation and gets them invested emotionally and intellectually.

So how do you take the tribe's pulse? You ask them questions or ask them to help you.

▶ Ask them which piece of merch they prefer.
▶ Ask them about the best venues in their area, why they like them, and if they'd prefer to see you there.
▶ Ask them what song they'd love to hear you cover.

▶ Ask them who their favorite artists are (this answer is great for other elements of social marketing, as mentioned in chapter 7).

▶ Ask them to judge the artwork on your next release. Then, when they respond, reward them. Give a free T-shirt to the first ten people who respond.

▶ Send them a secret link to download a track that's available only to them.

▶ Give a personal shout out to some of the best responses.

All of the above makes them feel special and great about belonging, and keeps the interest of the tribe high.

Also remember that the tribe is composed of both leaders and lurkers. These two subgroups usually fall into the familiar 80:20 ratio (80 percent of the participation is provided by 20 percent of the tribe). Leaders are the first to respond and are always eager to participate. Lurkers remain in the shadows—interested, but not enough to engage the tribe. Getting the lurkers to participate is essential in growing the tribe. Let them know that there are benefits (such as free show tickets, after-show party invites, and exclusive CDs or downloads) for being more active. Above all, let them know that they'll be sorely missed if they decide to opt out of the tribe.

Even though you want the tribe to expand, don't focus on the number of members; it's not the numbers that count, but rather it's the quality of the experience. Focus on the members themselves, and they'll bring others to the tribe. Remember that a tribe's rate of growth is dependent upon two things: the level of passion of the members and the leadership's involvement. Have a high level of tribal passion and leadership participation, and the tribe will grow quickly; but have a lower level of either of the two, and the tribe will be faced with slower growth. When the tribe no longer benefits anyone, it will die.

MARKETING TO YOUR TRIBE

Be extremely careful about how you market to your tribe. Chances are that your tribe wants everything you have to offer, but they don't want to be hyped about it. Make an announcement about a new release or a piece of swag, but don't oversell it. Members don't need to know that you think your new music is the greatest thing you ever did or that it's better than the Foo Fighters' last release. They'll decide for themselves and then sell it for you in their own conversations if they like it.

The way to market to your tribe is by simply presenting your product to them. Just make them aware that it's available, and they'll do the rest. You can take it a bit further by offering them information about the product—the more exclusive, the better.

Instead of a sales pitch:
▶ Give them a behind-the-scenes story about the making of the product.
▶ Tell them where the idea for it came from.
▶ Tell them about all the people involved, especially other tribe members.
▶ Provide interviews with others involved in the project.

▶Give them all the trivia involved in the project, no matter how small. True fans will eat it up. If it's a new song, tell them where it was recorded, who the engineer and producer are, how many Pro Tools tracks were needed, how long the mix took to finish, how many mixes you did, how the final mix compared with the rough mix, and all of the hundred other fine details that go into producing a song. If you just produced a new T-shirt, describe where the design came from, why you chose the manufacturer, what the shirt is made of, why you chose the color, and so on. Get the idea?

Giving them insight that no one else has makes them feel special, will keep them loyal, and will show mere fans and lurkers the benefits of tribal participation.

Marketing to Your Tribe

Present your product, don't sell it.

Give them lots of information and trivia.

Absolutely no hype!

Sustaining Your Career

The way to sustain your career in M3.0 has changed significantly from previous eras of music. The formula is simple: maintain your connection with your tribe. This could mean by putting out frequent releases, blog posts, email blasts, tweets, or anything else in social media, but you've got to keep your fan base engaged on a consistent basis. While long periods of time between releases (such as six months or a year) are not recommended, they can be overcome by constant interaction by the artist. It's only when communication grows cold that the tribe begins to dissipate.

A typical consistent communication schedule might look something like the following:

- ▶ **Tweets:** a few times a day or every other day
- ▶ **Blog posts:** once or twice a week
- ▶ **Email blasts:** once a month with tour schedules, release schedules, or just general info
- ▶ **Music releases:** once every six to eight weeks

Online communication isn't the only way to stay in touch with your tribe. Touring will always be a part of being an artist, and it's an especially important ingredient in not only sustaining your fan base but also growing it. The more you have contact with your fans, the more opportunities there are to reach out and touch them. Don't forget some of the items mentioned in chapter 5, such as meet and greets, after-show parties, backstage passes, and the like. Online and offline contact must all be part of the same strategic plan.

THE "1,000 TRUE FANS" THEORY

The "1,000 True Fans Theory" by *Wired* magazine's "senior maverick" Kevin Kelly states that all an artist needs is 1,000 true fans (the members of his or her tribe) to maintain a fruitful, if unspectacular, career, thereby relieving the artist of the need for some of the nastier things in life as a regular job. True fans are sometimes called superfans or uberfans, depending on whose theory we're talking about.

Kelly wrote the following:

> A creator, such as an artist, musician, photographer, craftsperson, performer, animator, designer, videomaker, or author—in other words, anyone producing works of art—needs to acquire only 1,000 True Fans to make a living.
>
> A True Fan is defined as someone who will purchase anything and everything you produce. They will drive 200 miles to see you sing. They will buy the superdeluxe reissued hi-res box set of your stuff even though they have the low-res version. They have a Google Alert set for your name. They bookmark the eBay page where your out-of-print editions show up. They come to your openings. They have you sign their copies. They buy the T-shirt, and the mug, and the hat. They can't wait till you issue your next work. They are true fans

The idea is that if each of the 1,000 fans bought $100 worth of product every year (the figure equals an arbitrary full-day's pay), you'd have an income of $100,000, which, even minus expenses, can still be a reasonable living for most artists. The trick, of course, is how you expand your tribe to that magic 1,000-fans number (providing that you buy the theory, of course).

> *I also see the rise of the musical middle-class artist that can make anywhere from a store-clerk living to $100 grand a year per band member. There'll be fewer superstars and a lot more mid-level artists as time goes on.*
>
> —Bruce Houghton

Like most theories on such things, the detractors of the 1,000 True Fans theory point out several relevant issues. They are:

▶ **The $100,000 amount is the gross income and doesn't take expenses into account.** Expenses for any creative endeavor can be quite substantial and must be accounted for in any income assumption.

▶ **Even if you reach the magic 1,000-fan number, that doesn't mean that each will spend $100 per year.** That's true, but remember that $100 is an average number. Some fans might spend $500, while others might spend only $20. Of course, you have to present them with the products and the opportunity to spend money. If you put out a single release and don't tour, it's unlikely that you'll hit your target. If you're touring, and a true fan attends three shows and brings five friends, that could easily account for $100 right there. And if you release two albums, a deluxe box set, and newly designed T-shirts, hats, mouse pads, and coffee cups, there's an even greater chance that the true fan will just have to have whatever you're selling.

▶ **M3.0 presents a worldwide marketplace, so 1,000 fans don't necessarily have to reside just in the United States.** Again, this is true and can lead you to believe that developing your fan base is a lot easier than it really is. Don't forget that true fans in some countries such as Russia, China, and Mexico might not be paying anything at all and still be enjoying your work thanks to the prolific piracy that those areas are accustomed to.

▶ **You can expect some attrition of your new fans.** Hopefully, the attrition of your tribe will at least be offset by new members, and perhaps even grow some in the process.

▶ **Other artists are competing for the same fans.** There's always competition in the marketplace for every dollar, sale, and item. You must differentiate yourself and your product from your competition to make the choice easier for the fan. For sure, you'll lose some fans during this process, but if done well, you'll make that number up, and more.

While the total number of true fans actually required to make the theory work (is it 300 or 1,000 or 4,000?) may be in question, the idea is that you need this hard-core group in order to sustain your career. Whatever the number that you're lucky enough to develop, be sure to take care of and nurture them, because they truly want you to.

Sustaining Your Career

Frequent online communication is a necessity.

Too little or too much communication can be detrimental to the growth of your tribe.

Touring and face-to-face communication are as important as your online presence.

Aim to develop a core audience (the 1,000 True Fans theory).

ELEVEN

CHAPTER

How to Make Money in Today's Music World

To be sure, making money in M3.0 is a lot trickier than it was in previous stages of the music business. When you're signed to a major label, there's an ever-changing sea of cross-collateralization between accounts, in which big sales by the record label might still result in small royalty payments to you. Yet at the same time, things are in some ways more cut and dried than before. As an indie artist who's without a label and is dealing directly with the fans, you know exactly how much money you're earning and where it's coming from. No longer tied to the fortunes of a record released by a major label and therefore the uncertainty of a royalty statement, what you see is what you get.

Although the exact recipe for making money in today's music world is different, the ingredients pretty much remain the same. If you're looking for a magic formula, however, you won't find one here, I'm sorry to say. It still comes down to talent and a lot of work, same as it ever did.

Hit the Road, Jack

. . . .

As said a few times earlier in the book, from the beginning of time in the modern music business, artists have always made the bulk of their money from touring, *not* record sales. Depending on who you speak to, this figure varies anywhere from 90 to 95 percent of a currently hot artist's total income, and even more for a former platinum-selling heritage act.

This means that for you to make money, you've got to play in front of people, and the more people you play in front of, the more you'll make. The problem is that large crowds hardly ever happen overnight, and if they do, beware. This can be a warning sign that they're interested in the spectacle of a media buzz or something other than the music. Any success that comes too fast will probably be short lived.

Unfortunately, developing an audience on any level is slow and time consuming. You still have to build your audience one show at a time. The formula is always the same: the more you play, the better you get at performing and the more the crowd will notice, generating bigger crowds as a result (see my book *How to Make Your Band Sound Great* for some performance and show tips and tricks). Things can snowball from there if you've got what it takes.

We often see bands that try to do too much too fast. A lot of indie labels will say, "We want the band to get in a van and we don't want them to get out of it for three years." At some point at the end of year one or 2 that runs its course. Virtually no band can keep on running around the country to try to build an audience indiscriminately. As much as touring is the most important thing, it has to be done strategically, concentrating on certain markets where you see the beginning of growth, then doing them often enough but not too often.

—Bruce Houghton

Are you playing in front of people and still not making enough money to keep it interesting or to even pay your expenses? Maybe what you're offering just isn't compelling, either musically or show-wise. People will gladly pay to see anything that they're passionate about, so perhaps they don't find you enthralling enough to pay for, or maybe even to come to see for free. Then again, maybe you haven't found your audience yet. If that's the case, use the marketing tools outlined in chapter 4 to build that tribe. Either way, growing your live audience is always a slower process than it seems it should be.

What you still never get away from is that it's still about a song and it's still about a performance of that song. Can you play that song in front of your audience however large or small and create the "WOW Factor?"

—Rupert Perry

First of all, an artist has to have the right attitude, which maybe is no different than it ever was. What's new is that the artist now must also have the ability to learn, adapt, and communicate.

—Derek Sivers

Describing just how to go about finding gigs, playing a show, and building your team with management and an agent is beyond the scope of this book. There are plenty of other books that focus on just that part of the biz. Suffice it to say that playing live has got to be part of your strategy for developing your tribe and making money.

Swag Is Your Friend

. . . .

Performing live is only one ingredient of the recipe, however. You've got to have merchandise (other terms include "swag" or "merch") to supplement your income. It's always been a huge part of the income of an artist, but until recently was considered just an ancillary revenue stream. Today it's an essential part of most artist's earnings.

It used to be that merch required a sizable capital outlay in order to get in the game. You had to buy enough to get some sort of economy of scale, but then you also had to worry about storing the inventory. And what if the item didn't sell? What do you do with 4,835 custom key chains or 492 pairs of branded underwear? Luckily, there are now alternatives that make the buy-in easier on the pocketbook than ever.

Today both Café Press (cafepress.com) and Zazzle (zazzle.com) make it easy to provide quality merch of all kinds without worrying about either the up-front money or the inventory. Both companies provide a host of items that they'll manufacture to order, and they'll even allow you to show examples of merch on your website or store. In other words, whenever an order is placed, that's when they'll make the item. They'll even drop-ship it to the customer for you so you don't have to worry about shipping and inventory. All this comes at a cost, and so your profit won't be as high, but it's an easy and inexpensive way to get into the merch business.

So what kind of merch should you have? You can now get a huge variety of items branded with your logo, but typical merch items are:

► T-shirts (probably the number one item ever for a musical artist)
► hats
► lighters
► sweatshirts
► coffee cups
► posters
► bumper stickers (a high-profit item because they're cheap to make)
► mouse pads
► bags (timely now, since people use them instead of paper or plastic at the supermarket)

Just about anything you can think of can now have your logo on it. Of course, that doesn't necessarily mean that just because you can make it available, it's a good idea. It's still best to narrow things down, since offering too many types of items can actually prevent willing customers from buying anything because they can't make up their minds. Keep the number of types of items to a maximum of 2 at first, and be sure that they will sell before you add more options.

Another interesting idea is to offer a tour book of photos (available from blurb.com) like the one the Grateful Dead did on their recent tour. Once again, it's on-demand printing, and the company offers a number of professional templates to make the design easy.

Don't forget that in the end, branded items such as T-shirts, hats, beach towels, and Frisbees are for marketing you as an artist, so be sure that the design looks professional. If you're going to spend hard cash, this is the place to do it. Find a pro or an advanced hobbyist to design it for you. Don't forget that the true reason for selling merch is that if enough people see your intriguing logo on a T-shirt, coffee mug, or bumper sticker, some of them will be interested enough to check you out.

PRICE IT RIGHT

Whatever you choose to sell, be sure to price it right. The obvious temptation is to price an item too high to try to make a large profit. Don't fall into this trap. Price things low enough to cover your expenses and make a reasonable profit. Remember, these items are promotional; it's better to sell more at a lower cost than a few at a higher cost.

Above all, be sure that your costs are covered. Make sure that any costing includes the price of shipping, sales taxes (don't forget those), and any labor or sales costs involved (many artists will pay someone 10 percent or more of the sale's gross for manning the merch booth). Also don't forget that some venues will also take a commission of between 20 and 25 percent. A good formula for pricing might be your costs (all of them) plus anywhere from 30 to 50 percent. If you're sure the market will bear a higher price than that, go there, but make sure that you test it first. Try a lower price at one gig and a higher one at another and see which sells better. Sometimes a higher price sells better because the customer perceives a higher quality.

Make sure you round it up to a reasonable number. If you use the formula of costs plus 50 percent and it comes out to $6.38, round it up to $7.00. Stay away from change. It's easier on everybody.

THE SECRET TO THE MERCH TABLE

Even though merchandise is a major revenue stream for the M3.0 artist, most musicians have a natural aversion to selling it (or selling anything for that matter). Yet one simple act that doesn't directly involve selling can help you greatly increase your nightly take from the merch table.

By just announcing during and at the end of the show, "After our show, we're going to be hanging out at the merch table, so come over and say 'Hi,'" without trying to specifically sell anything, you bring your fans that much closer to an impulse buy.

By getting people the ability to casually chat with you, it becomes a low-pressure way of getting people to look at your merchandise, which is always half the battle.

This one simple act can make a big difference in your merch sales, and that's the one place that you can be assured of making money these days, especially if you're just starting out. Remember, you don't have to physically sell anything yourself, just be there and talk to fans. Can you imagine what the sales would be like if Bono did that after a U2 concert?

CREDIT CARD TRANSACTIONS MADE EASY

More and more we're living in a cashless society. People are more likely to make a purchase with a debit or credit card when they want something, especially if they're short of cash. Of course this can be a drag at a gig when you're selling CDs and merch and have to rely on the Benjamins because of the hassle of taking credit and debit cards.

While the ability to take credit cards for merchandise purchases at a gig can make transactions easier, it can also eat into your profits. First of all, you have to enter into a long-term contract with a bank, then pay for the card reader, and in many cases pay a monthly subscription fee. Then, after a purchase, you have to wait for the money to hit your account, with the bank taking its piece through processing and transaction fees that are like the phone bill—lots of small fees for each transaction that no one can seem to explain.

Transaction costs are frequently overlooked, and they are the secret expense that eats your profit. All credit cards charge you multiple fees. First of all, there's a monthly transaction fee that's a minimum of $20.00 (usually more), a "gateway" fee of between $5.00 and $20.00 for ecommerce, an authorization fee, a customer service fee, and a monthly minimum transaction total. Slip below that total and you're charged a penalty.

Then there's the transaction costs per sale, which can go from $0.20 to as high as $0.35 (it's usually higher for an Internet transaction), plus a charge of between 1.5 and 3 percent of the total of the sale. Add all that up, and it means that if you only make a dozen or so song sales a month, you've actually lost money. Even if you've met your monthly minimum, you still may be only making less than half of a dollar per sale, thanks to the transaction costs involved.

But this has all changed recently as a service called Square (squareup.com) has slowly but surely made a big impression on large and small touring merchandising entities alike. With just a $10.00 reader that attaches to any iPhone 4, iPad, or iPod Touch (there's a $10.00 rebate so it's actually free), you can now have your customers easily pay by the card of their choice. What's more, it's paperless. You swipe the card, the customer uses a fingerprint to sign to the purchase by touching the screen of your IOS device, and the customer receives an email receipt later. Square takes a flat 2.75 percent transaction fee, which winds up costing less than most traditional credit card processors.

Swag Is Your Friend

Merch is an essential part of your income.

But don't forget that it's promotional too.

Invest the money on a great design.

Use Café Press or Zazzle to avoid upfront costs.

Limit the number of items to one or two at first.

Make sure that all your costs are covered.

Price to cover your costs plus 30 to 50 percent.

Meet and greet at the merch table
to increase sales.

Use Square for credit card transactions.

The novelty of signing with your fingerprint is so cool that many acts report that their sales have increased just by the fact that people want to try it out! The best part is that you can now get the Square reader from the Apple online store, and it's reported that it will be available soon from their retail stores as well. The transaction software is free.

The New Publishing Paradigm

Despite popular belief, the ones who have traditionally made the most money on the sale of music have been the songwriters and publishers, not the performers (unless they were the songwriters or owned the publishing companies). The songwriter and publisher make money in two ways: mechanical royalties are paid whenever a digital download of a song or a physical CD is sold, and a performance royalty is paid whenever a song is played on radio, on television, in a film, or streamed over the Internet. This payment mechanism hasn't really changed all that much in M3.0 from previous music eras.

What has changed is that during this period in which music sales continue to take a beating, publishing is the one area of the music industry that has held its own. How does that happen when sales, and therefore mechanical royalties, are down, you ask? While it's true that mechanical royalties are not nearly what they used to be now that CD sales are so low, they're offset by the tremendous increase in performance royalties, because music is now played on so many more broadcasts than before. The 500-channel cable and satellite television universe, along with satellite and Internet radio, provides more opportunities for music to be played, and as a result, more performance royalties are generated.

In aggregate, people are still watching as much television as ever if not more, but they are watching it across more channels. They're watching the cable channels more and the broadcast channels less.

—Larry Gerbrandt

As record company sales have been going down since the year 2000, publishing company income has actually been going up. What's happened is that performance income (when a songwriter gets paid whenever the song is played) has gone up because there are many more places where music is played and used. Now you have tons of little cable stations and they have to all pay a small fee. As a result, you have the increase in synch fees offsetting and sometimes exceeding the loss of mechanicals. Publishing is still one of the few ways left to monetize intellectual property.

—Richard Feldman, CEO
of ArtistsFirst Publishing

While publishing is sophisticated enough to easily fill an entire book (and there are many books specifically on the subject), here's a simple breakdown of how the money is paid:

ROYALTY TYPE	AMOUNT PAID
Mechanical Royalty	
Physical product (CD, vinyl)	9.1 cents per song.
Digital download	9.1 cents per song.
Performance Royalty	
Radio	Depends on a sample survey of all radio stations, including college stations and public radio. ASCAP, BMI, and SESAC use a digital tracking system, station logs provided by the radio stations, and recordings of the actual broadcasts to determine how much a song earns.
Internet Streaming	Commercial broadcasters pay $0.0019 per performance, which will increase to $0.0021 in 2012 and $0.0023 in 2014. Webcasters such as Pandora pay $0.00102 in 2011, $0.00110 in 2012, $0.00120 in 2013, $0.00130 in 2014, and $0.00140 in 2015.
Synchronization Fee	**Music against picture**
Television	Subject to negotiation or survey from cue sheets that program producers provide to ASCAP, BMI, or SESAC, as well as program schedules, network and station logs, and tapes of the broadcasts to determine how much a song earns.
Commercials	Subject to negotiation or survey from cue sheets that program producers provide to ASCAP, BMI, or SESAC, as well as program schedules, network and station logs, and tapes of the broadcasts to determine how much a song earns.
Movies	Subject to negotiation.
Printed Sheet Music	Subject to negotiation.
Ringtones	$0.24 per sale.

Can you make money from publishing if you're an indie artist? Maybe. If you're the songwriter on your own CD or digital release, then separating the songwriting money from the recording money only makes sense if you're sharing royalties with bandmates and getting paid separately for writing. Otherwise, it's irrelevant.

To receive any kind of significant royalties from streaming or radio airplay, you really have to have a huge hit that gets a lot of plays. So expecting any significant income is irrelevant for all but the extremely lucky indie artists.

Where you can make money is through synchronization fees. Anytime music is played with a moving picture—either on television, in a movie, or on the Internet—it requires a synchronization license. If your song is considered for a movie, you'd negotiate with the producer for a fee, which could be from 0 to $100,000 or more, depending on the placement in the film and its budget. As with everything in the entertainment business, the higher your profile, the more you'll get paid. But if you have a song that uniquely relates to the movie, television show, or commercial (e.g., the hook of your song is the title of the movie), you can usually get a higher rate. You'll also receive performance fees whenever it's played on television.

Bottom line, your income from digital publishing will remain a tiny grain of sand on a beach of potential income for the foreseeable future. There is real money in synch fees, and that's what you should be aiming for. The problem is, how do you get your songs to the people that will license them? Unless you live in New York, Nashville, Los Angeles, or Chicago (mostly for commercials) where you can network and sell yourself, your only options are to have either so much airplay or so much online visibility that you get noticed, or you get a publisher. Part of what a publisher does (besides collect the money) is to promote your work. Once again, there are lots of books and articles about this to check out. If you want to self-publish, it's also a good idea to become a member of the Association of Independent Music Publishers, where you can network with other publishers both large and small. It's well worth the $60.00 per year. See aimp.org for more information.

WHY USE A PUBLISHER?

While many artists feel that they want to control their own publishing and just hate the idea of dividing any income, a publisher can provide a number of useful services that can make that 50 percent (the highest rate that is used when splitting your royalties with a publisher) well worth it.

Besides giving you an advance against earnings if the publisher feels your songs warrant one, a publisher does the following:

► Registers the copyright for your songs so you don't have to do it
► Licenses the songs to commercial users
► Collects money from the licensees
► Pitches songs to music supervisors for film, television, and commercials
► Pitches songs to record companies and other potential users of songs
► Introduces the songwriter to artists looking for material

Having a publisher is just like having someone take care of your social networking: they'll free up your time so you can make more music, and they'll probably do a better job at administering your publishing than you can because they're pros at what they do. What's best is, in the right hands, they can even make some money for you.

COLLECTING DIGITAL MONEY

Unfortunately, collecting performance-fee money for digital music streams is a lot more difficult than it should be. There is no standard way of electronic accounting yet, which means that online radio stations and subscription services account to publishers in hard copy (though that's beginning to change). This hard copy (usually the size of several phone books for a busy publisher) must then be manually entered into the publisher's system so the songwriters can get paid, which sometimes costs more than the entire amount collected. To make matters worse, it's possible that a publisher is not being paid because it can't be found by the digital broadcaster (or so they say), or it's impossible for the publisher to obtain an accounting of what was played. And after all that, it takes a huge number of streams and an equally large amount of accounting to show any substantial money, because the songwriter is earning only $0.0023 per stream and then has to split that 50/50 if a publisher is involved.

That being said, every artist should be registered with SoundExchange, a service created by the US Copyright Office to collect performance fees for musicians featured on a recording and a song's copyright owners. SoundExchange collects money for the actual performers on a recording, not the songwriters. It's not much (from .015 of a cent in 2009 rising to .025 of a cent in 2015), but it's a good thing any time a performer makes money. Go to soundexchange.com for more information.

Yes, but there are challenges. It turns out that streaming doesn't really work as a model for selling music. In terms of collection, the statement that the publisher gets might be as big as a phone book yet amount to only 12 bucks in royalties. The problem is it might cost the publisher $100 to input it. If the publisher is getting 50 percent of the $12.00, it's cost them a lot more to input it than they're making, but they're obligated to account to their clients, who are the songwriters. That's a big new problem for publishers.

—Richard Feldman

The New Publishing Paradigm

Publishing is still making money in M3.0.

The mechanical royalty is the same for a song on a CD or a download—9.1 cents.

There's not much money in streaming for anyone yet.

The real money is in synch fees.

Register with SoundExchange now.

Crowdfunding

One of the most difficult aspects of being an artist is finding funding for your project. Regardless of where you're at along the ladder of success, if you don't have the resources for recording or marketing, you're severely hampered in the process.

A new trend in social media called crowdfunding (sometimes called fanfunding) is becoming a popular way to finance a recording project, thanks to sites such as Kickstarter, MyBandStock, indiegogo, Rockethub, and Sellaband, among others. Regardless of which site you use, the idea is the same—it allows your fans to pool their money in order to fund your project.

The way this is done is that the artist sets the amount-of-money goal, then the length of time to reach it. There are then different levels of rewards that vary based on the amount a fan contributes towards the project, very much like the multitiered product offerings by Trent Reznor and Josh Freese as described in chapter 4.

While this sounds like a great way to fund your project, it does take a moderate amount of planning and effort, as well as a significant amount of time before you see any cash. More importantly, most funding platforms require that the entire goal be hit before the artist sees any of the money. It does work though, with high-visibility artists such as Public Enemy, Jonathan Davis from Korn, Rockwell, and Marillion having been successfully funded.

THE FOUR TIERS OF A CROWDFUNDING CAMPAIGN

In crowdfunding, a funding tier is a level of investment, going for as little as $10 to increments such as $25, $50, $100, $500 and more. One of the most important elements of a crowdfunding campaign has to do with the rewards that an investor receives for putting money into the project. Just getting credit and money back usually isn't enough, but Yancey Strickler of Kickstarter had these suggestions in a blogpost on Hypebot to make the campaign a bit more enticing:

1. The Basic Reward: If nothing else, the investor should receive a copy of the recording, be it a CD or a free download, along with a written credit on the project.

2. Limited Editions: For either the first 100 investors or the next-higher tier, the investor receives a deluxe edition that's individually numbered and personally signed.

3. Share the Story: The next tier investor would receive something even more exclusive, such as pictures or videos from the studio, used guitar strings, or drum heads, the coffee cup used by the artist, or some other personal item.

4. The Creative Experience: Bring the investor into the process itself by asking for his or her opinion on which version of a song or photo to release, bringing him or her into the studio for background vocals or handclaps, or just inviting him or her to sit in on a recording, photo session, or video. The idea is to give an investor at the highest level a once-in-a-lifetime thrill.

None of these cost very much, yet they could mean the difference between someone investing or not, or investing in a more costly tier.

THE FOUR RULES FOR CROWDFUNDING

If crowdfunding is something that you'd like to pursue, here are four rules to help your campaign be successful:

1. Choose an attainable goal amount. Everybody would like a $100,000 budget to work with, but unless you have a large fan base to begin with, you're probably dreaming if you think you can raise that amount. Even a once huge-selling band such as Public Enemy had to cut their goal from $250,000 to $75,000, so be realistic in both what you need and what you can raise.

2. Concentrate on low price-points. Kickstarter's data indicates that $50.00 is the optimum investment point, closely followed by $25.00. While most artists include amount in the thousands as well, don't count on these being filled.

3. Make sure the investment reward is sufficient. Remember that you're not getting a donation, it's an investment, and your investors will expect something in return. Check out this list of incentives from Hind, one of the finalists of Netherlands Idol, as an example.

Marketing Manager = 1 Part (€10): The album plus my eternal gratitude, hugs, love and kisses. And the kudos you'll get from your friends and family for discovering the fastest funded artist on Sellaband ever, in less than 11 days . . . i raised €40.000 with the help of my believers ;-)

Marketing Promoter = 2 Parts (€20): All of the above plus my personal autograph on the album mentioning your name. Plus a chat through KyteTV.

Marketing Guru = 10 Parts (€100): All of the above, plus a pro rata share of 10% in the sales revenue from 10 parts and up, for a limited period of 18 months after releasing the album. If you already have bought parts in the album this will be added to it. Plus a genuine silver Hind keychain made of the Hind logo.

Marketing Department = 25 Parts (€250) All of the above, plus a limited version Hind Crew T-shirt.

Marketing Director = 125 Parts (€1250) All of the above, plus a personal performance through Kyte TV, where u can chat with me after the performance.

Marketing Executive = 250 Parts (250x €10= €2500) All of the above plus an additional pro rata Publishing rev share of 0.01%.

Marketing President = 500 Parts (500 x €10 = €5000) All of the above plus an additional pro rata Publishing rev share of 0.02%.

Each investor also received a free CD and download of the album, and was entitled to participate in 10 percent of the revenue from the album.

4. Keep the campaign short. Kickstarter has found that the optimum campaign is 30 days, with longer campaigns performing significantly worse. The largest periods of investment come right in the beginning and right before it closes, with everything in the middle a somewhat "dead period." If that's the case, you might as well make the campaign short, since there's no advantage to dragging it out.

Kickstarter also has some great additional info and data on their website that's worth checking out.

THE CONCEPT OF "FUELERS"

Rockethub has a separate site that provides some insight into crowd-funding and how to take advantage of their service, and on it they introduce the concept of "fuelers." In Rockethub parlance, fuelers are contributors to your crowdfunding project and can be broken down into three categories. According to the site:

The vast majority of your Fuelers will be people you already know. They are your friends, family, and fans. These are people who already know and trust you. For most projects, the number of strangers who become Fuelers is fairly low. That being said, all Fuelers will fall into one of the following three categories:

1. **The Committed**—already committed to supporting you when they arrive
2. **The Inspired**—become inspired to support you after they arrive
3. **The Shoppers**—will shop (and tangentially support you)

Category #1, the Committed, will be populated with your First Degree Network of friends and family. These are folks who will support you every time, regardless of the project, or its quality. Your parents are likely a good example.

Category #2, the Inspired, will be populated with other friends and family members, your Second Degree Network. These are people whom you invite to the project page. They are not committed to contributing when they arrive, but after watching your video or reading your project description, they decide that you are up to something great! They become inspired to support you. Some strangers may fall into this category, but a friend you see occasionally is likely a better example.

Category #3, the Shoppers, will be populated with everyone else (i.e., your Third Degree Network). In order for your project to grab friends-of-friends and strangers, you'll need to grab the shoppers as well. The best way to do this is by creating rewards that are interesting and/or a good value.

If you think about it, the fueler concept also applies to an artist or band's audience.

▶ The **Committed** are your "tribe" (as best-selling marketer Seth Godin calls them). These are your most passionate fans that will go to any lengths to attend a show or buy a product.

▶ The **Inspired** are your "casual" audience: the ones that like you but don't love you. It may only take a single great song to push the casual fan into the committed category.

▶ The **Shoppers** are the part of the audience that really like your genre or even subgenre of music, but either hasn't been properly exposed to you or just hasn't caught the fever yet.

Your first job as an artist is to take care of your most passionate members (the Committed or your tribe) first, since they frequently bring the Inspired or casual fan into the tribe just with their enthusiasm.

Spending too much time on the Shoppers of the audience can take too much attention away from the fans that really matter, and you may never win them over anyway. In short, take care of the fans that are already in your corner first. If treated well, they may be your fans forever.

Crowdfunding

Allows your fans to pool their money to fund your project.

Set an attainable monetary goal.

Make the incentives enticing for investors.

Embrace your "fuelers."

When You Need a Label

. . . .

This entire book so far has been about getting along in the new music world without a record label, but there does come a time when having a label is worth considering if you want to jump to the next level as an artist. Record labels are not intrinsically bad; it's just that you have to weigh the advantages versus the disadvantages to determine whether or not the time is right for you to be associated with one.

> *It's easy to look at them as buffoons (like we do politicians), but most of them are surprisingly smart. This last ten years has been humbling for them. It's shaken out the people that were only in it for the money, so most of the people at labels today are in it for the right reasons and are more entrepreneurial.*
>
> —Derek Sivers

You might want to consider a label if:

▶ **It's offering you a staggering amount of money.** If this happens, either you must be hot enough for a bidding war to have broken out or they really, really believe in your future. Just remember that this might be the last money you'll ever see from the label, and it may have a significantly negative impact on any credibility that you have with your fan base. Best to test the notion of signing with a label with your tribe just to see their reaction first, since they won't buy anything from you if they feel you sold them out.

▶ **You need money for recording, touring, or any other needs.** One of the things that labels do really well is to act like a bank by using your music as collateral. Major labels still do this as skillfully as ever before, but is it worth the price you're going to pay in terms of the freedom that M3.0 offers?

▶ **You're spending too much time on certain aspects of a career.** A label can take some of the burden of marketing and distribution off your shoulders. You still have to be involved on some level, though, or you run the risk of things getting way off course before it's brought to your attention. If you don't have a manager already, that might be a better association to make at this point than to start working with a label.

▶ **You need expanded distribution.** If distribution into the remaining brick-and-mortar stores is beyond what a small indie label can provide, a major label can be your friend. Major labels have the relationships, the sales force, and the means to collect the money. If you're distributing by yourself, you'll get paid if and when the stores feel like it because you have no clout. In some cases, you won't even be able to get into the remaining chains and retail stores because you don't sell enough to get on their radar. A major label or large indie sells the stores a lot of product, and they're trusted, so it's a lot easier for them to get the retailer to take a chance. Further, the label has some leverage in that they can always threaten to withhold in-demand product if they don't get paid.

▶ **You want to expand into foreign territories.** Let's say that you have a huge following in Germany via your online efforts, but you can't service them properly because you live in Kansas City. A major label can use their overseas resources to promote you and get product in the stores there. It saves you the hassle of reinventing the distribution and marketing wheels.

▶ **You need economies of scale.** Sometimes the power of a big label can be used to your advantage since they can cut a better deal with a service (YouTube and MTV come to mind) than you ever could as an indie.

In the video business, there was a conscious decision made that video was no longer going to be free anymore. How can it be promotional if MTV doesn't play it? It has become a product, so we're going to make money out of it. It turns out there's a tremendous demand for music videos, and they can be monetized. Now we're the biggest channel on YouTube. But it's better for us to deal with YouTube on a centralized basis than as individual labels.

—Howard Soroka, Vice President of Media
Technologies of the Universal Music Group

▶ **You need major marketing.** Another thing that a major label does well is to market you traditionally. If you want airplay on radio and appearances on television, a label may be your only hope. If you want reviews and articles in mainstream media, they still have the clout to get it done.

► **If you feel that you've gone as far as you can go as an indie artist.** If you need help to push your career over the edge to stardom, then a major label or major label imprint may be the way to go. This is what they do—sometimes well, sometimes not.

Unless you have a specific need for any of the above that you're sure you can't fill any other way, it's best to stay independent for as long as you can as long as M3.0 is around. Who knows how long it will last? Maybe a year or two if we're lucky, but maybe a lot less than that, which might be lucky, too, since it will spell the latest music-business evolution.

TWELVE

CHAPTER

Music 3.1—
The Future

o many in the business, the future is now. Yes, you can say that we're already in Music 3.1 and well on our way to M3.2. So what's the barrier that we crossed? Was it a date, a technology, or an event? Yes, it was all of those, but also a change in attitude. Let's look a little into the very near future. Chances are that much of it will have already come to pass by the time you read this.

Making a Living Is the New Success

Musicians and artists will begin to see success in a different way as making a living replaces stardom as the big score. To some degree that was always true. Most musicians are only too happy making a living by playing music, but thanks to the excesses of M2.5, far too many felt that stardom was well within their reach.

This has changed as a new realism takes place

▶ The realism that DIY takes a lot of work and the rewards aren't as great as in the heyday of the major labels. There's not as much revenue in the music industry pie to split as there was before.

▶ The realism that social networking has limitations just like traditional marketing, so traditional marketing and promotion can't be completely abandoned. You still need both for effective branding and marketing.

▶ The realism that the touring market is not nearly the gold mine that it once was during better economic times. Fewer venues, less money, and more competition makes gigging more difficult than ever.

▶ And the realism that some things in the music business never change. You still need talent, great songs, lots of hard work, and a little luck to make your mark.

THERE'S NO SUCH THING AS A DEMO

If you're an artist or band recording your own songs, erase the word "demo" from your mind. In these days of increasingly better recording gear at ever lower prices and great information on just how to use it, a demo will always keep you in the "good enough" mindset. Each song has to be approached as if it were a finished master because these days it's easier than ever to make some really excellent recordings, and that's what nearly everyone expects to hear. The days of a producer or publishers being able to "hear through the song" (hear the final product in their head) is over. So forget about demos. They're just an excuse for a recording that's inadequate in some way.

The idea of the demo came out of practicality, since up until about the year 2000, you just didn't have the ability to make a record that sounded like a major release anywhere but in a real recording studio. Yes, it was done occasionally, but the vast majority of songs that you'd hear on the radio had real pros with real pro equipment involved. What would happen is that you'd make a "demo" that was just good enough to get a label or producer interested in taking you to the next level. Because studios were so expensive to record in (typically $100 to $250 an hour, plus engineer, tape, etc.), it was usually impossible to spend enough time to make a recording that was up to snuff with a major label release. And if you weren't located near a reasonably high-end studio, you were forced to use whatever was available, so as a result, almost everyone made a demo before moving on to a deal with a label where they got to make real records in real studios with some real pros who knew what to do.

Most of that has changed with the last few generations of affordable recording gear that are now readily available, and with the fact that the listening public doesn't care as much about audio fidelity as they once did (maybe they never did, but the record companies sure thought so). So now it's easy enough to record for not a lot of money and distribute it for next to nothing, but people expect every recording to be as good as you can make it.

Major Label Deconstruction

Among the many recent changes in the music business is the total disruption of the major label paradigm. Where once the music world revolved around six majors, the number may be soon reduced to just two as of the writing of this book. What's more, the influence of the majors has dwindled considerably in just a few short years. To most young artists or bands, the majors now represent the idea of indentured servitude rather than the path to fame and fortune.

The path to major label deconstruction has been rather swift. The Big 6 of Warner Music Group (WMG), EMI, Sony Music, Bertelsmann Music Group (BMG), Universal Music Group (UMG) and Polygram reigned for only ten years, from 1988 to 1998. The group decreased to five in 1998 when UMG absorbed Polygram, and further consolidated to four in 2004 when Sony Music and BMG merged and became Sony BMG. In October of 2008, Sony acquired Bertelsmann's 50 percent of the venture, and the name returned to Sony Music. Bertelsmann wisely retained many of the publishing elements it maintained prior to the merger and was renamed Bertelsmann Rights Management, understanding that the record business was floundering but publishing still remained strong. In 2009, the private equity firm Kohlberg Kravitz Roberts, also known as KKR, acquired 51 percent of the company, a sign of things to come.

THE SAD CASE OF EMI

In May of 2006, EMI attempted to buy Warner Music Group, but the bid was rejected. WMG then returned the favor and tried to buy EMI, only to have it reject a $4.6 billion offer. Then in 2007, EMI was acquired by Terra Firma Capital Partners, a private equity firm, for £4.2 billion (about $6.8 billion) that was largely financed by a loan from banking giant Citigroup. After buying at the top of the market, EMI began to hemorrhage money almost immediately after Terra Firma takeover, as their sales and market share fell through the floor, and several important artists such as Paul McCartney and Radiohead walked away when their contracts ended. Shortly thereafter, Terra Firma was no longer able to make payments on the debt service, and sued Citi essentially for "forcing them to take the money." Terra Firma lost the court case in short order, and as of February 1, 2011, Citigroup became the owner of EMI, immediately writing off £2.2 billion of the debt. While EMI continues to run as a record label, the future is highly uncertain as Citi pounders its next move, with its main objective now of recouping some of the equity for its shareholders. The Big 4 may become The Big 3 as a result.

THE SAD CASE OF WMG

Warner Music Group (WMG, previous known as Warner/Elektra/Atlantic) was one of the most respected labels by both the music industry and among artists. Once helmed by music-industry pioneers such as Mo Ostin, Joe Smith, Ahmet Ertegun, and Jak Holzman, the label was known to stick by artists it really believed in, regardless of whether the first few albums sold or not, as was the case with Jackson Browne and Fleetwood Mac.

From the time that Seagrams (the Canadian liquor giant) purchased a small piece of the company in 1994, WMG has been in increasing disarray, which was exacerbated in 2004 when a group of investors lead by Edgar Bronfman Jr. (who became CEO) purchased it from the Time Warner group. Since that time, it's been all downhill.

WMG has struggled, with sales, market share, and revenue dropping in spite of excellent digital sales. In a surprise move, WMG recently put itself up for sale and was purchased by Russian billionaire Len Blavatnik and his Access Industries. It's too early to see how the sale will affect the record label. The bottom line is that with two of the majors in such a state of flux, the end of the major label era as we knew it is certainly gone forever.

In the end, even though the remaining major labels will lose even more influence, they won't go away. There will always be needed for what they do best—taking successful artists and making them superstars.

Four Steps to a New Music Business

We live in a technological world that moves so fast it's nearly impossible to keep up. That said, there are advancements on the way that will change not only the way we do business but also how we think about it.

STEP 1: NEW BLOOD FOR THE INDUSTRY

The music industry was creatively at its best when the pioneers of the business (Berry Gordy, Ahmet Ertegen, Mo Ostin, Jac Holzman, and so forth) were actively running their companies. They were fans first, businessmen second, and they intimately knew their audience well because they were part of it.

Everything changed in the '80s when the increasing music industry revenue became so attractive that these entrepreneurs were bought out by multinational corporations. From that point on, the quarterly bottom line was king, not the music. Where previously a label could wait as many as four or even five albums for an artist to break (as in the cases of David Bowie, Alice Cooper, Fleetwood Mac, Hall & Oats, and Red Hot Chili Peppers, among others), soon the policy became one and done if sales were not immediately up to expectations. To make matters worse, MTV became a primary music-promotional tool, so the development cycle soon spun around image rather than music, which further depressed creativity.

But that's beginning to change as we witness a big shakeout in the music industry right before our very eyes. With the music industry no longer the cash cow that it was, the big business that controls the industry will soon drop away, as will the old guard that ran it. In their place will be a new crop of music entrepreneurs, who, like their early predecessors, love the music that they sell just as much as their customers do. They'll nurture talent because they believe in it, just like before, and music will become vital and exciting again, and with that, will come back healthier (though probably not as profitable) than ever.

STEP 2: MICROPAYMENTS MAKE SALES A SNAP

Ninety-nine cents per song download is a barrier. Even $0.69 is a barrier that gives a consumer pause before purchasing, which takes the impulse buy away. That's because consumers are more keenly aware than ever that those amounts add up quickly, so as a result, there's a built-in incentive to download the same file illegally or not buy it at all. But what if the cost of a track were mere pennies, like a dime or a nickel, or even less? Would you be willing to purchase it then? And what if it could be easily charged to your phone bill or an online account such as Paypal so the transaction was so easy, or even automatic, that you didn't have to think about it? Would you go through all the trouble of finding it on a torrent and illegally downloading a file that might be corrupted?

I think the answer is that you'd take the easiest way and pay the few pennies. History has shown us that when the consumer is given the choice, convenience nearly always wins.

But there are a number of problems with this scenario. The first is that the transaction fees with banks are so high (supposedly $0.10 of every iTunes transaction, and even higher with other online purchases), that transactions in cents are currently not feasible. This barrier seems as though it will be broken soon, as rumor has many of the new smart phones feature Near Field Communication (as spoken about in the interview with Ken Rutkowski) that enables a new mobile payments system that will allow low-cost direct transactions directly with your personal bank account. In essence, your phone will soon be your wallet.

But other barriers exist as well. A deal still has to be worked out with publishers, as mechanical royalties of $0.091 still apply to every download, although it's way lower ($.0019 or even less) for a stream. And you can bet that a major label will never go for a low-price transaction with any of their artists unless it can be proven that it's driving the piracy factor down and sales numbers up.

That being said, if you're an indie DIY artist, micropayments can be a great way to make at least a little money on your work.

STEP 3: SUBSCRIPTION IS THE NEW DOWNLOAD

Music subscription has been talked about to death, but the bottom line is still true—consumers are beginning to see the value in subscription music, and their interest will only grow. There's both a lot of hope and a lot of record-label resistance to subscription music. On the one hand, everyone likes the idea of a steady monthly income that $10.00 a customer (the reported target price) might bring. On the other hand, how that money gets split up has labels, publishers, and artists all wringing their hands in simultaneous anxious hope and fear.

But consumers are seeing the value of not condemning 20-plus gigs of hard drive real estate to a library that provides you no discovery options, and where you only listen to a few hundred songs anyway. An all-you-can-listen-to, anytime, anywhere option that subscription promises is beginning to make more and more sense to more and more people. As stated previously in this book, someone will get music subscription right, and the world will beat a path to their door.

STEP 4: A NEW APPROACH TO PIRACY

To date the RIAA's approach to piracy was to fully punish anyone caught indulging in illegal music downloading in order to make a nasty example that would deter all others from even thinking about participating in such a heinous crime. Didn't work, did it?

Let's try another technique instead. How about taking the same approach that countries often take when they catch a spy?

When spies are caught they're given the option: come and work for us as a counterspy, or be prosecuted. What if the industry used the same mindset? Register with a music subscription service (assuming that a widespread subscription service is in place) for a minimum number of years (say, five), or be prosecuted. I bet you already know which one everyone would take. This way, you turn illegal file sharers into customers, you take the incentive out of illegal file sharing in the first place, and the artist, publisher, and labels get paid. Everyone wins.

Will these advances and ideas completely change the music business? Probably not by themselves. But they're a good start to reinvigorating the industry and finally bringing us into the new music age—the age of Music 3.1.

THIRTEEN

CHAPTER

Interviews

Ted Cohen

Known throughout the technology and music industries as being part ambassador and part evangelist, Ted Cohen has been on the cutting edge of digital music from its inception. As a former senior vice president of digital development and distribution for EMI Music, he led the company's next-generation digital business development worldwide and was instrumental in crafting the licensing agreements upon which the Rhapsody subscription service and the iTunes Music Store were built. Prior to his role at EMI, Cohen served as executive vice president of Digital Music Network and held senior management positions at both Warner Bros. Records and Philips Media. Currently the managing partner of the industry consulting firm TAG Strategic, he is one of the most influential voices in digital music today and can be seen speaking on the subject worldwide.

What's the state of digital music today?

I recently wrote a blog about how the industry was making a horrible mistake if they increase their prices at this really critical time. This isn't the time to try to figure out if they can extract another pound of flesh from the consumer, while most households have at least one kid in the house who can figure out how to get it for you for free.

The idea of variable pricing, when I was promoting it at EMI, was to put new artists on sale, to create special bundles, to create value, to create differentiation, and to get a premium out of certain artists only where it was appropriate. If Coldplay came out with a new track a month before the new album, sure—charge $1.49 for it. But the buyer might get $0.50 or even $1.00 off the new album when it comes out.

One of the things that I think is missing in digital retail is any sense of merchandising. I refer to iTunes as a digital 7-Eleven, and Ian Rogers from Topspin refers to it as an Excel spreadsheet that plays music. I think we're both right, in that there's nothing appealing about iTunes. It doesn't really market music effectively. Most people go to iTunes and see what's in the Top 10, and it becomes like picking up a digital quart of milk where on the way out you buy something on impulse at the checkout counter. For the most part, it's not a Border's [Books] experience, where you curl up in a chair and read for a while.

The good thing that has happened is we've moved from digital being a possible part of music's future to being the inevitable basis of music's future. I think the real mistake that a lot of people are making outside the old school is that they chant with glee about the fall of the majors and the loss of control and the breaking of the stranglehold on distribution. In a digital world, it's not about distribution, because everyone has it. In the physical world, you used to have 25,000 SKUs [or stock-keeping units—the individual numbers that each item in a store has for the purpose of inventory control] competing for attention. But now you have 5 million SKUs competing for attention in the digital world. So when someone says, "I released my record on the Net," how many people know you put it out there? How are you reaching anyone? How are you creating not only a fan base but people that are compensating you in some way? Maybe you're giving your music away, but they're signing up for your fan club or they've bought a season pass for your shows. But just saying that your music is being distributed on the Net doesn't mean anything.

Digital is a new phase of the industry, and it increases the need for really targeted marketing, really clever promotion, or anything that you can do to stand out. Whenever anyone says that the Internet creates a level playing field, I have to laugh. The fact is, it creates a ridiculously level playing field. It's so level that it's really difficult to stand out among 5 million entities struggling for attention. The question is, how do you get noticed? How do you reach your constituency? How do you make people aware? How do you create targeted mailing lists without people deleting them when they come in?

So how does an artist do that?
The other thing that's critical is "recommendation," because in that level playing field of 5 million songs, I need something to make suggestions of new songs to me. If I have an hour today to listen to 15 new songs, please tell me what to listen to and I'll pay you for that. I need somebody to recommend and personalize that music experience for me so that I'm not listening to 15 new songs going, "I hate that. That sucks." I want to go, "How did they know that I'd like this? This is wonderful."

Who's doing that now?
Companies like Echo Nest out of Boston [the.echonest.com]. Pandora does it very well. Music IP has done a pretty good job. GraceNote has a recommendation engine. AMG Macrovision has a pretty good recommendation engine.

Are any of them gaining critical mass?
Pandora is getting to critical mass, but I think Echo Nest is the coolest technology out there in that it combines music recommendation with social recommendation. It's not only "If you like this, you'll like that." It's "If you like this, you'll like that because your friend likes it." It's a combination of collaborative filtering and music recommendation. So on the same exact criteria, the recommendation I would get this week would be different from what I'd get a month from now.

Do you see everything going to subscription?
I've had a slide in my deck for the last three years that says, "For $10 a month, you can get 10 songs on iTunes or 10 million songs on Napster." Access trumps ownership. I totally believe that in a

360-degree connected world where I have pervasive connectivity (we're still not there yet but we're getting there), I don't need to own music. As long as I have my music whenever I want it, I would always pay for access over ownership. There's a point where we get past that fear of "It's music rental."

How close are we to that?

If iTunes announced subscription tomorrow, we'd be over the hump. We need some sea-change event. GraceNote is working on some cool stuff with the car companies where the head unit on a 2010 car will have a built-in 3G or 4G communications module, so wherever I am, I can stream whatever I want—whether it's coming from Rhapsody or my home hard drive. It's just not a cost-effective value proposition to fill up an iPod with 10,000 songs at $0.99 a track. No one's going to do it. I would pay 10 or 15 bucks per month to Apple to download a playlist of beach music, a playlist of dance music, or whatever, and just keep that thing filled. And as it gets to know me each time it's filled, the music selection gets better and better.

Is that going to be better for the industry?

Right now as an industry, we're thrilled if an artist sells a couple of hundred thousand records. We have 200 million people of buying age in the US, and let's say that half of them want to pay to access music. That's 100 million people subscribing at 10 bucks a month!

But how is it going to filter down to the artists?

We need a really good micropayment system to make it work for everyone. One of the things about digital is that it provides some really granular and really accurate play/event data. Rhapsody can tell you how many times a song was played and by what artist, so they can tell if an artist is owed 27 points against whatever the total pie is. We've never had that before. We've had BMI and ASCAP audits, where they come into a station and see what they do for a month, but we now live in a totally granular world where we can keep track of what happens.

Which companies that aren't record labels are doing the best job?

Ian Rogers is doing an amazing job, at least initially, with Topspin. I also believe that ReverbNation does a good job. I think TuneCore's model is really interesting, where it's just a flat fee to get your music distributed. But again, that's just the first step. They can get your music onto iTunes, but you still have to let people know it's there. There are companies like TheBizmo [thebizmo.com] and a few others that are providing widget tools for artists to put their music onto pages and have their fans act as their distributor for them.

Which of the record labels are doing the best job in digital music?
I think that one of the brightest people I know in digital is Syd Schwartz at EMI. But I would have to say that Warner is doing the most interesting stuff, because they have really good people at the label level and really smart people at the corporate level.

You have these two things happening at a record company: you have corporate who's asking, "How do we get paid?" and you have the labels going, "How do we get our artists discovered?" They're working on opposite objectives. When music leaks and they find out that the new U2 album [for example] is out before its release date, chances are it's someone at the label level that leaked it because they wanted the publicity. Of course, they'll deny it later that they leaked it.

So you have the label trying to expose artists and trying to make some noise, and you have corporate going, "Are you going to pay us for this?" You might argue right now that Google should be paying U2 to feature them on the front page of their music section. Or should U2 be paying Google to be featured on the front page? The answer to that question might determine digital music's future.

Richard Feldman

For as long as I've known Richard Feldman (more than 20 years), he's been trying to get out of the music business to pursue a business career, only to get pulled back by more success. A very successful songwriter and producer who has platinum and Number 1 records to his credit, Feldman's 2005 attempt to leave the business ended with him winning a Grammy for producing Toot's and the Maytals' *True Love*. His latest foray into getting out of the business finds him with a successful publishing venture, a music library/placement agency called ArtistFirst Music. Feldman comes to publishing from the point of view of a musician, producer, and songwriter, and he has a unique perspective on the changes that M3.0 brings.

What's the difference between music publishing today and the way it used to be?

There are many differences, but you've got to look back at publishing from the beginning to understand them. Publishing meant receiving a percentage from the sale of sheet music at first, then [later] from other physical products like piano rolls, and [most recently, from] vinyl to cassette to CDs to MP3s. This is called a *mechanical royalty* and results from a sale of a song. Another source of revenue for songwriters and publishers is performance income. This started out as a payment for a live rendition of a song, then evolved into payments from broadcasting the song on radio and television. The performing rights organizations (PROs) collect this money from the various radio and TV broadcasters and distribute it to their writers.

There is another source of revenue that has basically saved the publishing industry, and this is called a *synchronization license*. A synch license is required if you use music in a production with moving pictures, and for that there is a negotiated fee. So mechanical royalties from record sales have gone down, but income from synch licenses has gone up, and performance income has been increasing as well.

Why has synch income increased?

There are many reasons, but the most obvious is that there are so many more broadcasters today. Where it used to be only the big three networks (NBC, CBS, and ABC), now it's more like 300 with all the cable networks, so there are more sources of income than there were before. As a result, you have the increase in these synch fees offsetting and sometimes exceeding the loss of mechanicals. Publishing is now the "last man standing" in terms of making money in the music business, and still one of the few ways left to monetize intellectual property.

Is there any money being made online?

Yes, but there are challenges. Besides the biggest eternal problem of competing with what people can download for free, streaming isn't really working as a business model for the publisher. It's making some money, but unless you're the guy getting megastreamed, it's just a game of pennies.

Here's how it works. If a song is played on the radio or television, half gets paid to the publisher and the other half gets paid directly to the writer, so there's no accounting expense for the publisher. But when a digital track is sold (or a CD, for that matter) or streamed, all the fees go to the publisher, and the publisher is responsible for paying the writer.

With streaming, a publisher might have lots of sources he collects from, but the total amount turns out to be very little because it pays less than 1/4 of a cent per stream. A publisher I know finished his accounting run with a report as big as a phone book, yet the total was only about 12 bucks in royalties. So a publisher who pays the writer 50 percent and then takes his or her portion of the publishing would end up with $3.00 in this case. It actually costs more to produce the statements than they are worth! Of course there are some artists who cut through with a huge volume of streams, and other sources like ringtones still bring in big money. But it's getting more like third-world countries, with a small upper class, no middle class, and a huge group that makes very little.

For a while, everyone thought digital distribution might be the answer to the industry's problems, but the problem is that streaming doesn't pay enough, even with no distribution or inventory costs involved. And what happens when you fill the bucket up with the long-tail items? It really doesn't make sense to a publisher from the accounting perspective, because what's going on online is a disruption of the longstanding idea that you have to buy a whole album to get the one song that you liked. That's over, since we're back to a singles business again.

You mentioned in a previous conversation about how synch fees are going down.
Synch fees are soft for several reasons. One is supply and demand. Record companies see the opportunity with film and television placements as both promotion and a source of revenue, so in some cases they are giving away music to get exposure. Also, there are more royalty-free sources for music where publishers give up the front-end synch-license fee and try to make it up on performance fees when the show is broadcast.

Another reason for the lower fees is the current economy. Advertising rates are down, so broadcasters have less money for music. And DVD sales are down, which affects movie budgets for music. As a result, for a known but not famous song used as an end title on a major picture, the fees used to be about 15 grand per side, but in some cases it's now down to about $10K a side. However, don't forget that if you have a piece of music that's unique (say, a Beatles tune), or if a director just has to have a particular track, you can name your price.

I should also add there's a chance that performance income could go down as well—again for several reasons. Firstly, the economy has affected advertising, which translates to less money collected by the performance-rights organizations and therefore less money distributed to publishers and writers. Then there's another trend that has some people within the PROs worried, and that's the migration of viewers away from the major broadcast networks. As people change their viewing habits from watching "their show" [on TV] at 8 p.m. on a particular night to [watching it] whenever they have time thanks to the DVR, it translates into less money collected from the big networks. The major networks make up the majority of fees paid to the PROs, as the smaller cable outlets pay a lot less because their ad rates are lower. For example, if your song is played on *Monday Night Football*, you might get between $150 and $200 from performance fees, but if it's on a cable channel, it could be more like $.017. It's that different.

How does a blanket license work?
Blanket licenses are issued on two levels. Music libraries like Firstcom and Killer Tracks will issue a network a blanket license for the use of their library on the broadcaster's shows. Think of it like an all-you-can-eat buffet. Instead of licensing each song, they can use as many songs as they like for as many times as they like for one fee. The PROs also issue blanket licenses to the networks for the performance income. For each contract period, the PROs negotiate a license fee with each broadcaster, which can be very large, like in double-digit millions for a network like NBC.

Then there is the notorious survey, which figures out how all the money is divvied up. The way an individual writer [or] publisher is paid is by a cue sheet, which indicates that a particular piece of music was used and is turned in by the producer of the show. Since it's presently impossible to survey all networks all the time to see what they're playing, there are survey periods, which cause headaches because of their randomness. If you have a lot of cues played during a survey period, then you'll make more during other periods, too, since your payout rate is based on the survey period.

I know a publisher who had a song used on a television series. There were two writers and thus two publishers—one with ASCAP and one with BMI. One of the credits over a quarter was for $19,000, while the other was only $1,200. It's not a good system.

The perception of success has changed in the business, hasn't it?
You bet! Maybe it's better, but now success can be measured in how many hits you have on your MySpace page or even how many Friends you have. With MySpace, bands and artists consider 12,000 hits like a gold record. There's less money to go around but still no lack of people wanting to make music. Where it used to take a $5,000 development deal with a label as a first step to making a record, all it takes now is a free software package like GarageBand and a desire. The traditional gatekeepers (like record company A&R executives) who decide what is good and bad have been banned from the temple.

In fact, the endgame isn't even a record deal these days. I recently talked with a big manager out of the UK, and he said he had a list of things that he tries to do for all his artists. Way down at number 8 was trying to get the band signed, where it used to be on the top of the list.

The truth is that music is still about passion, not money. People need music like oxygen and food, and people who make it *have* to make it. Where this all ends is uncertain as the industry searches for the "New Model," but you can bet people will keep making music whether or not a model is ever found.

Larry Gerbrandt

. . . .

An expert on entertainment analytics, Larry Gerbrandt's Media Valuation Partners advises its clients on the economics of media and content on traditional and emerging technology platforms. Formerly a senior vice president with research giant Nielsen Analytics, Gerbrandt provides a wealth of experience in entertainment market research that we're pleased we could tap for this book. Get ready for some interesting and insightful facts and figures regarding sponsorships, branding, and advertising—all the things necessary to monetize M3.0.

Why does television have less of an impact on music than it used to?
What's happening is that the numbers for traditional broadcast television are dropping dramatically. In a 500-channel universe, viewers have a lot of choices, and a lot of the programming is simply not compelling enough. Reality programming isn't as compelling as scripted drama, and [yet] there's more and more of it.

Does that mean that the aggregate is going down, or is it the per-channel viewing?
Per-channel viewing. In aggregate, people are still watching as much television as ever, if not more, but they're watching it across more channels. They're watching the cable channels more and the broadcast channels less. What's also happening is that people are using new technologies to increase their overall consumption of video.

What's the digital reality of actually monetizing that?
The problem is that on cable, you have a 500-channel universe, but on the Internet, you have a 5,000- or 50,000-channel universe, and there is no central place to aggregate information as to what all of them are doing. Having said that, sites like Hulu are starting to gain some traction, although YouTube is still the 800-pound gorilla.

It used to be that an act appearing on *Saturday Night Live* could expect a sales bump of 100K units the next week, but that's no longer true. Why do you think that is?
First of all, *SNL's* viewership is down. It used to be that it did a 12 rating, but now it might do a 2 or a 3. What that means is that only 2 percent of the households are viewing it, or to put it another way, it's not being viewed by 98 percent of the available households. So there's been some dramatic drops in viewership, and as a result, traditional media becomes a lot less effective.

The demo for TV has grown older as well, hasn't it?
The US population is aging, so we as a nation are growing a bit older as a result of the baby boom [generation]. What's happening on

television is a bit more complex, however. Young adults watch significantly less television than their older counterparts. They are busier with education, careers, raising families, socializing, and have less leisure time as a result. That's why advertisers are willing to pay a premium to reach the younger demographics—they are simply harder to target. There's also a continuing belief that individuals make lifelong brand choices as young adults.

How do you see television changing in the future?
The first thing is that the DVR is going to have an ever-greater impact. Secondly, we're going to see online content come to the big-screen TV. And third, we're going to see greater consumption of television outside of the traditional sources. You'll see more and more content on mobile devices, for instance, as well as portable display screens connected to wireless broadband. Television will have to adapt to the new zeitgeist: that whatever video content they want should be available whenever and wherever they want.

How will everyone monetize video online as compared to broadcast?
The models are not that dramatically different. The difference is in the commercial loads. Fox has begun to experiment with less clutter [shorter commercials] and charging advertisers more. We're probably going to see a reprising of the program sponsorship model. Part of that is in response to the DVR.

Can the consumer be driven to the network's online shows, and can they monetize it to a level that makes it worth it?
All the online numbers are still tiny compared to broadcast. If you took all of YouTube's views in a 24-hour day, it's equivalent to about an hour of a single prime-time show on any of the four major networks. Now that YouTube number is growing, and one of the things that makes it so attractive is that the demographics of that viewer tend to be younger and a little more affluent.

You'd think that the prime demo would be the boomers who have more money.
Yes, but what brand advertisers continue to believe is that people make up their brand choices in their 20s and early 30s. By the time you're

a boomer, you've already decided that you're a Dove Bar--eating, Chevron-using, Charmin-wiping fan, and that's what you like. So the advertising is really designed to affect the young.

Let's talk about sponsorships. Is the sponsorship spend getting wider or more targeted?

What I think we'll see a lot more is much tighter integration with the program, because then you can control the message. What we're seeing with *American Idol* is incredibly tight integration with the products. They're almost shameless. At every turn they're integrating the show with a sponsor's message. This is still virgin territory, and we're still trying to figure out exactly what works. What they do know is that over time, consumers develop advertiser-aversion techniques. For instance, they're increasingly finding that banner ads don't work because we've come to ignore them. Billboards became the same way, so now they wrap entire buildings and use them as giant billboards and use the new digital signs that are much more compelling and attention grabbing. It's a constant battle between advertisers and viewers in terms of making the advertising message get through the visual corridor that we're confronted with.

What seems to work online these days, then?

There's a new set of ads that pop up with the content (not pop-ups as a separate window, like before) that take over your screen, as well as mouse-over ads that integrate movement into it. We all hate it, right? But for the Web to continue to be free, commercial messages have to continue to work in some fashion. It's going to continue for the rest of our lives. There will be escalations and different techniques, but it will continue.

NASCAR is probably an extreme example. Every car and every driver is covered head to toe with messages, so affiliating yourself with something that people positively associate with definitely works. It's all branding and identity. The problem is that it's getting harder and harder to tell a story, and there's still nothing like a 30-second commercial to do that.

Two of the emerging forces in advertising are the power of the blog and of social media. Word of mouth has always been critical to spreading brand awareness. With the viral nature of online communications, the near-instantaneous methods for information and opinion dissemination, and the ability to rapidly influence large groups through social media, learning how to harness the power of these new recommendation "chains" of interconnected individuals may be the single-most important challenge for brands and advertisers going forward.

Bruce Houghton

. . . .

Bruce Houghton started his highly influential Hypebot blog because he wanted to better understand the changes in the music business in order to help educate the clients of his Skyline Music agency. Since then, Houghton's blog has become a must-read for anyone at any level in the music industry. His keen observations come from being not only a highly prominent blogger but also a booking agent working in the industry trenches every day.

Has your booking agency been affected by M3.0?
We have some problems that we never used to have because there's a fractured media landscape, and the major record labels are not as well staffed or well financed as they used to be. The old paradigm was that the promoter bought the band and figured out which radio station to copromote with, and after that, the record label came in and did a lot of the rest. The label was the publicist, they bought additional advertising, and they put up posters in local record stores to help promote a show. None of that happens any more. The promoter or the artist themselves are left as the promotion machine, and the promoters are, for the most part, pretty ill equipped to do it. Like the labels, they're also understaffed and don't necessarily understand the digital age. Most of them are starting to try, but overall, there is no formula anymore that they can follow.

So what we see is that it's tougher and tougher to break a band live because too many of the dates are not well promoted. We find ourselves working harder to educate the promoters and the artists so they can figure out how to reach out to their audiences directly themselves.

How many artists are equipped to do that?
Honestly, not many—and that's the problem. If they have a really good mailing list, a really active social-networking presence, and

some kind of way to mobilize the uberfan to put up posters and that sort of thing, then they have a chance. How many have that or are equipped to use it properly? Probably less than 20 percent. Part of that simply is that there are only so many hours in the day, because they're trying to be musicians. Some of it is also that what works is changing so rapidly that unless they really have a propensity to keep up with things, they'll have trouble.

For example, a few years ago, MySpace was everything. Now, depending upon who you are and the age of your audience, MySpace may mean nothing, so those kinds of things are very difficult for a band to grasp. If they work really hard to master a craft over here, suddenly the playing field changes, and they have to go over there instead. You see an increasing number of companies trying to deal with that problem on behalf of the artist.

What are the most effective promotional tools that you see?
Right now it's that combination of having a great email list and a great website that's constantly updated and gives the fans a reason to come back. If it isn't updated every day, it's updated two or three times a week, with news, pictures, free stuff, and links to other bands they like. Also, some kind of presence on the social-networking sites, depending on who you are as a band and who your audience is.

In terms of growing an email list, I'm a big fan of the tools that Topspin and Bandcamp have, where it's something like, "Give us your email address, and we'll give you this MP3," or "Here's an easy way to send this MP3 to your friends." I'm a big fan of anything that encourages viral growth.

Have you seen any huge shifts in the business in the past few years, or has it just been evolutionary?
I think that the end of music retail is in sight, and it really has accelerated in the last 2 years. What that means is we're only a couple of years away from not caring at all about getting records into stores. That's huge, because it eliminates a marketing opportunity where a clerk in a record store who likes your record will tell people about it, so it's a little sad, because that point of contact at the record stores is going to be gone in a few years. On the other hand, it's really exciting, because that barrier where a band feels that they needed a nationally distributed release is gone.

That being said, we may never get to the point where we don't want to press physical product. In fact, I'm a believer that physical product acts like a souvenir of the band. If bands think of a CD that way and package it as such, they might find some increased success with it.

What are the trends in the business that you see today?
I see more and more niche markets finding more coherent audiences. You can be into Hungarian death metal or central Canadian bluegrass and easily fill your iPod with songs of that particular genre. Then in your spare time, you can read blogs pertaining to only that subject.

I also see the rise of the musical middle-class artist that can make anywhere from a store-clerk living to 100 grand a year per band member. There'll be fewer superstars and a lot more mid-level artists as time goes on.

I also see the marginalization of major labels outside of pop and hip-hop.

What do you see happening with venues? Are they healthy or in trouble?
It's really market to market, but in general they're pretty healthy. People still want to go out and have fun and see a band live. The larger the big promoters like Live Nation get, the more it opens up the opportunity for the guys underneath them—and we're starting to see that trend. The venue business took a real hit when the drinking age went from 18 to 21 in 1984, but since then it's been pretty steady.

What's the best way to break an act today?
It depends on the act and musical genre. For hip-hop it's entirely about the record and finding a powerful enough team to sort of ram it home on the radio in the mainstream media. If it's not rap or hip-hop, it's probably more about touring and doing the work you need to do build your fan base so that they become your promotional army, telling their friends about you and helping you grow.

It used to be that if a DJ talked about you in afternoon drive time, then there'd be 300 more people at the club that night. Now you need 30 people talking about you on their blogs and to their friends so that each of them will bring 10 more people to the club. So it's doing whatever you have to do to build an audience, which usually includes touring to some degree.

That's how everyone makes money now, right?
Yeah, that's true, but there's also a misnomer about that. We often see bands that try to do too much too fast. A lot of indie labels will say, "We want the band to get in a van, and we don't want them to get out of it for three years." At some point at the end of year one or two, that runs its course. Virtually no band can keep on running around the country to try to build an audience indiscriminately. As much as touring is the most important thing, it has to be done strategically, concentrating on certain markets where you see the beginning of growth, then doing them often enough but not too often.

What's the most effective DIY promotion tip?
It's figuring out what excites your fans and doing more of it, and that means spending some time getting close to them.

I remember going to see a mainstream country act, the Blackhawks, about 15 years ago. They were on their second gold record, and each of the members had a lot of success apart from the band. There they were at a little county fair in the middle of nowhere, standing in the rain while 400 people lined up to get their autograph and their picture taken with them, and nobody made them feel like they had to buy something. If every band would do that, they would be a lot more successful and have a lot more loyal fans.

To some degree, what we're all trying to do online now is a digital version of that. How can we keep the fans excited? How can we give them the tools to tell their friends about us? Are we worth having them tell their friends about us? [Laughs.]

What do you see as the most important things that contribute to an artist becoming successful these days?
Great music. That's the one thing that really hasn't changed.

Ariel Hyatt

· ·

A PR person is vital to any artist's visibility, but the right PR person can make all the difference in the world to an artist's career development. That being said, Music 3.0 is a completely different PR world that few publicists know much about. Enter Ariel Hyatt, one of the few true experts in the field of online publicity and social media. Ariel and her socially-based Cyber PR agency specializes in teaching artists the ins and outs of the brave new world of Facebook, Youtube, Twitter, and social media so that the artists can take control themselves. As you'll see, her story is as unique as her service.

You're so much more than a PR person. What are some of the other things that you do?

I do four things. The first is I run a digital PR firm for bands and musicians. What we do is get them featured on blogs, podcasts, and Internet radio stations, and at the same time coach them to become empowered around social media, so we're part education company and part PR firm. That's Cyber PR®, campaigns for musicians.

To facilitate Cyber PR®, I've become a software developer, which is the second part of what I do. I did this because I couldn't find anything online to disperse my educational materials and, more importantly, to track our various campaigns. I think the biggest problem when you hire publicists is that you never really know what they've done for you. They take your money, you don't hear from them for a while, then they send you a report that doesn't make sense. You want them to be a bit more accountable than that, so my Cyber PR® software makes the campaign experience transparent.

Because I was a traditional publicist for ten years, I understood the frustrations coming from clients, but giving them result-oriented answers wasn't always possible. I was working really hard, but my work was not reflected in the reports that said, "Left message. Left message. Left message." It was really painful for me to send minimal results to clients. Hilariously, I was Internet dating at the time, and I liked the interface of an Internet dating site because I could see which men were checking me out. I could make a profile of myself and be as open or as not open about anything. I thought, "Wouldn't it be great if I could make a portal like this for my clients? We could make a profile for them, and then they could see for themselves who was checking them out."

I wanted to create a site where my clients could see which blogs, which podcasts, which Internet radio stations, and which publications were reacting so that unanswerable question that you always have when you hire a publicist, "What the heck did she do for me today?"

gets answered. It's a Web-based solution where everybody gets a user name and a password. I invested a lot of my own money to build it, because I realized that if didn't do it, I was never going to be able to satisfy clients and produce a scalable business.

Part 3 is I write books. I've written two: *Music Success In Nine Weeks* and *The Musician's Roadmap*. Those books relate to part 4 of what I do, which is teach master classes and mentor artists at conferences. I think I'm one of the few music business professionals at some of the conferences I go to who really loves to talk to artists one on one without feeling like it's an obligation. When an artist sits down in front of me and goes, "I don't understand a Facebook personal page versus the fan page," or "Please explain the Twitter retweet to me," or "How do I convert my ReverbNation posts to my blog," and all the questions that they struggle with, that's how I learn what their problems are. I'm constantly curating information to help artists either one on one, on my blog, in my newsletter, or in my books.

How did you make the transition from traditional PR to Cyber PR®?
September 11 is the answer. In my opinion, journalism as we knew it changed forever from that day onward. I was born and raised in New York City and had been a traditional publicist since 1996. I went to work a few days after September 11 and was sitting at my desk just crying. I picked up the phone to do what I'd always done, which was to pitch music journalists and fax releases and email and call and leave messages. I got a journalist on the phone and he started crying too, because what had happened was so moving, and he knew I was in New York. Then we both started laughing because of the ridiculousness of having to pitch a release or a show, and at that moment it just seemed so absurd.

Soon afterwards, all the entertainment editors at the local newspapers who were my lifeblood and who helped support my artists turned all of their focus and column inches to 9/11 tributes. Also, people were not feeling too good about going out, we were going to war, and it was a very, very dark time for entertainment. Then it got even worse when those editors began to get fired.

My PR firm was the canary in the coal mine because my client base was all independent musicians, and they did not have the support that most artists on labels were getting at the time. They didn't have major distribution or even management in some cases; they had only me, and all of a sudden, I couldn't produce the results we were both used to. I started going to bed every night feeling horrendous. I'd have to show up at work and say, "Okay, for $3,000 a month I got you 8 calendar listings and a small photo inset," when five years before I would've gotten 50 features, 20 CD reviews, 10 calendar listings, and 4 cover stories in local newspapers. I thought to myself, "This is untenable," so I turned to the Internet and started to find things like listservs and groups (a lot of the stuff that we're used to online today didn't exist yet).

Then MP3.com and Napster and similar sites and new technology started to take over. I realized that someone was making money online because I was seeing all of these Viagra and mortgage spam flooding into my inbox, so I took myself on a two-year journey to Internet marketing conferences, and I learned about the science of online marketing. As I was doing this, it dawned on me that no one in the music business was in the online marketing space yet. No one was teaching artists about the science of how to send an email. I thought, "If I'm just getting my head around this after all of these seminars and workshops, then what are the artists doing?"

That's the genesis of how Cyber PR® started. In the beginning, it was painful to convince my clients to come on board.

Because they weren't hip to it?
Yes, and because there's a checklist that you put forth in your mind if you're an artist trying to succeed. Letterman, Conan, Rolling Stone, SPIN, New York Times, LA Times, LA Weekly—you hired a publicist to get you exposure there. These were all the goals that every artist knew to have.

At first when I said, "I'm sorry, but we're just a digital PR firm. We've given up traditional press," the artists did not understand what I was talking about. That's when I started writing articles (which turned into my books), because I had to begin explaining not only what I was doing, but how artists could be more effective as well.

Why were all the editors fired around 9/11?
A few factors contributed. The Internet was taking over, and more people began reading their news online, so advertising revenue started dropping. We see it now in that 24 out of the 25 top newspapers have experienced record declines. If they looked at all the journalists on their masthead, the first jobs that got consolidated were the dance

editor, the arts editor, and the music editors—they all became the same person. Suddenly my contact that used to be just the jazz writer was now covering every type of music, as well as dance and theater. Then it got worse when those journalists lost their jobs altogether because the paper just started to use the AP wire services for their music articles to save money.

Most of my clientele were touring artists, so I knew every single newspaper in secondary and tertiary markets, even the little ones built around weddings and funerals. I somehow managed to find angles and get feature stories written, but suddenly those avenues were closed because those editors that were left that had always covered my artists started to tell me, "I'm sorry but we're interviewing Elton John," or "I've got Gwen Stefani." I'd think, "But you only have a circulation of 20,000. How is this possible?" What happened was that all of the major publicists started to focus on the smaller cities and papers, because many of the major publications that used to be available to them were scaling back their entertainment coverage as well, so I was no longer getting the results that I was used to.

What did you focus on when you first started Cyber PR? Blogs didn't exist then.
No, they were called "fanzines," but there were lifestyle sites, portals, listservs, groups, AOL message boards, and those kinds of things. If we had a hippie jam band touring through Chicago, we'd find a local jam board and post there. Of course, Internet radio started to take off, and there were quite a few stations. Live 365 was taking off back then. There were thousands of DJs, and we'd approach them each individually.

I hired a social media expert from San Francisco when I started pivoting my business, because I was lost and confused. The blogosphere was not warming up to me, and the podcasters were mad at me because I was communicating to them like a publicist. I was sending releases, and I was calling and formally pitching them. So she came in and said, "You have to start to use these resources yourself. You've got to get on Twitter, and you must blog regularly." I told her that I wasn't the commodity, my clients were, but she told me that the only way the bloggers would respect me is if I spoke their language. That's what artists need to get. If you want a blogger to respect you, then blog yourself. It's that simple.

What do you think is the best way to break an artist today?
If anyone had the answer we'd all be a lot richer [laughs]. I think that the only answer I can come up with is authenticity. The Internet is one of the biggest BS filters in the world today. If anything, there may be too much importance placed on Internet marketing and social media, because if you don't have a live show that grabs people by their souls, you're really in trouble. As Seth Godin says, "Are you remarkable?" If 10 people come on Tuesday, are there 20 coming on Wednesday because you were that remarkable? Being remarkable on stage now has to be backed up with a great recording that people want to hear and an engaging presence on social media. All of these things work in tandem, and it seems that artists just focus on one. You need to have a strategy about what you're trying to accomplish.

How did you learn the art of music PR?
I worked at a tiny independent label, What Are Records?, where we were completely DIY. Rob Gordon, the label founder, understood direct-to-fan way before Topspin or Nimbit ever coined the phrase. He understood that the Samples from Boulder, CO, was a band that everyone loved and wanted to feel connected to. There was no social media at the time. We did it with live performances, postcards, and street teams. He understood the "1000 True Fan" theory perfectly before it was coined. We created CD carrying cases, beer cozies, and VHS tapes of a documentary we self-produced that took fans on a journey with the band. We had multiple CD releases, cassettes, tons of different T-shirt designs, baseball hats, and it went on and on. What Are Records? grossed that band over $1,000,000 by having a brilliant direct-to-fan plan in place.

Rob did the same thing with media, and that's how I got trained. "We're gonna hit the same market four to six times a year. You go back to the reporter in the local newspaper, and don't let up until you get your feature story." It might have taken us four times through a market to get our story, but that was okay. He taught me to go to the Irish or Jewish newspaper or the obituaries or the wedding paper to find the local angle. It's that mentality that still succeeds today. It's leaving no stone unturned and understanding your audience even if your audience is a journalist.

The artists that I see succeeding today have the same mentality. It's that one-on-one model that works. That's how Amanda Palmer does it. She signs CDs until her hand falls off after each show and so does Taylor Swift.

What would you recommend for a new artist who's beginning to build a fan base as compared to an artist who's been doing it for a while who already has a fan base?

The core message is the same. Unfortunately or fortunately, depending upon how you see things, success now lies in engaging your audience. If you are a band just starting out, you're going to need to engage one person at a time. Start with a goal of ten. Most musicians have this really backward-looking concept that you have to engage millions of people on radio or with world-wide distribution. Just go for ten first.

I was on a panel recently when a guy was so frustrated when he asked a question. He said, "I don't know about Facebook. It's the same people all the time. It's only my friends and family." I asked him, "Have you ever gone to listen to other people's music and commented on it? Have you ever reached out to ten perfect strangers or moved them in some way?" Stop thinking about yourself and start asking about how you can help. It will come back in spades.

So that's the baseline. Now an artist who's already established or has "made it" has to reverse engineer that stuff. It's something like, "Oh, I didn't know that Bonnie Raitt was online. I want to be part of her community." She might not be tweeting or doing everything herself, but at least I get to feel special when I see what she's up to. That's okay. It doesn't have to come directly from the artist, although I think that's very helpful. If Britney Spears can tweet, anyone can.

So it's all about engagement. If you can afford someone to help you with social media, hire them to help you with that relationship, but the bottom line is: you still have to care about your audience enough to want to communicate with them.

Why do you take the approach of training your clients to help themselves instead of charging more to do everything for them?

I took that approach because I realized that if they weren't responsible for themselves, I couldn't help much. I'm really good at Twitter, but you can't just sit back and watch me. You have to learn how to use these platforms effectively to get results, and you have to take control of your business.

Traditional media doesn't mean as much as it used to, and I wish more artists understood that. They think that one article in *Rolling Stone* is going to make them. I've been on *Oprah* and it didn't do anything for my career. She showed my logo and talked about my business and said that I worked with independent artists in front of 40 million viewers. Not one person called. Why? Because independent musicians looking for a publicist aren't watching *Oprah*. It's the wrong niche, just like very few people watching *Letterman* are signed into iTunes ready to buy music. They're watching *Letterman* to decompress and laugh a little bit after a long day at work.

At the end of the day, my clients want two things: fame and fortune. But there's two things they don't have: time and money. Unfortunately it costs some money and some time to learn all this stuff. The fame part is in their own hands.

You can get more info about Ariel and Cyber PR at arielpublicity.com.

Thom Kozik

. . . .

A seasoned tech-industry executive of more than 25 years, Thom Kozik began in digital media in 1990 while at Microsoft by helping to engineer the beginning of both the multimedia revolution and interactive television. He later cofounded the leading media agency MindShare Media. Along the way Kozik has spent most of his time on the gaming side of the tech industry, having served as president of gaming search engines Wazap and All-Seeing Eye (which he sold to Yahoo in 2004), before he became director of business development for Yahoo's Media group, then executive vice president of online gaming at Atari. He is now president of Nüko Games.

What's changed in gaming in the last couple of years?
There are two big things that have changed: the explosion of online gaming in the Western markets (predominantly driven through

Facebook), and the music games that we were talking about two years ago have sunsetted with the change in appetite among gamers.

As far as console games like *Rock Band* and *Guitar Hero*, there's a feeling by video game publishers that they've milked that cow as far as they could and can no longer sell tracks endlessly into those franchises. They haven't turned them off completely, and there's still an effort to continue to sell into their installed base, but we're not going to see another *Beatle's Rock Band* on the horizon. The economics just aren't there.

For an artist who wants to produce for this space, I think there's actually more opportunity than there was a couple of years ago. Back then the focus was on the music games, but the publishers really didn't worry about new music at all. They just wanted old back catalog to throw into the channel.

Now browser-based and mobile gaming (which I still consider to be online gaming) is where the action is. The truth is that the biggest growth area is based around games that depend upon and live via an online connection. In mobile games in particular, most of the early games in this area were self-contained experiences, where titles like *Angry Birds* and *Doodle Jump* had the audio assets for the entire experience, along with all other elements, in the download package that the consumer purchased from an App Store. That's shifting quickly to games like *Infinity Blade,* which uses a traditional console gaming engine and has taken the iPhone and iPad markets by storm. No one expected to see a game of this breadth and quality on a mobile device. It wasn't because of the limitation of the device, but more about the nature of the product being released by the game developers. What's most important about a game like *Infinity Blade* and those that are going to follow is that they're structurally more like console games, in that different levels load dynamically as the player progresses. What's important for musicians is that there's a need for more soundtracks and audio assets as the publishers continue to sell and ship those new levels to players. This trend in mobile gaming is much bigger than the equivalent of "map packs" that publishers put out for console and PC games in years past.

From a creative standpoint, now you have a few leading indicators of what can really be done on these mobile platforms. We're opening up a really cool opportunity for the composer, artist, or publisher to do the same kind of grand scoring and creative expression of music on a mobile device that they would have done on a console as recently as a couple of years ago. That's a big opportunity.

On the browser-game side, one of the things that we're going to see is that the game developers and studios have had their eyes opened to what can be done in a web browser, so the games are getting much bigger in scope. What's important is that in the *Angry Birds* or *Doodle Jump* world, the ability to create a score or the amount of music available in the game is fairly limited. Contrast that to the kind of games we're used to seeing on consoles or PCs or massive multiplayer games like *World of Warcraft*. The music is epic—it's a lot more than some
catchy loops.

It's soon going to be easier to have great epic scores on mobile games than on the browser because of the nature of the way that a browser talks to the Internet. There is technology out there that can make it easier on a browser, but it will be a question of how smart the game developers are with this.

How large are the audio assets in a game like that?
If you were to look at all of the audio assets in *World of Warcraft*, you're probably talking on the order of dozens if not hundreds of megabytes. If you've developed a browser game, you haven't had the ability in a typical session to be able to dynamically push those kinds of assets through to the player, nor have you had the ability to pre-cache it so it's already there when the player enters that next dramatic moment in the game. As a result, most of the audio assets, even when you do have pretty good scoring and epic soundtracks, have tended to be very short. It's been considered okay, because most of the sessions in browser games tend to be short, where a player plays for only a few minutes or even seconds.

There's not been a lot of creative room for the composer, but knowing that the experience is repetitive, the player is going to come back again and again and again. In fact, many come back every day and sometimes many times a day. They'll clock in many more hours of game play than even on an X-box or PC title. These experiences are just as engrossing. In the aggregate, as this market continues to grow and the development models mature, we'll start to see music and audio libraries for browser games equivalent to, or even larger than, traditional console and PC games. A good example of this is the *Battlestar Galactica* browser-based game from Bigpoint.

Have the budgets changed?

Yes, the budgets in the legacy models have changed. A couple of years ago, there wasn't a lot of money in the budgets for music for online gaming. What's happened since then is that the microtransaction model has been validated, not only by the game publishers, but the studios as well.

One of the trends that I see that's occurring is we're getting away from the traditional console or PC game business, where the studio just licenses a set amount of work from an artist, and instead allows the artist's work to be incorporated along with a new level in-game item, or a new character, which are themselves sold via an in-game microtransaction. That means we now we have a really straightforward model to track how much value is created by that artist's music. This will make it easier to compensate the artist as a percentage of the revenue gained by that microtransaction sale. If a player comes in and buys a new map and that map has a unique score, the game studio and publisher know precisely how much revenue is generated. As a result they'll be able to pay the artist a royalty on that specific transaction, instead of a flat license fee.

The old flat-fee models came into being because nobody could say precisely how valuable the audio was, or more precisely, what percentage of the game play it was experienced in. In the old models, if the majority of players never got beyond, say, level 5 out of 30 in a game, why would a publisher want to pay a higher amount to the artists? In these new online models, the studio and publisher can see exactly how much of the revenue was generated by each level, and pay out the talent accordingly. The great part is that the opportunity exists where artists could make substantially more in this model than they could in the past, now that the contribution of their work on the bottom line is known.

The initial budgets might still look small in the short term, but longer term it's much fairer. It's going to take a while to change the majority of publishers and the guilds' ways of thinking though. I'd say three years on the outside.

It's a new distribution method for the artist.

Look at it from the iTunes model. The artist gets paid each and every time the track is purchased on iTunes. It's not like Apple got away with saying, "For the privilege of putting it in the iTunes catalog, we're going to pay you a one-time licensing fee." No one would ever sign up for that, but that's exactly what gaming has historically done. But now that gaming has moved to this microtransaction model, the game publishers are going to be hard pressed to hold the line on the old model.

As a studio or publisher, I can afford to get a much stronger artist to do more creative work now, since they're going to be paid as we go instead of there being a massive line item up front in my budget.

That also means you can also use a variety of artists, instead of only one.
Right. There was a model that showed up in a few games about a decade ago where the player was offered an option on the music. Because the licensing models were what they were at the time, that didn't work as well as hoped. Now all these decisions about taste that you can express in an online game puts the control in the consumer's hands instead of the game studio or publisher. We'll see the return of the "choose your own soundtrack" model, with direct, immediate payment by the consumers at the time they hit play.

Gregory Markel

One of the pioneers of search engine optimization (SEO) and marketing, Gregory Markel's company, Infuse Creative, touts major entertainment clients such as Gibson Musical Instruments, New Line Cinema, the National Geographic Channel, Led Zeppelin, the Rolling Stones, the television show *24*, and many more. As a recording artist and great singer formerly signed to Warner Brothers, Markel has a deep empathy for the plight of today's artist and provides an abundance of good advice in the following interview.

What is search engine optimization exactly?
SEO these days has a broad definition. It means optimizing anything and everything that a search engine is going to return. That means a Web page, a video, a news feed, a blog, a product, a book, an article; it's paying attention to all those areas.

We have three basic types of clients. The first is a client that wants branding awareness. A good example of that is a theatrical release where they can't measure the number of people who might have visited the website who later went on to buy tickets, but they feel that it's something they have to do in order to get the word out.

The second is a client that does e-commerce, where they sell a toaster or something with a specific fixed cost. If you can choose and effectively set up the right keywords with the right ads, with the right landing pages and at the right cost, then if your cost is $15.00 and you deliver a sale at more than that, it's a positive outcome.

The next type of client wants lead generation, which can be extremely effective if your product has a moderate to large margin. There are companies like mine helping to generate leads to companies that need them, where they can turn that into $20K to $100K per day.

Turning to music, if your music's good, there are so many opportunities available with social media, free technologies, and methodologies that you can definitely get a large number of people to find you. Whether you do these things for yourself or have someone who partners with you as your designated online communicator and extended member of the band, there's lots that you can do now without paying for media. Of course there are a lot of paid options that are very powerful and immediate, but they might not be cost-effective for someone who has a limited budget, or even none at all.

What would you suggest to a new artist who's trying to break and who wants to use SEO to get the word out?
Everybody knows to set up a Facebook page. Beyond that, regardless of if you're offering your music for free or not, you want to utilize the rest of the Web that doesn't cost you anything, meaning all the Web 2.0 and social media stuff like personal profile pages, bookmarking and tagging, and an official Twitter channel. It's figuring out a way to broadcast to your fans and affinity groups, which are groups of people that like the type of music that you play. For example, if I sound a lot like John Meyer, then I want to reach out to John Meyer fans. You can do all that at no cost by simply putting the time in.

Now the ones that do well with this are either going to have a Webmaster as a partner or be a new type of musician. Most musicians are abstract and creative types and don't really have an entrepreneurial or measurement-oriented brain, so a new kind of musician who thinks this way, or has a Webmaster, is essential.

What's the advice you'd give about optimizing their Website and SEO?
The first thing I'd recommend is research, which means finding some artists similar to yourself and examining their online presence. See how they're communicating, where they're communicating, and what they're offering, then see what appears to be working and what they could be doing better. Look at some obscure acts that you've not heard of but that have a lot of listens, as well as at the better-known acts.

The second step would be to educate yourself on the working of social media, or have someone outside the band as your digital-communications partner so you can address these areas. You have to figure out how to put down some kind of footprint online for people to find you. If you're a serious artist, that might dictate one approach, while if you're kind of pop oriented, then that will denote another kind of approach. So you have to educate yourself about social media and what approaches are available and what approach is right for you.

The third step is to put some thought into being disruptive. There's a constant with a lot of independent artists now in that they've figured out how to do something that gets people's attention. There's online chatter and buzz that will cause the press to talk about the fact that it's different, which is like free advertising. It's pretty easy to realize that the people that are successful do more than just put their CD online: for instance, something like what Radiohead did with the video contest on aniboom.com. For a $10,000 prize, they got these jaw-dropping videos for their songs that were every bit as good as if they'd paid some creative house $100K or $200K. The same thing with Prince and his idea to put a CD in the newspaper over in the UK. You've got to figure out a way to be disruptive.

The last step would be understanding the supply chain and the economics. You have to understand your startup and labor costs, as well as your gross and net profit, in order to measure the income you're generating. This has changed a bit from the days when I was an active musician. My eyes would've gone sideways on this last one. [Laughs.]

What did you do for Led Zeppelin?
Believe it or not, Zeppelin never had an official website all these years. When Atlantic was releasing the *How the West Was Won*

DVD, we did all the search marketing for that effort. It was a branding-awareness campaign, so it wasn't tied to directly selling the DVD off their website. We were really just broadcasting to the world that this was coming out and was available. We did it through nonpaid search (sometimes called organic search) and website optimization, going after all of the affinity keywords or key phrases, making sure that the website was built correctly and had all the content to address all the keywords that they liked to be found by. Then we helped build links to the site and build up link popularity. We also ran a paid search campaign for all of the obvious and not so obvious keywords to get the word out about the DVD and website launch. What was unfortunate at the time was that the site was way too overtly commercial, and there was a minibacklash from the hardcore fans who were initially so excited.

Can we talk about keywords for a bit? I think that's something that sometimes confuses people. You mentioned affinity keywords before. What exactly are those?

That's an ultrageneric phrase meaning the universe of keywords and key phrases that would likely be used by a person or a group that would be interested in your stuff. If the primary phrase was Led Zeppelin—for instance, we'd look all the way out to British blues rock and all points in between, which means every phrase that would have some affinity to the content and to the profile of people interested in the content. I'll bet a percentage of the people landing on a page on ledzeppelin.com who are interested in the blues would find Zep's admiration for old bluesmen interesting. There might be someone interested in Jeff Beck who would enjoy landing on a page on ledzeppelin.com talking about Jimmy Page's time in the Yardbirds when he was playing with Jeff Beck, and so on.

You could come up with hundreds of keywords, so how do you determine which are the most important?

With a branding-awareness campaign, keywords are less mission-critical because you're really just getting qualified people to your content. With sales it's entirely different. Let's say that you launch with 500 keywords, to just pick a number. In a very short amount of time, you're turning off whatever isn't resulting in a sale because you're measuring everything within an inch of its life. So in that type of campaign, you know painfully what works and what doesn't because you might've spent $500 on a single keyword and never got a single sale from it.

For organic search, it's all about being relevant to your content, so in a sense, you're going to be limited by your content. In the Jeff Beck example that I just mentioned, unless you have the content on the ledzeppelin.com page that mentions Beck, then you don't stand a chance in hell in getting a ranking for that keyword. Nothing would prevent you from adding Jeff Beck into your keyword tags on ledzeppelin.com, but it's so irrelevant compared to the content that supports that keyword that you're never going to rank for it organically.

So keywords are joined at the hip with content. Supporting content is as important as keywords and vice versa. In the old days you used to be able to fool the search engines. You could get a ranking for Jeff Beck without having any relevant content, but it was argued that's not a good user experience since you'd get a percentage of people who resented landing on the page and not seeing anything about what they were looking for. Everything's changed with the search engines, and now you have to have the keyword and supporting content or you just won't rank.

When we have SEO conversations with clients, there's always that surprise in their eyes when we start talking about content. That's usually only a conversation that they have with their developers, but there's a direct one-to-one relationship these days. You have to have the content to support the keywords.

Rupert Perry

. . . .

One of the most respected and beloved executives in the music industry, Rupert Perry held a variety of executive positions with EMI for 32 years. He went from vice president of A&R at Capitol to president of EMI America to managing director of EMI Australia and, later, of EMI Records UK, to president and CEO of EMI Europe to, finally, the worldwide position of vice president of EMI Recorded Music. During his time at EMI, Perry worked with a variety of superstar artists such as The Beatles, Blur, Duran Duran, Iron Maiden, Nigel Kennedy, Robert Palmer, Pink Floyd, Queen, Radiohead, and Cliff Richard. Such were his contributions to the British music industry that in January 1997, he was appointed CBE (Commander of the Order of the British

Empire), a position of British order of chivalry that is just below knighthood. He is also coauthor of the fine book *Northern Songs: The True Story of The Beatles' Song Publishing Empire.*

Despite having worked for one of the "four ugly sisters," as he so affectionately calls the major labels, Perry is well up on the latest technology and trends within the music business, and shares some surprising contrasts between the old business and the one we're in right now.

You have a unique perspective on the music industry. In your eyes, how are things different today from the heyday of the record business?

One big thing was that the record labels of that time were making those things called gramophones and record players and radios, and they would also be recording content to play on these pieces, so it all fit together. But in the mid-'50s, the technology got away from the recorded-music business and got into the hands of third parties, and from that time on, everything that happened technologically that affected the music business was driven from outside the business. Record labels were no longer technologists. They understood the recording process, and they understood the manufacturing and distribution process—whether it be vinyl, cassette, or CD. But that was the extent of their technology knowledge.

The other thing is how people consumed content in those days, which was that people mostly listened to the radio. Then the Japanese came up with the transistor radio, which was portable. Suddenly [the idea of] portability meant that consumers didn't have to sit in their living rooms in front of that radio. That was the start of something else from a distribution point of few. You can look at all the things that changed, but then you look at the transistor radio and think, "Gosh, the portability was so important."

Don't we have the same thing today with Steve Jobs and iTunes-driven digital media?

Exactly. And then the other great moment of portability came when Sony came up with the Walkman. It's amazing that Sony let it slip through their hands and let Apple come up with the iPod, which to me is just the next stage of the Walkman. Sony's engineers understood the portability aspect between the cassette Walkman and the CD Walkman, but thereafter they missed out on what became the iPod.

Then when the reel-to-reel tape recorder was introduced, that changed things forever because it had a "Record" button on it. It was that "Record" button that really started to change things.

But what really people forget is that by the end of the '70s, the recorded-music business was in deep, deep trouble. There was a recession and a couple of years of downward trends, and a lot of people thought, "This is the end of it." There was a lot of piracy, thanks to the cassette player and that issue of the "Record" button, and people just weren't buying vinyl records anymore. The issue of people making their own copies was a pretty big one even in those days. People were copying music for free off the radio or from another cassette or a record. We reckoned that we were losing at least 25 percent of our business to home taping. So when people talk about "free" today, there's nothing particularly new about it—it's just a different version of the same thing.

The other big thing that happened was the compact disc. When it came along, there was a big upsurge in the growth of the business, and a lot of large corporations began to take notice. When CBS, which was the king of the business at the time, sold their record business to Sony—that was huge! It was a momentous happening, because CBS decided they wanted to exit the music business, which they had been in for years.

I guess that people forget that there were a lot of big changes and issues in the music industry before the Internet.
Yes they do, but the arrival of the Internet was just as big. If we roll forward to the start of the Internet in 1993, people in the content industry didn't get just how monumental the change was. To have any form of content available through a computer was a totally new form of distribution, but the difference was that the record label had no control over it. Up until that point, any of the media distributors (film, television, or music) were always able to control the distribution, and when you did that, you could decide where it went, who got it, and what people paid for it. With the Internet, that went out the window fast. That's the big, big shift caused by this new form of distribution.

The other big issue that the Internet brought was that everything became global. You could be anywhere in the world and you could access Napster, so all the ways that companies tried to segment the market (the way the film industry did with its regional DVDs) were over.

Yet another issue that was a problem, is a problem, and will continue to be a problem going forward is that the laws that govern intellectual copyright are national, as opposed to global, laws. The US has its own copyrights laws, as does Europe, as does Latin America, and so forth. But the nature of the business now is that it's totally global, so it is going to require a more global approach to copyright law as opposed to the parochial approach.

All that being said, how do you see record labels evolving? How will they evolve into something that monetizes content adequately yet is helpful to both the artist and consumer?
I think that's what we're gradually starting to see now. They're starting to come to terms with the fact that they don't have the same control and that online distribution is not something they're part of anymore. They might become part of it at some point in time, but for the moment they have to resign themselves to the fact that they're not. Who are the new distribution kings? ISPs, telecoms, mobile. Look at Nokia with its phones coming preloaded with music.

That's not always good for the artist though.
It's not very good for the artist because the other problem with this is the fact that in the physical world, you're selling a CD for $10.00, and in the digital world, you're selling a song for $1.00. If your business was built on a $10.00 model with your overhead built around that, it's very difficult to go to a $1.00 model. If you or I started off with a digital label today, we would build and operate it in a very, very different way. We'd look at each other and say, "Okay, fine. We need a couple of product managers sitting in front of computers instead of a big staff, and we need one or two rooms at the most in an office in North Hollywood instead of Beverly Hills." It's a totally different overhead structure and approach.

So when you think about that, you go, "Wait a minute. That sounds just like in the early '50s when it was pretty much a singles business." People bought a song at a time then, as they do in the digital world. In some ways we have gone full circle.

What's the future of the major labels? Do you think they'll survive?
I think they'll survive because they and a lot of smaller labels have catalogs of recorded music, and someone always wants to consume it. But they also have to consider what kind of business they're in now.

They're not really into artist development anymore or signing lots of new artists like they used to in the past. What they're really involved in is the business of rights management. They're managing the rights in the same way that publishers are managing rights. The music-publishing industry and the recorded-music industry—two industries that grew up side by side—are now coming together a lot faster because it's a business of rights.

If you're an artist, you will decide if you can manage your rights yourself or, if you've become successful, need someone to manage them for you on a global basis. Then maybe you go to one of these entities. Either way, you're going to have a much greater degree of flexibility in how you deal with those rights going forward.

What would be the best way to break an act these days?
It's back to immediately being able to build your website first, then communicating and interacting with your fans. Even if you only have 50 email addresses when you start, if you're any good, that will increase. Create your MySpace and Facebook pages, because someone will see you and want to go to your website. When they get there, you want them to be one click from anywhere they need to go. If they want to buy something, it's one click. If they want a ticket, it's one click. If they want to read the bio or see the photos, it's one click. But in the end, it's your songs and your performance that's going to drive the traffic.

What you still never get away from is that it's still about a song, and it's still about a performance of that song. Can you play that song in front of your audience, however large or small, and create the "WOW" factor?

What do you think of the "Economics of Free," where the more you give away, the more you sell?
I don't know if I agree with that premise. People argue the same point about pricing [the lower the price, the more you sell], and it's not necessarily so. Creators need to be compensated for what they create, however that may manifest itself. But in the early stages of a career, you will find that you have to make your music free to get attention and develop a following.

Is a CD necessary these days?
It still may be. People tell me that they sell 50 or 100 CDs at a show. If you control your content, sell X number of CDs and X number of

T-shirts and merch, and stay on the road, you can make a pretty good living. You may not be a household name, but you'll have a really strong fan base, you'll know who they are, and you'll be able to communicate with them. The fan/consumer is the piece of the puzzle that you really need.

Ian Rogers

. . . .

Formerly the general manager of Yahoo Music, Ian Rogers is now the CEO of Topspin Media, one of the premier direct-to-fan services currently available. A frequent panelist at industry conferences worldwide, he is one of the most respected and widely quoted voices in the music business today. Ian was kind enough to look into his virtual crystal ball as to what he sees for the future of the industry in the next few years.

Let's talk about the state of the industry. What are some of the opportunities and challenges you see right now?
The opportunities and the challenges are all wrapped up in the how the physics of the space are changing. The good news is that the barrier to entry is gone, and for the first time, the majors [major labels] have no intrinsic advantage anymore. Just let that sit for a second. The advantages were that they owned both the distribution and marketing channels. They don't anymore. They still own marketing as far as radio is concerned, but that's not even a thought for most artists. You and I could start a website tomorrow and be the next Yahoo or Google, or we could be the next My Morning Jacket. That's all within our grasp, and no one is standing in our way.

A great example is Odd Future, who are a group of 19-year-olds who only have a website. Those guys were the stars of SXSW this year, yet do not have a single track at iTunes, so something like that is possible, and that's the good part of where we're at today.

The challenge is that you're competing with more things than ever for people's attention, so the marketing side of it is harder. You have to be careful not to sell an artist a bill of goods that there's a technology that will make people listen to crap, but if you have something that people really want, it's easier than ever for them to get it.

So generally speaking, that's the landscape of the business today. The good is the lower barrier to entry as the cost of product and distribution has come down, but at the same time, the cost of marketing has gone up. Or it's gone to zero depending upon how you look at it. Odd Future spends zero dollars on marketing, so maybe the hard costs haven't gone up, but the challenge of it certainly has.

Where do you see things heading a couple of years down the line?
I really see things crystallizing. The industry has been in the way of what consumers wanted for the last 15 years, but it's finally getting pushed out of the way. The way fans are consuming music will change again in the next five years' time, which should really scare the industry. They just got used to the idea of digital downloads, and now they're going to see their distribution format change yet again. Five years from now you won't connect your computer by a wire and transfer tunes to it. CD sales will continue to decline, but they won't decline to zero, because some people will still want collectables. Things like box sets or 12-inch vinyl will still exist.

Then you're going to have two types of services. One is the subscription services, which are the Spotifys of the world, like Spotify, Rdio, MOG, and Rhapsody. I don't think you'll see many new entrants there, and in fact, the weak ones will probably get bought by a company with an existing subscriber base, such as a cable or wireless company.

And then you're going to have Apple, Google and Amazon, with these more sovereignty-based services. You buy the track in some form so you own it, and then it's lockered, and you can access that track from any device. That's what it's going to look like.

Companies like Topspin are going to be dealing with the direct-to-consumer channel which will be for the higher end goods. Digital is 50 percent of our volume and 25 percent of our revenue right now, but it's possible that ratio will decrease over time.

Let's talk about Topspin for a moment. When you started, the service was for established acts, but recently you just opened things up to everyone. What brought that on?
It was always our intent to make Topspin available to all artists. To be honest, we were a year and a half later than we'd planned, but we waited because we wanted to have the right depth of functionality. My

fear was that if we opened up broadly too early, we would never get some of the advanced features in the platform. Last year we made a strategic decision to remain in private beta while we built our ticketing and fan-club platforms, which were not small or simple features. I felt that if we could hold back until we could build those products and then go self-serve, then we'd have a competitive advantage. But we always intended to go self-serve.

Our vision from the beginning was to be like Pro Tools. To me, a number of other services available today are more akin to Garageband to our Pro Tools. We don't want to be iMovie, we want to be Final Cut Pro.

Do you find that your clients utilize a third party to use your tools?
Many do. I think that this is where the Final Cut Pro or Pro Tools analogy works well. For instance, I know that the Beastie Boys know their way around Pro Tools and do a lot of recording on their own, but when they're really making their record they get an engineer, and when it's time to mix, they get a professional. It's the same thing here. We have a lot of artists that use our tools themselves, and we're happy about that, but a lot of people at the high end use professionals.

The most exciting thing is that some of the marketing pros have become so competitively priced that a small artist can now actually afford them. At SXSW this year, we invited our partners to speak at sort of a miniconference during the day, and two different marketing services companies, Oniracom [see the interview with Jacob Tell] and Eyes and Ears Entertainment, told a couple of great stories. The Eyes and Ears guys have a $1,300 product, and for that they give you a website, a store, and some digital marketing.

What they're saying is that instead of spending a grand pressing up some CDs, spend that money setting up an excellent and professional web presence, including a store. It's better than giving a bunch of CD copies to family and friends and having the remaining 950 copies sitting in a drawer somewhere.

Then Oniracom said that they now actually prefer to work with smaller artists because of how easy it is for them to take the Topspin tools and add the graphic design and web development to provide a an extremely useful yet cost-efficient site for an artist without having to reinvent the wheel.

So the answer is that a lot of people are doing it on their own, but a lot of small guys can now afford to hire someone too.

Can you give me a breakdown of your clients—established to nonestablished?

We have a bit more than 5,000 total clients, and probably 150 of those are what you'd consider top-tier artists; another 30 to 35 percent are people in the middle; and the rest are smaller artists. I expect that ratio to change now that we've opened up self-serve.

Even though it seemed like we were always closed, we were in this state where we just weren't marketing. We still gave an account to anyone that just sent us an email. You had to show some interest, but we didn't chase you down.

What's the best way to break an act these days?

I'm not sure that it's changed all that much. More than ever you have to have something that people are passionate about, and you have to build awareness through great recordings and touring. Step 2 is different in that you now have to build real fan connections and a real relationship with those fans. If you're lucky enough to do both of those things, then you can talk about selling something.

I think another difference between the proverbial yesterday and today is that we're moving from a mass market to mass niches, so you have to know what the first niche is that you're targeting and then go after it. You don't put the music out there and see who adopts you; you have to know when and how and where you fit. Square peg, square hole, you just go straight into it.

If you look at the way that Yeasayer did it, it wasn't about an all-out blitzkrieg. Their manager said, "I know exactly the audience that is going to like this. I'm going to tailor our approach to fit that." It wasn't that he changed the way they looked or anything, but he didn't let any photos of the band get out for the first 12 months. He had a specific way that he wanted people to experience the music and the art that went with it. He knew it would resonate with a certain audience, and that's the way he let it unfold, naturally but still really deliberate. Once he saturated that niche, then he moved on to another audience that would likely dig it, and treated it like it was a brand new band and pulled all those levers again.

The typical scenario is more of a shotgun approach, that "If only I can get it out there, someone is going to find it" kind of thing. That may have worked in the past, but not now.

Yeah, you're right, but if you look at Odd Future as an example, those guys didn't really do anything. They literally did just put it out there and the right people did find it, and then some magic happened, but that's the exception because it's proven that the way your awareness unfolds really matters.

There's a great study that someone sent to me that found that the influence of people on other people matters a great deal. Having someone say "You're going to like this" is really important. That speaks to the fact that trusted filters really mean something when it comes to marketing music. I think we'll have more of that happening in the future, and getting music to those new trusted filters in the right way will become increasingly important.

What's the best way to do that?

I'm not sure, but I think this is where the relationship game goes in the future. Having a relationship with the right bloggers and things like that is really going to matter. I think that there will be a "relationship with trusted taste makers" business somewhere down the road, which is something different. Getting introduced to those sites in the right way will soon be an important part of marketing.

To find out more about Topspin, check out topspinmedia.com.

Ken Rutkowski

. . . .

Ken Rutkowski is considered one of most broadly informed and connected people in the media, entertainment, and technology markets. His daily radio and Internet show, *World Tech Round-Up* at kenradio.com, is a source of inside information for listeners in more than 40 countries, often scooping the major media and giving perspective to emerging trends, developments, and industry maneuvers. His *IQ Report* newsletter is distributed five days a week to the technology, entertainment, and business elite. Rutkowski is also the creator and guiding force behind the Media Entertainment Technology Alliance (METal), a members-only group of alpha influencers.

What do you think is new in the digital music space?
One hundred percent of my music discovery today comes from social networks, meaning that I watch what everyone that I connect to via Facebook, Skype, Twitter, and other social networks is listening to or watching, and discover from that. Last year my discovery was from music portals like last.fm, iLike, Slacker, and Pandora. The year before I was listening to niche radio on the Web, utilizing things like Shoutcast and the radio stations provided by Microsoft through the Windows Media Player. Now it's completely community driven for me. I think that's a radical change, in that I used to discover only what the labels controlled, but now it's what the community proliferates among their networks.

For example, inside things like Skype, their status shows what people are listening to and watching. I have certain friends who I really respect for their musical taste, and I really discover from them on the network level. I never would have expected that before, because at one point in time it would have been a CD or a tape exchange or, in the early 2000s, we'd open up our own FTP areas and send our friends there. None of that happens now because it's who's doing what on a social media tool or an IM client. And it's much more lasered. Bam! I know whatever Ian Rogers (president of Topspin) is listening to, and I know that there's a 90 percent chance that I'm going to like it. If he listened to it, I'm going to go listen to it. That makes it a much more pleasurable experience and an interesting connection point, in that I now go to him and say, "I know you love this band, and now I love them too." It fortifies my social network even more, because we have common likes through those discoveries.

How typical do you think that this is?
I would say that it's becoming more typical, especially with the push mechanisms like Twitter and Facebook. The other social media tools are realizing how important it is too. The irony is that the labels aren't getting as active as they should in this avenue of discovery and still think that a fan site is good enough. A fan site is a destination, but people don't go to destinations anymore—they're pushed information. Everything is an RSS kind of push from your Facebook status, to

a Twitter push, to even the next-generation text messaging, which in theory are tweets. This is where it's all at now.

What's the next great technology that's going to change everything?
There's a new technology in Asia that's trickling down here called NFC, or Near Field Communication. It's like Bluetooth in that it allows us to synch with other devices, but it's more specific. If I walk into a room of 20 people, my device will know which of those 20 people I want to synch with and what areas of their device that I want to synch with. For example, say five of these people are trusted friends that have trusted libraries on their phones. When I walk into this group, my phone, through NFC, might intelligently connect to all my friends' phones and download a playlist or certain types of content. It's all invisible to me. So the next form of communication and technology is the personalization of my community while I'm with my community. Anytime I'm with you, I get to experience the music that you're listening to, for example, without having to go download it off the Internet. When I get back after hanging out with you, I'll see my phone blinking and realize that I just exchanged content with you. It's a new type of discovery that you don't have to manually engage. That makes meeting people one on one more important than having that distance that we have today. It's more about "I want to discover, but I want to be with my friends when I'm discovering." It's hard to wrap your head around it, but I believe that it's going to make people want to get together more.

What have you seen recently that's cutting edge in music?
There are sites popping up all over the Web that use Google and Yahoo to find links to free music, like Groove Shark. You go on the site and type in an artist, and instantly all their songs show up with all the lyrics next to it as you're playing it. I love it. You don't need to download anything, because it's instantly there for you to listen to. Everything's there—from cartoon themes to cutting-edge new music.

The other one is Microsoft's new search scheme called Kumo. It's fairly interesting in that it's in a three-pane window, so if I search for U2, the first pane would be the standard pane that you'd see on Google or Yahoo or any other search. The second pane would be a universal search, which is video, audio, and pictures. The last pane would be any form of commerce, which would be CDs, videos, apparel, or tickets.

That can change the face of discovery, because now it's not just finding the music, but also the personalities, the places, and the commerce around it—all on one single search.

In terms of social media, have Facebook and MySpace run their course? Are we on to something new yet?
The first thing to remember is that they're a destination, and I really need to stress that. Let's take the Counting Crows, who are now doing business without a label. If a Counting Crow member puts something up on their MySpace site, it's really hard for that to be discovered outside of MySpace. That pertains to anything the band or their fans put up there. If you post a video on Facebook, it's not seen by any of the search engines that are out there because it's very walled garden. So social networks aren't to the point where they're 100 percent useful. What has to happen with all the major social tools is that they have to be searchable externally in order to have a presence on all of them. It has to happen, because the walled-garden approach is just not sufficient anymore. It's going to change just like music discovery.

Derek Sivers

· ·

Derek Sivers's life has certainly been interesting so far, from working as a musician/ringleader of a circus, to a stint at the publishing giant Warner/Chappell, to being on the road as a touring musician, to creating and running CD Baby, one of the most widely used music-distribution services today. After selling CD Baby in 2008, Sivers now spends his time thinking of new ways to help musicians. As you'll see, his insights are as thoughtful as they are cutting edge.

What trends do you see today that you think will influence the distribution and consumption of music as we go forward?
Now that there's absolutely no barrier to entry for every person on earth to release every noise they make, there is a huge flattening of selection. Instead of 100 people making $1 million each, the future music biz may be 1 million people making $100 each.

How do you think the audience has changed?

They've changed because they can't be spoon-fed anymore, and they can't really be sold or persuaded as much as before. Because they have endless selection, they only receive and act on recommendations from trusted sources, usually friends.

Radio used to be one of the things they trusted. But now it's transformed into something that music lovers can't even tolerate, so real music fans don't expect FM radio to turn them on to new music like it once did. Therefore, for new artists, radio is moot.

What's the best way to break an act today?

First of all, an artist has to have the right attitude, which maybe is no different than it ever was. What's new is that the artist now must also have the ability to learn, adapt, and communicate.

You've got to touch lots of people. You've got to resonate emotionally with them, then communicate sincerely. A lot. Fans really do like using their favorite artist as a bonding, cementing group maker. It's part of your job as an artist to encourage your fans to talk to each other and make a "tribe" (to use Seth Godin's word) around you. And after breaking, you have to solve problems and improve your skills weekly to keep your career developing.

That being said, to be a great musician you have to learn how to focus. You have to look at yourself objectively to notice what needs improvement, and have the dedication to improve that even when you think you can't.

But to be a successful professional musician, you have to learn how to look at yourself through others' eyes. You have to understand why the venue owner is really booking artists, why this person really signed your mailing list, and why people really go out to a bar at midnight on a Thursday night. It's an amazing learning experience, and as you've noticed, I'm endlessly fascinated by these things.

Do you have any promotion tips?

Hundreds. Please see http://sivers.org/pdf, where I took a few months to write them all down and share them all for free.

As for tools, I'd try to find ones that aren't already saturated with music: maybe an artistic use of Twitter or Improv Everywhere. But whatever I used, I'd really make sure that I was always in a real three-way conversation with my fans. It's three-way in that I'd encourage them to talk with me and with each other and make my success their success, just like Obama did in his election campaign.

What are your feelings toward the major record labels today?
It's easy to look at them as buffoons (like we do politicians), but most of them are surprisingly smart. These last ten years have been humbling for them. They've shaken out the people that were only in it for the money, so most of the people at labels today are in it for the right reasons and are more entrepreneurial.

If you look at the current biggest sellers, they're almost all on major labels, so it's just bad logic to say that the labels are doing everything wrong. They still may do many things wrong, but not everything. Their different expectations change their costs, so they have to get incredibly lean and efficient so they can actually profit off something that sells only 10,000 copies. Most indies can profit off of 10,000 sales, but majors simply can't right now.

Do you think an independent artist needs an agent or a manager today?
Most musicians feel if they just had a good manager, agent, or promoter they'd be all set, but most managers, agents, and promoters will tell you that most artists aren't ready yet.

I think it's the artists' responsibility to develop themselves to the point where they've proved their persistence and ability to make music and to put on a show that people love. Once they've got more bookings than they can handle, it's a good time to hand that job to an agent.

As for a manager, I think that should be like a business-minded band member whose sole job is to handle the business and marketing. It doesn't have to be a professional manager. But yes, someone of that mindset should definitely be included always. Don't go too long without one!

Visit Derek Sivers's website at sivers.org for lots of ideas and inspiration.

Howard Soroka

. . . .

I first met Howard Soroka when he was the primary programmer for the famed GML recording-console automation system some 25 years ago. Since then, he's gone on to being more an executive than a programmer, rising to vice president of Media Technologies at Universal Music Group's eLabs. Always on the cutting edge of technology, Soroka had some great insights to share on the digital workings of the world's largest record label, as well as a look into the future of the music business.

What do you do at Universal?
I use the term *geek* generically, but what it means is that I work on deals that come in and out of the company. When a new company wants to do business with us, we're always going to look very hard at their technology because we want to understand it very well. We want to be sure that we know what we're getting into and that the other company knows, too, so there's a lot of due-diligence work. We put a lot of paper behind the deal, including a lot of technical paper, to make sure that it's all well understood and we're not putting our content or artists at risk and there's a logical business model behind it.

We also do a certain amount of what I'd loosely call R&D, which is to say that we participate in the development of new technologies. Most of them don't see the light of day. Sometimes they're things that come in from outside the company that want our participation. Sometimes they're things done on an industry level from RIAA or IFPI, for example.

How does Universal maximize the digital presence for its artists?
What we are trying to do is have a lot more context around the music, so you just don't download a file and listen to it and nothing else. We want the customer to have a relationship with the artist, and we want that to be as well coordinated as it can be so that they're not wasting time. Customers will know that if they buy a U2 record, they should get a very full experience with it. The true fans want to get everything about the band, so buying the record should get them connected to the artist, and to each other. Coordinating that community around an artist is a lot of what we have to offer. We see a need and an

opportunity for a lot more interactivity between the listener and the artist, and we're working toward that.

Couldn't an artist do that him- or herself, or get a third-party company to help?

Most artists don't know how, and getting a third party involved can be problematic. There are other companies out there that offer services to the independent artist. I'm aware of at least one very good one that we like a lot. You might think that we look at a company like that and think, "Oh, my God. They're the enemy. How can we kill them?" But it's not like that at all. In at least this one case, we're actually very friendly with their CEO and we look for opportunities to work together. They lean toward more of an indie market, but we think that's just what those guys need. There's no doubt that we can, and should, help each other.

But doesn't Universal have a department just for social media enhancement for the artists?

Typically, each label has their own new-media department. Some functions of the company are centralized, and a lot are not. But that's bound by tradition, because at one time a lot of these were stand-alone labels and they did everything themselves before they came under the UMG umbrella, and they're still treated as stand-alone labels.

We do see some appropriate internal centralization now. In the video business, there was a conscious decision made that video was no longer going to be free anymore. How can it be promotional if MTV doesn't play it? It has become a product, so we're going to make money out of it. It turns out there's a tremendous demand for music videos, and they can be monetized. Now we're the biggest channel on YouTube. But it's better for us to deal with YouTube on a centralized basis than as individual labels.

There's more consumption of music now than there ever was. Our numbers are bad only if you look at physical product, because CDs are clearly in decline. But a lot of our other numbers are going up—some a lot, some not so much, some are flat—but overall, music is not a bad business to be in. And even the physical business, shrinking as it is, is a really big business. We still sell millions and millions of CDs; it's just that the year before it was more millions. Vinyl is exploding, but it's exploding from a microscopic thing to a tiny thing, and is pretty unlikely to ever be more than a niche. Happy to fill it, though.

Where do you see digital music going?
I think what we'll see eventually is the prevalence of a model where people will say, "I own this much music. Give me access to it everywhere," or "I don't need to own any music. I'm just going to rent it and have access to it whenever I want." Those two things might blur into one.

What's missing is the range of content. Almost nobody releases only on the Internet, except for unknown artists and amateurs. Anyone signed to a label has made a CD, but you can't necessarily get their stuff on the Internet. And you can't necessarily get it in the same place as all the other music on the Internet. You need to be able to go to one place to get all of the music that you want, as well as all the other ancillaries like the booklet and pictures, info on upcoming shows, tickets, and T-shirts. There may be more than one of these places that you can go to, but if you need to go to more than one source, there's probably something wrong.

Is piracy any different from the way it used to be?
It's certainly different in ratio. You'd sell a million, and that would mean that there'd be a million plus x copies out there, because people made tapes. Now, because it's so incredibly easy and convenient, it might be a million plus $10x$ for every million sold.

How do you digitize and archive your digital files?
We keep PCM [pulse-code modulation] quality copies of masters in our library. We actually make compressed files to order for each customer. Amazon gets whatever Amazon needs, for instance. We do the encoding, but they choose the codec and bit rate, and we deliver to them. The encoding's done on the fly, and we don't archive any encoded files. We started doing that a few years ago, and we've found that it only gets hairy when the demand is really heavy. That's because the process takes a while, and there's a lot of complexity in delivery of, say, 250,000 tracks at a time to 50 or 100 partners. We also only deliver over the Internet with a secure transfer protocol; it never goes out on a disc. I can't tell you how many times we've been begged to ship stuff on hard disc, but we essentially never do.

There's a lot of bits coming out of the encoding farm every day. Most companies farm it out, but we made a conscious decision a while back to do it in-house, and there's absolutely no doubt that we made the right decision. A major label should absolutely own and control that process. The theory is that we need to do as much of the heavy lifting as possible in-house, for cost reasons, efficiency, quality control, and frankly, to be able to offer the services to smaller companies.

If you put together the list of services that we provide and the things we do, it's a lot, man. There's no one place that an artist can go to get it all. We can probably do more of it for an artist than anybody else, and we'll be able to do a lot more in the future because we'll get better at it. The evidence is around me every day at work, but it'll take a while to make it out to the public. It takes a long time and a lot of effort to turn around a ship this big; but I promise you—it's turning.

Jacob Tell

. . . .

Jacob Tell's Oniracom is a new breed of company that provides a full line of digital media services to artists, labels, and management. Starting his career running the computer systems on the road and coordinating the merch for Jack Johnson, Tell put the big picture into context by watching the interaction between artist, label, management, and promoter in different venues around the world. Helping artists in the digital space before there was a YouTube, MySpace, or Facebook, Jacob has watched the development of Web 2.0 and learned how an artist can best take advantage of it along the way.

What does your company do?
What we do is develop monthly, yearly, and tour-cycle campaigns based purely around our clients' music. There are basic monthly maintenance plans that include updating MySpace and Facebook pages with tour dates and things like that, but going a bit further, we also develop real content or campaigns that engage the fans. We manage everything from their mailing list to their official website to their social media, social networks, MySpace, Facebook, iLike, imeem, Twitter, YouTube—you name it. We provide a framework for all of it so the artist and management don't have to think how this needs

to be organized and disseminated out to the fans on all the various platforms.

This is so needed. It's something the record labels should be doing. The artists that I know don't have time to do all that, even if they're capable.

What we like to do is provide some clarity to the artists that do have time. If they say "I have time three days a week," or "I have time once a day to do a Twitter post," then we'll walk them through how to install the application on their iPhone or Blackberry and show them how to use it and when to do it. We offer suggestions, like when they're onstage to say, "Hey everyone, smile. I'm going to take a picture of this great crowd and put it up online," and then you have a couple of thousand fans going online after the show to see if they can see themselves in that picture. Very basic ideas like that go a long way. Engage the crowd. Give the crowd a reason to find the artist on the Web and move [him or her] from the back of [the crowd members'] minds to the front of their minds, even after the show's over.

The labels are missing this stuff, and as soon as we show them what we can do, they say, "We can do that in-house." But the management groups say, "Well, no you can't. We see what you do with other artists, and it's pretty cookie cutter." That's the difference. We're more of a boutique shop. We really get into the artists' music because everyone here is completely passionate about music. We get into the artists' mentality so we can suggest things. For example, Jack Johnson's more of a private guy and a surfer, so we come up with things in his ideological makeup that both his fans and Jack would be okay posting about. Now someone like G. Love is more about promotion and is willing to do just about anything, so that's easier for us to work with because there are fewer limitations. It just depends, because every artist is different. You really have to get to know the artist and go from there.

How does an artist monetize the music, considering that one of the current thoughts is "The more you give away, the more they buy"?

For the smaller bands, I completely agree that the more you give away, the more you have the opportunity to sell. For example, there's a local artist here in Santa Barbara, Matthew McAvene, who's a singer-songwriter and has an incredible visual show, since he has puppets and props and large creatures. The idea is that he's giving the fans more of a live experience, so he gives the music away for whatever they want to pay. At the merch booth, he has a sign that says "CDs—name your price." If you want to pay $1.00, go ahead. At least that music has gone out to a fan who desires the music. Some people feel they had an incredible time at the show and they pay $10.00 or even $20.00, but it's their choice.

I believe that you're going to keep a fan longer if you build it that way and give them more of an experience around a live concert. The music should be more of a promotional tour tool the way stickers used to be in the '70s, '80s, and '90s, where they were handed out for free and posted on things by your personal street team. It's the same kind of thing with the music, which is what goes out for free like a sticker. Your live show and merchandise is where you're making your money. The paradigm has already shifted. People are now expecting to get music for free, or at least not in physical CD form, so embrace that. Let your fans take a CD away from the show for whatever they want to pay for it.

Do you see a strong Web presence as an effective way of monetizing an artist?

Yeah, because it's all about creating a loyal fan base. But I think that the fan base really picks up on the time and attention that the artist takes on the Web. It's all about how much content and how frequently that content is flowing, and most importantly, the artist's visibility. You want to be moving from the back of the mind to really getting the artist to come up in the front mind of people so that they are brought up in day-to-day conversation. When somebody is reminded of another thread in their day-to-day lives, they go, "Oh, by the way, I just saw G. Love posted a new picture," and then they go Google for it. The more people that are searching for them, the more visibility the artist has on the Web, and it just spirals. We really believe that merch sales and ticket sales are a direct reflection of that. It's all about continuous visibility.

Is there an optimum number of times that an artist should post or tweet? Is there a point at which it's too much?

I think each medium has an answer to that. Mailing-list blasts have a definite point where it's too much. We like to limit those to a couple of times a month, or once a week at most if you're really doing something special or have unique content. If it's just announcing tour dates or trying to sell something; you shouldn't do it more than once a week, but we find once or twice a month works best. If it's unique content (like G. Love's Thursday 12:07 video blog, where you get a glimpse into his life every week no matter where he is or what he's doing), that could be cool to blast weekly. That's a campaign we designed with him. On the other hand, if you're Twittering, the more the merrier—because that's the kind of minutia that people are into. That platform is great for 3 to 10, even 20, times a day.

Can a friend or a surrogate connected to the artist work just as well if an artist isn't into it or doesn't have the time?

If they have direct access to the band and the content is close enough to being unique from the band and not a reinterpretation filtered through some promotional dollar-sign lens that a major label might do, yes it can work. If whoever is doing the posting is into the mindset of the artist, it can be just as effective as if it were from the artists themselves. The distinction is not who it's coming from, but the type of content that matches the ideological makeup and worldview of that artist.

Michael Terpin

. . . .

Michael Terpin is the founder of SocialRadius, a social media marketing company focusing on social media outreach and strategy. The company is a spin-off of his Terpin Communications, which is a high-technology public-relations firm specializing in emerging technologies. The projects that his firm has worked on include the outreach for recording artist Will.i.am's "Yes We Can" video for the Obama presidential campaign [which won 2008 Emmy, Global Media, and Webby Awards]; social media event marketing for Live8, LiveEarth, the Green Inaugural Ball, and the David Lynch Foundation; and the social media launch of startups ranging from Software.com to Shapeways. Terpin also founded Marketwire, one of the world's largest international newswires.

PR is really changing, isn't it?

So much of the PR, publicity, and promotional arena have become dependent upon social media that I decided to start another company, called SocialRadius, that just does social media marketing. Social media is different from traditional media in that it still accomplishes the same objectives, but it really reflects the way the world is changing and the way people consume information. It used to be that the most important thing you could do was get written up in *Rolling Stone,* but now it's a very different marketplace. Every year people consume more and more content on the Internet, and more and more of that is social.

If you look at where things were 20 years ago versus 10 years ago versus today, they're totally different universes. For example, we had a couple of clients in a *USA Today* article last week. Twenty years ago that would've been earthshaking in that it would have gotten a lot of people buying their products and sending them mail (10 years ago it would've been email), but now we'll probably get as much traction with a well-placed Twitter tweet.

When you say the term *social media,* do you mean Facebook and LinkedIn and those kinds of sites?

No, most of what we do involves the blogs. That's also social media. Most of the social networks have limited impact outside of one's group friends, so they don't have the same kind of impact on search engines or the same rapid viral growth of more open social vehicles.

Tell me about the strategy for the Will.i.am "Yes We Can" video.

What we did there was not do any traditional media whatsoever. In order to have an impact on the California Primary, we started giving it to enthusiasts in the blogosphere on Saturday, shortly after we received it from Will and when the traditional media are pretty much sleeping.

The blogosphere is really divided into a lot of different areas now. Most people know the editorial part of the blogosphere, but a lot of it is technology, and it's a form of editorial, too. It's sometimes misperceived as being a lot of angry guys in their pajamas, but *TechCrunch* has more readers than the *Wall Street Journal.* There are 50 times more thought-leaders and enthusiasts than editorial bloggers around a specific topic.

There are several hundred bloggers who blog about online video trends and topics; that's a group we've worked with a lot, so we gave them the "Yes We Can" video first. They started posting it, and people started picking it up. On Sunday, we started going out to the political bloggers. We wanted to make sure that there was already a lot of stuff on the Web so that the political bloggers would see it as important.

By the time Monday came around, we had incoming emails from the *Today Show* and *Larry King Live,* and the *New York Times* saying "Whoa, what happened over the weekend? How do we talk to this guy?" We ended up getting 47 million views and half a billion impressions on traditional media without even making a single outbound traditional media call.

So that means you go to traditional media after social media?
From the public-relations standpoint, particularly as it relates to the entertainment and music industries, the rules have all changed. You can find and aggregate your audience very effectively online, and then when you get to a certain level, the traditional media looks to the online trends for news.

There's also a lot of interconnection between the two. For example, we recently did something with the David Lynch Foundation for the Paul McCartney and Ringo reunion at Radio City Music Hall. They have a large, traditional entertainment company that they hired to promote it to about 20 places like *USA Today,* the *New York Times, People, US Weekly* magazine, and those kinds of things. They hadn't really considered doing anything on the blogs, so we were brought in. We're running an onsite social media pressroom, we're giving access to bloggers who are not able to attend, and we'll be managing those bloggers who are onsite attending. We're going to be doing live streaming of interviews in ways that they can pick it up and post it on their site, and we're going to be doing a Twitter feed and live blogging of the event. Those are the things that we find go over well on the larger entertainment events.

Depending upon the client, would you identify different blogs as being important?
Yes, the same way as in traditional PR, where you would identify different publications as being important. If you've got an automotive product, you're going after a different part of the media than if you have a computer-based product.

How do you identify the blogs that are important?
We have a research department. In traditional media, there are directories that have been out for years, and every PR firm subscribes to at least some level of these $10,000 databases and directories. In the

blogosphere you have to build your own, since there's no commercial directory of bloggers out there yet. There are some open-source things that we track and aggregate, but for the most part, we just interact with bloggers and add them to our own database.

We follow about 15,000 bloggers to where we know what their likes and dislikes are and what types of things they're interested in. It's a lot more one on one than with the traditional media, where you can say, "These 30 publications all kind of act the same way" and then send them a press release. It's so much more fragmented and specialized. A lot of bloggers don't even consider themselves journalists. The thought-leadership and enthusiast sites don't take advertising, and all they want is to be tipped off early. For example, with the Paul McCartney concert, there are a number of very large Beatle fan blogs that are read by tens of thousands to hundreds of thousands of people, so we made sure that we got information to them early and often, which is great for the people that are reading the sites.

So you don't send out a press release to the blogs? You're doing more personal contact?

Correct. It's kind of ironic, since I started a press release newswire. They've been saying for 20 years that the whole phenomenon of the press release is dying, but it keeps on getting larger every year. Right now most press releases are not put out to get written about; they're put out with the idea of getting into search engines. There are a lot of easier and more impacting ways of getting into search engines by using social media instead of press releases. There are 30,000 press releases that are issued a month on the major wire services, but maybe 5 percent get picked up by anybody in terms of actually getting written about. It's funny; there's less and less media every year, yet there are more and more press releases.

Then what's the best way for an artist to approach a blogger?

Quite frankly, if you're trying to court a blogger who covers your space, the best thing to do is to first start reading them. The nice thing about blogs is they all have RSS feeds, and most of them link their most important posts to their Twitter account, which is mobile and a lot easier to deal with than a large RSS aggregator. You can follow all these bloggers on Twitter, and it'll be on your iPhone, Blackberry, or anything that has a Twitter client, and they'll sort of recognize you as you become a Twitter follower and are watching what they say. You can comment on some of their posts, and all of a sudden, you have a bit of a relationship, so that when you come out, you don't come across as a salesman who's trying to spam 50 sites with the same information. It's better to come out and say, "Hey, I read your site frequently, and here's what I'm doing."

I know you're high on Twitter.
It's very effective right now, even thought the number of users is a lot less than Facebook or MySpace. A typical Twitter user is going to be posting several times a day, because you're only posting 140 characters at a time. The beauty of Twitter is that you don't have be "Friended" by somebody. You can follow anybody you want (thousands of people if you want), and they can follow you unless you're blocking your profile. And if you're following each other, that constitutes a friend relationship, and that means you can direct message them. It becomes a very sophisticated way to search and have conversations with a wide array of thought leaders. It's a very sophisticated crowd now, but it's starting to expand to the masses. It's not real big in music promotion yet, but it will be.

How would you use it to promote a client?
We'll be following people who we want to contact, and we'll also advise our clients to have their own Twitter accounts and do the same. We'll have certain things that we'll do as an agency, and we'll have things that we'll have the clients do on their own. You're both involved in the conversation.

Do you have any advice for an artist who wants to get ahead in this space but doesn't have enough money to hire a firm like yours?
It's something that you can absolutely do yourself if you put the time in. Follow the top bloggers, read a few books on social media marketing (although the books are outdated as soon as they come out), follow guys like Seth Godin and Malcolm Gladwell, look at artists who are Twittering and have blogs, go to some conferences, and experiment and see what works.

Appendix 1: Online Tools

Below you'll find all of the sites, tools, and applications mentioned during the course of this book.

BAND-ORIENTED PLATFORMS
ReverbNation (reverbnation.com)
Band Camp (bootcamp.com)
Sonic Bids (sonicbids.com)
Nimbit (nimbit.com)
RouteNote (routenote.com)
WHOOZNXT (whooznext.com)
Ning (ning.com)
The Ultimate Chart (ultimatechart.com)
Ditto (ditto.com)
CD Baby (cdbaby.net)
Tunecore (tunecore.com)
RouteNote (routenote.com)
Topspin Media (topspinmedia.com)

BLOGS
Blogger (blogger.com)
Typepad (typepad.com)
Wordpress (wordpress.com)
Tumblr (tumblr.com)

CROWDFUNDING
Kickstarter (kickstarter.com)
MyBandStock (mybandstock.com)
Indiegog (idiegog.com)
Rockethub (rockethub.com)
Sellaband (sellaband.com)
Pledge Music (pledgemusic.com)

FACEBOOK

Rootmusic (rootmusic.com)

My Band App (facebook.com/rn.mybandapp)

iLike (apps.facebook.com/ilike/)

Damn the Radio (damntheradio.com)

Facebook Insights (facebook.com/help/?search=insights)

My Band (facebook.com/rn.mybandapp)

MAILING LISTS

Fan Bridge (fanbridge.com)

Mail Chimp (mailchimp.com)

Constant Contact (constantcontact.com)

iContact (icontact.com)

MEASUREMENT

PeopleBrowsr (peoplebrowsr.com/)

Sysomos (sysomos.com)

Radian6 (radian6.com)

Google Analytics (google.com/analytics)

Who's Talkin (whostalkin.com)

Google Alerts (google.com/alerts)

Band Metrics (bandmetrics.com)

Google Alerts (google.com/alerts)

Twitter Search (search.twitter.com)

Stat Counter (statcounter.com)

Tynt Tracer (tcr1.tynt.com)

Next Big Sound (nextbigsound.com)

Music Metric (musicmetric.com)

RockDex (rockdex.com)

Fame Count (famecount.com)

MERCHANDISE

Zazzle (zazzle.com)

Cafe Press (cafepress.com)

Blurb (blurb.com)

Square (squareup.com)

QR Codes (qrcode.kaywa.com)

Kunaki (kunaki.com)

MUSIC BLOGS

Hypebot (hypebot.com)

Music Think Tank (musicthinktank.com)

Seth Godin (sethgodin.typepad.com)

Music 3.0 (music3point0.blogspot.com)

PUBLISHING

Association of Independent Music Publishers (aimp.org)

Sound Exchange (soundexchange.com)

SOCIAL MEDIA MANAGEMENT

Artist Data (artistdata.com)

Dijit (dijit.com)

Ping (ping.fm)

STREAMING VIDEO

UStream (ustream.com)

LiveStream (livestream.com)

SURVEYS

Survey Monkey (surveymonkey.com)

PollDaddy (polldaddy.com)

TWITTER

Search.twitter.com

Twellow (twellow.com)

Tweetstats (tweetstats.com)

Tweetstats Trends (tweetstats.com/trends)

Trendistic (trendistic.com)

Klout (klout.com)

Blast Follow (blastfollow.com)

Tweepi (tweepi.com)

twAitter (twaitter.com)

Tweetdeck (tweetdeck.com)

Tweetchat (tweetchat.com)

TweetWhen (tweetwhen.com)

TweetReach (tweetreach.com)

YOUTUBE

YouTube Trends (youtube.com/trendsdashboard)

YouTube Insight (youtube.com/
my_videos_insight)

TubeMogul (tubemogul.com)

Appendix 2: Glossary

360 deal. A record deal that enables the record label to share in the income of other aspects of an artist's career beyond recording, such as ticket sales and merchandise.

A&R. An abbreviation for artist and repertoire. A talent scout at a record label.

AAC. An abbreviation for Advanced Audio Coding. A standard compression encoding scheme for digital audio used exclusively by Apple's iTunes store.

Adsense. A Google service for supplying advertisements to a website based on many factors, such as the website's content and the user's geographical location.

after-show party. A party directly following a show that is for the band's friends and associates.

airplay. When a song gets played on the radio.

Arbitron rating. A measurement of the number of people listening to a radio station.

art. A creative endeavor that you do for your own personal satisfaction.

artistic control. Control of the creative aspects of a recording. Artistic control usually lies mainly in the hands of the producer, with input from the artist.

backlink. An outside link on another website that's connected to your page.

bar code. A series of vertical bars of varying widths in which the numbers 0 through 9 are represented by a unique pattern of bars that can be read by a laser scanner. Bar codes are commonly found on consumer products and are used for inventory control purposes and, in the case of CDs, to tally sales.

bootleg. An unauthorized recording of a concert, a rehearsal, an outtake, or an alternate mix from an album.

brand. A name, sign, or symbol used to identify the items or services of a seller that differentiate them from their competitors. A brand is a promise of quality and consistency.

branding. The promotion of a brand.

breakage. In the days of vinyl, a certain percentage of records would break in transit. This number was subtracted from the artist's royalties.

brick-and-mortar. A physical retail store usually composed of building materials such as bricks and mortar.

cobranding. Two firms working together to promote a product or service.

catalog. Older albums or recordings under the control of the record label.

collectible. An item (usually nonessential) that has particular value to its owner because of its rarity and desirability.

conglomerate. A multi-industry company or a large company that owns smaller companies in different businesses.

container. With regard to music, the package that allows the listener to consume it. Vinyl records, CDs, and MP3 and AAC files are all containers.

consultant. A person who advises a radio station about what to play, when to play it, and what on-air personalities to use.

craft. A creative endeavor that you do for someone else's approval.

cross-collateralization. Royalties from one agreement used to cover the losses or advances of another agreement.

crowdfunding. A method of raising money for a project by offering incentives for fans to pool their money.

DJ. An abbreviation for disc jockey. A term used in the early days of radio for the on-air radio person who played the records that the station was broadcasting. Later replaced by the term on-air "personality."

distribution network. The various retail sales outlets or, in the case of M3.0, digital music download sites.

DIY. An abbreviation for do it yourself.

DRM. An abbreviation for Digital Rights Management. An antipiracy measure that limits the number of legal copies that can be made.

FLAC. An abbreviation for Free Lossless Audio Codec. A lossless file format used to make digital audio files smaller in size.

four-wall. When one management individual or company uses the clout of a larger management company in return for a percentage of the income. The manager of the smaller company sometimes shares an office with the larger management company, or is "four-walled" within the company's offices.

fuelers. Contributors to a crowdfunding project.

gatefold. An album cover that folds out.

heritage artist. A superstar act that is still active. Madonna, Tina Turner, the Rolling Stones, and The Eagles are examples of current heritage acts.

IFPI. An abbreviation for the International Federation of the Phonographic Industry. Represents the recording industry worldwide, with some 1,400 members in 66 countries and affiliated industry associations in 45 countries.

independent promoter. A person or company not employed by a record label, but hired by the label to persuade a radio station to play a record.

ISRC code. An abbreviation for International Standard Recording Code. An international standard code for uniquely identifying sound recordings and music-video recordings. An ISRC code identifies a particular recording, not the song itself. Therefore, different recordings, edits, and remixes of the same song will each have their own ISRC codes.

jewel case. The standard plastic case that holds a CD.

kbps. An abbreviation for kilobits per second, or the amount of digital information sent per second. See also **bandwidth.**

leader. Initiates contact with the tribe and leads the conversations.

loss leader. An item priced at a loss in order to entice people to buy another more costly product, usually at full retail price.

lurker. One who reads a blog but doesn't participate or post him- or herself.

meet and greet. A brief meeting with an artist to say hello, answer a few questions, and take pictures.

metadata. Data about other data or content.

micropayment. A means for transferring very small amounts of money in situations where collecting such small amounts of money is impractical, or very expensive, with the usual payment systems.

millennial. A member of the generation of children born between 1977 and 1994.

MP3. The de facto standard data-compression format used to make audio files smaller in size.

M0.5. See **Music 0.5.**

M1.0. See **Music 1.0.**

M1.5. See **Music 1.5.**

M2.0. See **Music 2.0.**

M2.5. See **Music 2.5.**

M3.0. See **Music 3.0.**

Music 0.5. The time before recorded music, when sheet music was the only form of music distribution.

Music 1.0. The first generation of the music business, in which the product was vinyl records, the artist had no direct contact with the record buyer, radio was the primary source of promotion, the record labels were run by record people, and records were bought from retail stores.

Music 1.5. The second generation of the music business, in which the product was primarily CDs, labels were owned and run by large conglomerates, MTV caused the labels to shift from artist development to image development, radio was still the major source of promotion, and CDs were purchased from retail stores.

Music 2.0. The third generation of the music business, which signaled the beginning of digital music. Piracy ran rampant because of P2P networks, but the industry took little notice, since CD sales were still strong from radio promotion.

Music 2.5. The fourth generation of the music business, in which digital music became monetized, thanks to the online digital-distributor iTunes store and, later, others such as Amazon MP3. CD sales plunged, the music industry contracted, and retail stores closed.

Music 3.0. The current generation of the music business, in which the artist can now communicate and interact with, and market and sell directly to, the fan. Record labels, radio, and television have become mostly irrelevant, and single songs are purchased instead of albums.

one-stop. A company that buys from major record-distributors and sells to small retailers who buy in quantities too small for major distributors to bother with.

paid download. A downloadable song that you buy and own.

pay-per-click. An Internet advertising model used on search engines, advertising networks, and content sites such as blogs, in which advertisers pay their hosts only when their ads are clicked on.

paid search. A type of contextual advertising in which website owners pay an advertising fee to have their websites shown in the top placement on search-engine results pages.

payola. Payment in exchange for airplay. The payment could be in cash, illegal substances such as drugs, or products such as televisions or paid vacations. The practice is illegal.

pay to play. In order to play at a club, the owner demands that the band buy a certain number of tickets, which they then sell or give away to their fans. The club owner is guaranteed a minimum cash presale, while the band usually ends up losing money.

peer to peer. A type of transient Internet network that allows a group of computer users with the same networking program to connect with each other and directly access files from one another's hard drives.

performance fee. A fee paid to the performer (as opposed to the songwriter) each time a song is played on the radio, over the Internet, or on television.

performance-rights organization. An organization that collects performance royalties from broadcasters or Internet streaming and distributes it to songwriters. Performance-rights organizations include ASCAP, BMI, and SESAC. See also **PRO.**

P2P. See **peer to peer.**

pirating. The sale of an illegal copy of a digital file, CD, CD artwork, or any other creative product where the record label, artist, and songwriter never take part in the profit or are provided royalties.

PRO. An abbreviation for Performance Rights Organization. Some are ASCAP, BMI, and SESAC.

producer. The person in charge of recording, from managing the budget to creatively guiding the project to completion.

promoter. A person who organizes a concert or show, including booking the venue and talent; arranging for advertising, security, and insurance; as well as a host of other duties. The promoter usually uses his or her own money to finance the project in the hopes of making a profit.

QR Code. A graphic code similar to a bar code that provides a link to a website when scanned. An analog web link.

rack jobber. Someone who leases floor space from a retail store (such as a department store or car wash) and puts in "racks" of CDs or other types of recorded music.

record. A generic term for the distribution method of a recording. Regardless of whether it's vinyl, a CD, or a digital file, it is still known as a record.

record club. An outdated way of obtaining prerecorded music at a discounted rate through the mail. Usually used by the consumer because there is no retail music store in his or her area.

RIAA. An abbreviation for the Recording Industry Association of America. A trade organization for record labels.

rotation. The playlist of a radio station.

RSS. An abbreviation for Real Simple Syndication. A family of Web-feed formats used to publish frequently updated works (such as blog entries, news headlines, audio, and video) in a standardized format.

SEM. An abbreviation for Search-Engine Marketing.

SEO. An abbreviation for Search-Engine Optimization.

shed. A large outdoor-concert facility.

SKU. An abbreviation for Stock-keeping Unit. The number allotted to every item in a store for the purpose of inventory control.

SoundScan. The company that measures record sales. Whenever a CD or a DVD is sold, the bar code on each unit is scanned and recorded by SoundScan.

superfan. A fan that is more passionate than the average fan. See also **true fan; uberfan.**

subscription service. A download service for which you pay a set monthly fee and listen to as much music as you want during that time without any limitations.

swag. Another name for merchandise, such as T-shirts, that is sold at a concert or on a website.

technology expense. A clause in a recording agreement that subtracts a portion of the artist's royalty if a certain new technology is used in the production or sale of product.

torrent. The latest form of Internet P2P (peer to peer) file sharing. Since 2006, Bittorrent sharing has been the most popular means by which Web users trade software, music, movies, and digital books across the Internet. Bittorrents (a term that is synonymous with torrents) work by downloading small bits of files from many different Web sources at the same time. See also **peer to peer.**

true fan. A fan that is more passionate than the average fan. See also **superfan; uberfan.**

turntable hit. A song that receives massive airplay but has few actual sales.

tweet. A Twitter posting.

uberfan. A fan that is more passionate than the average fan. See also **superfan; true fan.**

vertical. A particular marketing or sales niche or demographic group.

WMA. An abbreviation for Windows Media Audio. An audio data-compression format created by Microsoft.

Index